Extending Thought in Young C

Extending Thought in Young Children

A Parent–Teacher Partnership

Second Edition

CHRIS ATHEY

Paul Chapman Publishing

First published 1990
Second edition published 2007

Paul Chapman Publishing
A SAGE Publications Company
1 Oliver's Yard
55 City Road
London EC1Y 1SP

SAGE Publications Inc
2455 Teller Road
Thousand Oaks, California 91320

SAGE Publications India Pvt Ltd
B 1/11 Mohan Cooperative Industrial Area
Mathura Road, Post Bag 7
New Delhi 110 044

SAGE Publications Asia-Pacific Pte Ltd
33 Pekin Street #02-01
Far East Square
Singapore 048763

Library of Congress Control Number: 2006933410

A catalogue record for this book is available from the British Library

ISBN-978-1-4129-2131-2
ISBN-978-1-4129-2132-9 (pbk)

Typeset by Pantek Arts Ltd, Maidstone, Kent
Printed in Great Britain by Cromwell Press Ltd, Trowbridge, Wiltshire
Printed on paper from sustainable resources

To Molly Brearley, CBE, and Joyce Bishop, DBE, who worked together to initiate, raise money and guide the Froebel Early Education Project. Their public lives were spent advancing educational ideas and policies. As teachers and as private persons, they transformed the lives of many staff, pupils, friends and others who were lucky enough to meet them.

Contents

Preface

Many professionals and parents have been influenced in their thinking by the Froebel Project findings. This is gratifying, after so many years of endeavour. Many professionals have added knowledge of schemas to their own considerable expertise and experience. What all the following people have in common is a search for a coherent and useful pedagogy for the early years of education.

As well as having an influence on teaching programmes, many publications in the early education field have acknowledged the influence of the Froebel Project findings: Arnold 2002, 2003; Roberts 2002; Meade and Cubey 1995; Meade 2005; Worthington and Carruthers 2003; Nutbrown 1994, 1999; Wood and Attfield 1996.

Margy Whalley (1994, 2001), Lynne Bartholomew and Tina Bruce (1993), Mollie Davies (2003), Pat Gura (1992), John Matthews (1984, 2003) and Rosemary Roberts (2002) are just a few of the authors, together with Tina Bruce (2004), who are advancing a pedagogy based on the identification of the positive aspects of cognition in young children. This is central to 'constructivism' which is still the most powerful and useful theory for teachers.

In 1994 (2nd edn, 1999), Cathy Nutbrown produced *Threads of Thinking*, published by Paul Chapman. This can be thought of as a companion to *Extending Thought in Young Children* in that it applies the Froebel Project findings in a wide number of early education settings, thereby taking the illuminative theory forward and showing that it has a wide application. She also produced new material on how to extend schemas with suitable curriculum content.

The findings of the Project have had a considerable influence on early education practice in many places. In New Zealand, for instance, one of the teaching programmes in a larger research study was based on extending patterns of thinking and behaviour in young children. Anne Meade, the New Zealand project director, found that the group that had been taught according to the schemas the children had brought to the situation were statistically ahead of other groups. The New Zealand researchers are elaborating a pedagogy based on diagnosed 'patterns of behaviour' in young children (Meade and Cubey 1995) and *Catching the Waves* (Meade 2005). Schema theory is alive and well in Portugal and in Germany.

The staff of Pen Green Children's Centre in Corby, England, have embraced the Froebel Project findings enthusiastically, and professionals belonging to a research group at Pen Green are taking the findings forward. They have had articles on schemas published by *Nursery World*. These have attracted genuine interest in different parts of England. They have also recruited parents in 'the search for schemas' with considerable success.

Of particular interest are the books from people who are starting with schemas and following the children to a more advanced level in some area of the curriculum. Worthington and Carruthers (2003), for instance, began observations on 3-year-olds and pursued the same children until they were 8. They 'bridged the gap' between the early years and primary education in relation to mathematics, spontaneous mark-making and speech.

John Matthews is well known for pursuing art as well as successfully applying various theories to the art of young children. Mollie Davies has pursued schemas to more complex concepts of movement education and dance, in which she specializes.

Yuelong Pan carried out a study applying schema theory to a group of children in Beijing University Kindergarten. She has also translated *Extending Thought in Young Children* and *Threads of Thinking* into Mandarin.

At a conference at Pen Green on Saturday 23rd October, 2004, Ainsley Simmonds and Angie Collins, New Zealand parents, under the watchful eye of Pam Cubey, read papers and showed a video of New Zealand children exploring schemas. There was a large contingent of teachers from Shanghai at the conference. They were being shepherded around England by Wendy Scott, who has been very supportive over the years.

It is difficult to know how many head teachers are employing constructivism with its component of schema theory in their schools. We know that Sara Holroyd is, because she has a website (www.werneth-infantoldham.sch.uk/homepage.htm) where she discusses schemas. Sara worked closely with Tina Bruce during the Froebel Project years.

Similarly, it is difficult to know how many local authorities and universities are employing schema theory in their courses. Lynne McKenna, programme leader of 'Learning in Families, Schools and Beyond' at Northumbria University is, because a group from Northumbria met the research group at Pen Green.

There is a lot to be said for projects which are generated from a bottom-up perspective. During the 1960s, Jean Ridge, a white woman living in Cape Town, South Africa, approached the boss of a transport union for money to set up a care and educational project for young African children. There are now dozens of similar projects called 'Grass-roots' in different parts of South Africa.

It is realized that the search for and cultivation of schemas is as much of a luxury as the provision of early state education itself in subsistence economies. In Barbados (although not a subsistence economy) during the 1960s, there was a thriving nursery school housed at Erdiston College. This was supported by charity. Important dignitaries sent their children to the school but denied its existence in public.

Early education will never be really safe until it is seen as an essential part of real lifelong learning.

Part I

Events Influencing the Froebel Early Education Project

In the Beginning

The idea of the Froebel Early Education Project (the Project) was conceived during the 1960s when Molly Brearley, CBE and Sheila Macleod were out walking together discussing educational matters. At the time Brearley was Principal of the Froebel Educational Institute (FEI, now part of Roehampton University) and Macleod head teacher of Ibstock Place Preparatory School (the demonstration school of the FEI).

Following a one-year pilot study, their idea evolved into a five-year intensive study that became known as the Froebel Early Education Project. Its aims were to observe and analyse, on a daily basis during a two-year teaching programme, children under the age of 5 in order to:

- identify developments in each child's thinking;

- describe the development of symbolic representation from early motor and perceptual behaviours; and

- identify curriculum content assimilated to developing forms of thought.

Two groups were studied and tested: one multi-ethnic and underpriviledged, the other middle class and privately educated. Evidence suggested that children selectively assimilated the curriculum content offered to them by developing forms of thought that are fed by experience gained from home and school. The resulting principles, methods and findings have since had a considerable influence on early education practitioners in the UK and elsewhere.

Very few people in education are able to combine successfully pedagogy and politics. The two domains stem from different motivations, use different strategies, employ different research methods and operate within different time spans. However, Molly Brearley could. She had an internally consistent set of values, was an indefatigable searcher for evidence of educational gain and an outstanding communicator, becoming an influential member of the Plowden Committee

(Liebschner, 1991, p. x). The Plowden Report (Central Advisory Council for Education, 1967) and her discussion with Sheila Macleod reflected some of Molly Brearley's persistent pedagogical concerns as well as more specific concerns arising from her work for Plowden.

The educational ethos of the Froebel Educational Institute (FEI), and the wider Froebel Foundation, always reflected its European philosophical and psychological heritage. Froebelian values, conceived within Europe, coincided with constructivist values, also conceived within Europe. The main value of Froebelian pedagogy and constructivism, the main system of educational research endeavour of the last century, is quite simple. It is based on the conviction that each individual learner contributes to, and collaborates in, his or her own learning.

The Froebel movement has often been associated with a 'child-centred' pedagogy, but this description has never reflected the wider concerns of the Froebelian view of learning. Worthwhile curriculum content has always been as important to Froebelian teachers as the teaching style by which content is conveyed. However, there are those who believe otherwise. During the 1940s, 1950s and 1960s, the main opposition to constructivism in Britain and America was 'behaviourism'. This view of learning maintains that teachers should teach and children should learn what they are taught, and tests will ascertain what has been learned. The behaviourist approach to teaching and learning disregards the contribution that each child makes towards his or her own learning. Although constructivism was a widely adopted model for experimental research during that period, behaviourism was the main teaching style in most schools.

The English are not famous for their pedagogical knowledge, nor for their interest in increasing it. This is a persistent problem in English education, as can be seen in two articles published 20 years apart. In 1985 Simon wrote 'Why no pedagogy in England?', and in 2004 Alexander wrote 'Still no Pedagogy' in which he examined principle, pragmatism and compliance in primary education.

Pejorative, anti-theory, anti-intellectual attitudes are often disguised or softened by the use of terms such as 'pragmatic' or 'eclectic'. 'Common sense' is often put forward as a preferred alternative to professional systems of explanation; professional concepts are more expensive to organize through training courses than appeals to common sense. Common sense implies that something good and shared is already in place. Some of the pedagogical concerns raised in the Plowden Report caused consternation, and it was perceived by many as an aberration from the usual English government reports.

COMMON SENSE, PROFESSIONAL KNOWLEDGE AND PATTERNS OF THINKING IN YOUNG CHILDREN

Professional pedagogical knowledge is not the same as common sense knowledge, although they are not mutually exclusive. Professional knowledge finds its evidence in the everyday world of home and school. It is 'sound' rather than esoteric, and uses ordinary language as far as possible. Professional knowledge in education is on a human scale and so, although professionals may study quantum theory or the big bang theory of the origin of the universe out of interest, such epistemological knowledge of physics at the outskirts of magnitude are not necessary for teaching except in higher education. However, from a very young age children make judgments about objects in the world being 'big' and 'little', and a little later 'fast' and 'slow' or 'expensive' and 'cheap', and so the recognition of concepts of 'magnitude' in children must be included in professional knowledge.

Most people can communicate within systems of commonly shared knowledge with anyone about almost anything, for instrance in a supermarket in relation to a particular product. This is communication based on common sense. There is a particular philosophical meaning based on inputs of sensory data attributed to John Locke, based on *phenomenological* or sensory experience. This has given rise to the idea that humans learn by experience, that is, by sensory data which, taken on its own, is a behaviourist notion. Sensory data do become integrated, and there is a whole complicated literature in integrations of a perceptual nature. Neurological studies are heavily into sensory integrations. So are many teachers who love colour tables (where several different objects share one attribute – colour). A cursery examination of the objects on display usually shows that the least important property of each object, such as a comb, a cup, a ball, a cube, a yo-yo, is its colour. The most important property is usually what a person can do with it.

A more useful meaning of commonly shared sense, however, is based on human understanding that sees what is shared as having a more conceptual basis. It is the human brain that does the combining. Our shared brains provide the link between common sense and professional understandings. Without professional understandings: the adult–child relationship is simply custodial. By custodial is meant that young children should be kept warm, fed, safe and contented (see Athey 1990, p. 24).

FITTING OR FLITTING

The most important findings of the Froebel Project were linked with the uncovering of 'schemas' – patterns of behaviour and thinking in children that exist underneath the surface features of various contents, contexts and specific experiences.

Naturalistic observations made on children will show them using different materials in different ways. They typically use the materials of representation such as pens, pencils, paint and paper to represent different objects in the world. If questions are asked about why particular content is represented, answers would normally be given within a common-sense theory such as 'this content reflects what has been experienced'. This still leaves particular or rather idiosyncratic selections unexplained. Why would a child select 'aeroplane landing', 'man', 'tree', 'my name', 'umbrella', 'elephant' and so on? These representations (see Figures 5.52 to 5.65) are from different children but, with the possible exception of the frock coat, they could have been from any portfolio of drawings from any 4-year-old.

One of the deficit accusations thrown at young children is that they are idiosyncratic and they 'flit' from pillar to post. The few examples above could be used to support this hypothesis. However, 'flitting' is demonstrated only if the surface content of experiencing is being analysed.

If the question is asked: 'What have all of these drawings got in common?', different conclusions can be drawn. Each drawing shows that the child is 'exercising' his or her latest graphic 'form' or schema which, in the case of these few examples, is the semi-circle. Viewed schematically, most of the apparent disparate behaviours of young children can be seen to have more similarities than differences.

SCHEMAS ON THE WEB

A word of caution seems necessary at this point. Feeding key word 'schema' into the search engine Google produces almost 60 million results. This is because of the adoption of the term for one of the great systems behind information technology. Feeding into Google the words 'schemas Piaget' produces almost 50 million results. This is because almost every university teaches 'constructivism', and 'schema' is subsumed within the Piagetian framework. Feeding in 'schema Piaget UK' produces almost 30,000 results, most of which do not accurately reflect the meaning of 'schema' (singular) or 'schemas' (plural) from a Piagetian or 'constructivist' viewpoint.

It might help to give some criteria for the meaning of 'constructivism' (and schema) as discussed in this book. The following are the essentials of Piagetian or constructivist theory according to Cambell (2002):

1 Knowledge has a biological function, and arises out of action. Making sure that 'schemas' (as discussed in the literature) are always biological and psychological is sufficient to 'see off' most contenders.

2 Knowledge is basically operative. It is about change and transformation.

3 Knowledge consists of cognitive structures (schemas and concepts).

4 Development proceeds by the assimilation of the environment to these structures, and the accommodation of these structures to the environment.

5 Movement to higher levels of development depends on 'reflecting abstraction', that is, coming to know the properties of one's own actions, or coming to know the ways in which they are co-ordinated.

It was changing cognitive structures rather than 'stage' characteristics which mattered most to Piaget. His book on *Structuralism* (1971) is difficult, but definitive on the issue of Piagetian constructivist meanings.

SCHEMAS AND COMMON SENSE

Can the recognition of schemas arise from common-sense perception? Apparently not, otherwise schemas would have found their way into research findings, books and classrooms a long time ago. However, 'discoveries' of schemas in early and primary education do not run contrary to common sense as do some scientific concepts: 'If someone says: "It's just common sense" I can guarantee he's got it wrong' (Wolpert, 2000). Many teachers being confronted by evidence of 'schemas', experience a 'shock of recognition' accompanied by some sort of comment such as 'Of course!'

Common sense is sometimes regarded as an impediment to abstract and even logical thinking. This is especially the case in mathematics and physics, where human intuition often conflicts with provably correct or experimentally verified results. A definition attributed to Albert Einstein states: 'Common sense is the collection of prejudices acquired by age eighteen' (from Wikipedia, the free encyclopedia on the Web).

INTUITIVE OR INFORMED

To say that he or she is 'intuitive' rather than 'logical' is not strongly pejorative; it can imply a sensitivity towards a child's concerns. However, it does imply that something is missing, in that between a premis and a conclusion are steps of a professional nature that cannot be articulated. 'Intuitive' knowledge can probably be best seen as partial professional knowledge that reading, course work and the search for empirical evidence can 'flesh out'. Research theses in higher education typically start as hunches or intuitions. These are then tested against more controlled observations that either support or refute those hunches. Since the early days of the Froebel Project, terms such as 'pedagogy' are increasingly being used by educators in England, but still not by politicians. One of the most important pieces of research on three teaching styles (pedagogies) was carried out by David Weikart in Ypsilanti, Michigan in 1962. The High/Scope Perry Preschool Project preceded the founding of the national Head Start programme in the USA by three years.

DISADVANTAGE, DEPRIVATION AND DEFICITS

During the mid 1970s, professional literature on education throughout the world had very little to say about cognitive development (or intellectual development, as it was then called) in children between the ages of two and five, even though there were hundreds of projects in the world studying young children. The bias of most studies then was to try to ameliorate poor intellectual functioning in school by tackling an assumed disadvantage and deprivation in the living conditions of the urban poor. Poor parenting was an associated assumption of the time. This is in contrast to earlier projects of the 1920s and 1930s, such as the Susan Isaacs Malting House School. There the children were privileged and the aim had been to find out more about children's positive thinking. Because Susan Isaacs' books were pedagogically sound and contained references to a wide range of international research studies and were about real children, they were used by nursery teachers for over half a century.

During the 1960s there were rich projects such as Weikart's High/Scope in the USA, poor projects such as those in the shanty towns of South Africa, where huts were built with rubbish and where there were no lavatories or running water. There were hundreds of reports on a wide range of projects collated by the Bernard Van Leer Foundation in Holland, which gave the impression that all the projects were tackling similar problems and experiencing similar difficulties. A type of deprivation-and-disadvantage-speak was used in reports of projects around the world. These reports acted as a smoke-screen to a real research problem. They obscured the fact that just about nothing positive was known about cognitive development in children between 2 and 5 years. Nobody was blowing whistles on this.

Weikart got near to revealing this problem. In 1972 he published a comparison and evaluation of three different pedagogical models – child-centred, behaviourist and constructivist – carried out in a real school situation. He anticipated that the constructivist programme would be the most successful in relation to the criteria he had laid out. He was a well-known constructivist at the time. His report in Stanley (1972) was interesting and illuminating and, unusual in research studies, entertaining. It honestly reflected the mess and muddle and misunderstandings of observational research while it was taking place in the real world. These issues tend to disappear when manuscripts are cleaned up for publication. For instance, because of unanticipated space problems in the research school in Ypsilanti, the staff of the child-centred programme found themselves next door to the constructivists and became increasingly aware of the large number of visitors the constructivists were getting. They became convinced that they were merely a control group and became depressed. This factor, rather than an unsuccessful outcome of a particular pedagogical approach to teaching and learning, could have accounted for third-year losses in the test scores of the child-centred group.

There were also unanticipated problems with staff in the constructivist programme. Put bluntly, some staff did not know enough about child development in general or constructivism in particular. This is not surprising, since Piaget himself had failed to find the positive characteristics of thinking in children from 2 to 5 (Paiget: *Play, Dreams and Imitation*, 1962, *Origin of Intelligence*, 1953, and *Construction of Reality*, 1959).

During the 1970s and 1980s there was much criticism of early years research. Derogatory comments were made on the application of inadequate theory to observations of young children with exhortation for greater rigour. Inadequate theory was frequently referred to as 'received wisdom'. Greater rigour usually meant that there should be more quantification and less description 'fleshed-out' with illustrative anecdotal examples. In spite of thousands of experimental studies on topics such as 'one to one correspondence', 'conservation', 'classification' and 'ordering' carried out within a constructivist framework there was no coherent system of constructivism which could be applied to spontaneous observations of children in the real world of home and school. This led to a proliferation of correlation studies. The trouble with such studies is that it is difficult to pin down factors that are responsible for change, for better or worse. Even the high and consistent correlation between smoking and cancer demonstrated for years by Richard Doll continued to be successfully challenged by the tobacco industry on the grounds that correlations are not causes.

The results of the Weikart experiments in different teaching styles were sufficiently equivocal for the Westinghouse Learning Corporation (1969) to threaten a shift in funding to studies of 'genetic determination' (Jensen, 1969). At this point Weikart managed to use correlations arising from his work in Ypsilanti to great political advantage. Political pressure for better education came from American politicians who were alarmed by Russian success in the space race. Also political pressure for greater equality of opportunity came from minority groups in the USA. Martin Luther King had a dream about racial equality. These were important political factors that led to the launching of the Head Start programmes in the USA. In 1965, President Johnson launched the programmes with the clarion call 'No American child shall be condemned to failure by the accident of his birth.'

In the UK as well as in the USA, political events rather than pedagogical aspirations determined the funding of projects following the High/Scope Project. However, the High/Scope long-term study documented the advantageous effects that high-quality early education can have on children's future lives. The long-term findings indicate that with a high-quality early education programme, children can achieve success in school and better economic and social status in adulthood. This was a message the politicians preferred to hear, rather than pleas for extra money.

PROFESSIONAL KNOWLEDGE AND THE EXPANSION OF EARLY EDUCATION

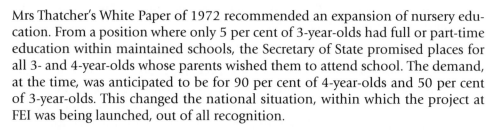

Mrs Thatcher's White Paper of 1972 recommended an expansion of nursery education. From a position where only 5 per cent of 3-year-olds had full or part-time education within maintained schools, the Secretary of State promised places for all 3- and 4-year-olds whose parents wished them to attend school. The demand, at the time, was anticipated to be for 90 per cent of 4-year-olds and 50 per cent of 3-year-olds. This changed the national situation, within which the project at FEI was being launched, out of all recognition.

2

Evolution of Early Educational Provision

This book is mainly about quality of educational interaction between teacher and child, parent and child, and parent and professional. Quality of educational interaction is very difficult to describe and illustrate, much less to measure. While discussions about quantity tend to be carried out against a shifting background of political and financial constraints, communication on high-quality education as opposed to high quality provision requires professional knowledge.

However, the emphasis on quality in this book does not imply that the *quantity* of pre-school services is unimportant. Although, theoretically, high-quality education can take place almost anywhere, it is more likely to be facilitated in enriched rather than arid environments.

OECD

One of the most important changes to have taken place during the past four decades regarding quantity has been the rise and rise of the Operation for Economic Co-operation and Development (OECD). The first signature to the aims and objectives of an OECD was the USA, on 12 April 1961, showing that the organization, with its main aim to help governments with their economies, was invented there. The UK joined the USA on 2 May 1961. By the end of 1961 there were 20 member countries, now there are 30. The OECD countries are the richest in the world.

What makes the OECD so important is that any economic aspect of society that can be quantified is quantified according to agreed-upon criteria. Originally the information was intended to be made available to governments; however, through the Internet this information is now available to anyone who types in appropriate search words. Just one example of what is now available will make clear the important shift from the statistical fumbling of individual countries in the past to the present global nature of international comparisons. Helping to spread economic progress and democratic forms of government are two important aims. On the face of it, this can only lead towards more open and democratic societies.

Asking Google, or other search engines, for 'OECD statistical profiles 2006', for instance, will make accessible 30 sets of statistical data. Each set consists of 40 statistical databases from the 30 member countries. Thousands of facts that Mr Gradgrind would relish are uncovered. Now comparisons can be made between quantifiable events in member countries. Implications arising from the facts are more difficult for all to accept as they depend on political and social theories. In the past, different events have been considered separately. Now different but related facets of society can be considered together. For instance, the burgeoning of ageing populations in some countries can now be related to government inducements to increase the number of children and to expand on child care and education which will enable mothers to work. The problem of pensions can also be considered against these other factors. Problems in society have to be solved in clusters otherwise there may be unintended consequences. Facts make good starting points for subsequent discussion. There are now, for instance, available facts about the actual size of immigrant populations as opposed to inflammatory fictions.

It is interesting to compare equivalences as well as differences. For instance, 49 per cent of people in the UK have access to the Internet compared with 52 per cent in New Zealand. The UK has a total population of 59, 422 million and New Zealand 4,009 million. There are cells in existing tables, collated in 2003, which are blank, presumably because data is either missing or not yet collated.

The future of early years provision in different countries is unknown, but it is likely that in the future facts will make for a tidier starting point than in the past because of the global and comparative dimensions of OECD. At present, for instance, there are hundreds of qualifications for early years workers in England. Length of training ranges from a few hours to several years. The mind baulks at the thought of any group of people attempting to sort out this mess. Whether tidier quantification of a training structure will automatically lead to higher-quality education will be discussed later in this chapter.

The extreme top-down perspective of OECD is historically recent and it is to be hoped that 'quantity' wars between countries with the inevitable lack of qualitative detail will not cut across bottom-up local initiatives based on values, and/or philosophy in any of the member countries. Some people will argue against any given set of values, but it is useful to remember that the two projects that unequivocally caught the professional imagination of the West during the past century would not have found much of a place in such international comparisons. One was Susan Isaacs' Malting House School. This was motivated and financed by a man who profoundly disagreed with the official educational policies of the time and the Italian Reggio Emilia projects motivated originally by Marxist Partisans who fought vigorously against the attempts of the Catholic church to take over their schools.

AN HEROIC REVIEW

Bertram and Pascal (2000) carried out an heroic review of early education and care in the UK for the OECD. Until very recently, Early Childhood Education and Care (ECEC) policies in England reflected ad hoc and usually short-term priorities of government and local authorities. The main motivations of the past have been social urgencies. These have led to practical measures involving young children, most of which seemed to be good ideas at the time.

Until recently, children from birth to age 3 were under the Department of Health, while the Department for Education and Employment (DfEE) (now called DfES – Department for Education and Skills) had responsibility for children of 3 to 5 years. This would reflect an historical fact that, until about one hundred years ago, the first two years of a child's life had more to do with physical survival than with quality of mind. Extending quality of mind through education was a concern of just a few reformers, such as Froebel and Susan Isaacs.

In England in 1873, the first Froebelian free kindergarten was established by the Salford local authority. One century later, the Froebel Project was just starting. Salford's local authority, in the north of England, responded to the voiced concerns of distinguished citizens who had been inspired by the values of the Froebel movement. They were protesting at industrial slum conditions in which young children were living. They wanted to improve the lives of young children through nursery education. This first kindergarten, free to parents, offered baths, meals, rest, play and parental training (Bertram and Pascal, 2000, p. 9). The broad 'mission statements ' behind Froebel initiatives then and now are not so different. However, because of information technology (IT) we are now in the so-called 'century of knowledge', so any discussion now on promoting quality of interaction must include children's thinking and cognition.

As we know, the world is an unequal place and any attempts to cultivate high-level interaction between parents and practitioners are less likely in some environments than in others. As a black South African colleague in one of the townships near Cape Town said to me: 'I would rather we were entering into a century of clean, running water.' He could equally have said: 'A century where one nourishing meal per day was guaranteed.'

The quantity of early years provision in the UK has never been linked with a widely shared cultural assumption that early education is a good thing for its own sake. Quantity has only been increased when it was socially expedient to do so. The expansion of state provision has, in the main, been related to keeping children off the streets, while adult populations (the parents of young children) were steered in directions considered desirable by people in power at any given time. An example of this is given by Bertram and Pascal (2000, Section 1:1). They point out that when the 1918 Education Act allowed local authorities to establish more nursery schools, the new powers were not extensively used by either health or education departments. Social circumstances between the Wars did not seem to warrant the expense of nursery schools. It took the urgencies of the Second World War to double the number of nursery school places. This was because women (mothers) were needed in the workplace.

Even before the Second World War ended, free state provision of nurseries began to close as the government encouraged women to return to 'hearth and home'. Many women were reluctant to do so because they had never had it so good. The present writer, for instance, was in a similar situation to Rosie, the riveter who had to leave her engineering skills behind when 'the boys came home'. Because of a shortage of workers, however, many women were steered into jobs with opportunities far exceeding those for women available before the War. The author of this book was steered away from engineering, into emergency teacher training. Apart from earning much less in teaching than in engineering, this was a 'steer' in a desirable direction.

Until recently, high-quality educational endeavours, such as the Malting House School, were privately financed, while governments have always had different agendas. Nanette Whitbread (1975) has given an interesting account of the differences between Robert Owen and Samuel Wilderspin. Owen believed in providing civilized and civilizing environments for the children of his mill workers. He focussed on quality. William Wilderspin was a reformer but he had a different agenda. He believed in 'rescuing' as many poor children as possible from the streets and putting them into school. He focused on quantity. The two men competed with each other as to who originated the English Infant School.

Right from the start of public education there has been a schism between the cultivation of high-level education as in the Bank Street School and Columbia University Kindergarten New York and the Malting House School in England. Most of the children studied by Piaget in Geneva were privileged. Increasing political attempts to tackle some of the urgencies of society by educational means has led many people to distinguish between 'education' and 'schooling', with good cause. 'Education' aims at increasing quality of mind, while 'schooling' appears to aim at increasing social control over populations, particularly underprivileged populations where poverty is the main problem.

THE CONCEPT OF EDUCATION

Earwaker (1973) suggests four ways in which the term 'education' is used in educational and non-educational literature:

- Concept A is the weakest. This refers to any process , not necessarily desirable, of 'bringing-up' or 'rearing' children, animals or even plants. As this concept is lacking in knowledge and value, it has no relevance to anyone working within the new legislature structures.

- Concept B is an improvement on Concept A in that it includes a concept of 'desirable states' (successful toilet-training would be an example), but it does not include 'knowledge' in the learner. Concept B might be 'worthy' from a desirability point of view, but 'woolly' from a knowledge point of view (Earwaker, 1973, p. 251).

- Concept C involves knowledge without specifying its desirability. The most notorious example of this type of programme was advocated by Bereiter and Engleman (1966) of the USA, who unrepentantly illustrated their attitude to pedagogy by giving a lesson on weapons. Bruner, in response, said: 'Just because children have a schema to do with "rotation" there is no need to give lessons on the history of the thumbscrew.' (The main features of this programme are reproduced in *Deprivation and Disadvantage*, Open University (1973) E 262, Block 8, pp. 52–8).

- Concept D is the most elaborated and complete concept of education. This may be defined as: Education is a process of bringing up children that develops their knowledge and understanding in depth and breadth in worthwhile directions. Whenever there is serious discussion about the nature and purpose of 'education' as distinct from 'schooling', 'upbringing' and 'rearing', it is Concept D that should be central to the search for evidence.

EARLY EDUCATION AND FEMALE EMPLOYMENT

As female employment began to rise in the late 1950s, part-time provision, either morning or afternoon, became the predominant form of state pre-school settings and generated a debate about whether provision should meet the child's needs or those of the child's parents and carers and their employers, where these needs were seen to be in conflict.

By 1972 (the year the Froebel Project started) the UK government was becoming more aware of ECEC comparisons. The Minister of Education promised a great expansion of free state nursery provision, but the reality of the mid-1970s oil crisis and the subsequent climate of economic rationalism militated against it.

As late as 1988, a memorandum submitted by the Department of Health and Social Security to the House of Commons Education, Science and Arts Committee on 29 June indicated that the government believes that in the first instance it is the responsibility of the parents to make arrangements, including financial arrangements, for the day care of pre-school children.

The differences between the organization of education and care began to be seen in a bad light, but it must be remembered that the recent process of co-ordinating services, now presented as an incontrovertibly good thing, had been initially motivated by administrative convenience. Implementing top-down policy with top-down planned outcomes does not necessarily improve anything except administration. Co-ordinating different levels of professional skill into a single administrative structure is not necessarily a good thing if training, wages and terminology are 'fudged' together into bland generalities. The terms 'helper', 'practitioner' or 'facilitator' may hide the professional aspirations and gains of the past. One important aspiration of the 1960s was to aim for a B. Ed. degree for all teachers.

Co-ordination of services is a good thing only if the organizational structures behind the co-ordinations allow for different but transparent levels of training and – this is most important – allow for a steadily ascending scale of qualifications as was the case with the old National Nursery Examining Board (NNEB) training.

RECENT DEVELOPMENTS

Since 1997, the government has launched an unprecedented effort to increase investment in families and young children, and to develop a wide-ranging plan of action that will expand and reform the early years system. In May 1998, a National Childcare Strategy was announced, to be implemented by locally-based early years development and childcare partnerships working in concert with the local education and social services authorities. Special funding for disadvantaged areas has been allocated through the Sure Start initiative. A pilot Early Excellence Centre programme was established in 1997 to test integrated approaches to care and education.

In the year 2000, *Curriculum Guidelines for the Foundation Stage (3–5 years)* were published, to help practitioners to plan how their work will contribute to early learning goals (see www.ne.uk.net). A Childcare Tax Credit (CTC) for parents working a minimum of 16 hours per week has also been instituted, targeted at low-income families. The Office for Standards in Education (OFSTED) will formulate national standards to ensure that all children receive good-quality service, and that providers are clear about the standards they must meet. Already the accumulation of these initiatives is radically altering the picture of early years provision in England, and 1.6 million new childcare places were created by 2004 with a further 80,000 childcare workers recruited. We are at:

> the mid-point of an ambitious government programme to develop 3,500 integrated children's centres across England. These offer an exciting vision for the future as centres where a range of multi-agency professionals will be drawing on the richness of their professional knowledge to work in the best way possible for children and families. (Wheelan, 2006, p. 1).

VARIATION IN PROVISION

Compared to most other European countries, ECEC provision in the UK started from a low base. In general, children of working parents from birth to 3 years of age are cared for by private childminders, playgroups and day nurseries. Until the recent CTC, children in these services were not eligible for public funding unless they qualified for special services or were considered to be seriously at risk. From 3–4 years, almost all children tend to join playgroups or nursery schools, moving toward reception class as they approach their 4th year. The majority of 4-year-olds are in state-funded primary school reception classes or in nursery school, operated mostly by local authorities. All 5-year-olds are in primary and reception classes.

CHILD–STAFF RATIOS

The regulation ratios are:

- 4:1 in opportunity groups and special schools;

- 4:1 and over in local authority nurseries, depending on the age of the child;

- 8:1 in private day nurseries, playgroups and nursery schools;

- 10:1 in nursery schools with trained teachers and nurses;

- 13:1 in nursery classes and early years units; and

- 30:1 in reception classes (but in practice, much less).

STAFFING AND TRAINING

A significant divide in training levels exists between early care (0–4 years) and early education (4–5 years) personnel. Only 20 per cent of care personnel, mostly in opportunity groups and day nurseries, have a university or tertiary qualification. In fact, the majority of childcare workers – and many classroom assistants in the reception classes – do not have formal training, except for some hours required by a few local authorities. On the whole, childcare staff have poor conditions of work, are paid much less than the average wage and do long hours with little access to training or support. The government has recognized these concerns: it introduced a national minimum wage which did improve the wage situation, and is attempting to bring coherence to the patchwork of recruitment approaches and training schemes. Teachers in the education sector are better paid and protected. They have a four-year university or teacher training qualification, some with a specialization in early years education.

The challenges of integrating all the different levels of 'practitionership' into a relatively smooth set of working relationships within each children's centre will not be easy. Human beings are territorial, and part of a person's territory is their knowledge. One aspect of knowledge on which most people will agree, if they think about it, is that all knowledge is partial – as Popper would have said, 'ultimately all systems of knowledge are falsifiable', but this does not mean that when knowledge at its highest level is falsified, that everybody on earth has to discard an existing belief system. Most systems of belief work quite well. Even creationism as opposed to evolutionary theory probably works quite well, as long as one is surrounded by people of a like mind and as long as no one asks for evidence in support of creationism.

Is there a lesson here? Should training start with a practitioner's views or belief systems? Should these be made more articulate? Should questions be asked such as: 'Did it work and in what circumstances. Where is the evidence for this belief? What counts as evidence in early learning? Are there better ideas around?' Do these ideas apply to most children? Do our theories allow us to predict what we are likely to find in most early years centres? Do we know enough about the processes of learning in young children? If we do not, how can we extend our own learning?

These procedures can be compared with a range of actions linked with obedience to a set of rules hatched out by people in power. People in power are always trying to 'push things through' by adopting the simplest method. Most simplified top-down edicts fail because they are over simplified and do not apply to most children. They do, however, waste a lot of adult and child time.

One of the main motivations behind the Froebel Project was to try to turn a corner in relation to professional knowledge and to pursue a more articulate pedagogy.

COURSES FOR AN EXPANSION OF TRAINING IN THE 1960s

When it was believed , in the 1960s, that colleges of education would have to run courses suitable for a large-scale expansion of the early years, it was realized what we had and what we did not have.

'Child development' can be roughly broken down into physical development, social and emotional development, and intellectual (or cognitive) development, which includes language.

PHYSICAL DEVELOPMENT

A lot was known about physical development, health and hygiene. Most people in England will know about the pioneering work of the Macmillan sisters working in the East End of London in the early twentieth century. Of course things change: in their day a great problem was under nourishment, now it is obesity. Obesity can, of course, and often does, go hand in hand with being under-nourished. In the Macmillan sisters' day, children needed fresh air; children still do, but in built-up areas there is so much lead in the air that it may have the effect of *decreasing* intelligence. Fresh air and nourishing food is still important for young children, but the air around the Froebel Project children's home area was polluted to such an extent that it could have been called 'emphysema mile'. Anyway, by the 1960s there was sufficient information on early physical development to run courses in colleges of education.

It always comes as a bit of a shock to realize how recent it is that parents could confidently expect their babies and infants to survive. Looking back on my childhood, there seemed to be more of a focus on physical wellbeing rather than other forms of functioning. I loved reading from the age of 4, and I battled with my Victorian grandmother for years: I wanted to read and she wanted me to walk around the block. Even today if anyone suggests walking around the neighbourhood just for the sake of the walk, my heart sinks.

SOCIAL AND EMOTIONAL DEVELOPMENT

When improvements in physical development, health and hygiene came about during the early twentieth century, parents were able to invest more emotional capital in their offspring. Reflecting this general improvement in society, researchers were able to investigate social and emotional development. The greatest of these innovators were Freud, Bowlby, Winnicot, Erickson, Anthony Storr, Susan Isaacs and many others, providing plenty of source material for teaching child development practices.

INTELLECTUAL DEVELOPMENT

In the 1960s and early 1970s, when intellectual (cognitive) development in children from 2 to 5 was examined, it was realised that very little was known about positive thinking in the early years. Piaget and his thousands of collaborators all over the western world had illuminated knowledge of infancy – from birth to about 2 – and knowledge of primary school children. Why, therefore, had Piaget been so unsuccessful with his studies of children from 2 to 5? Why did he not discover the positive patterns of behaviour which children of those ages were using in their exploration of the world?

One reason may be because he changed his method of study. Originally he closely observed the spontaneous behaviour of each of his own children. He then compared his observations and, most importantly, his interpretations of those observations with the findings of other researchers. He had, for instance, a detailed correspondence with Susan Isaacs over her Malting House School observations and interpretations.

At a certain point he shifted from this successful observational method to a different method, usually called a cross-classificatory approach. This meant that he tested older children to see whether they had understood certain ideas. He wanted to see whether 6- and 7-year-olds, for example, were able to conserve number, quantity and space, whether they could classify and put things in different kinds of order. Unfortunately he used younger children for purposes of comparison, so the literature on the intellectual development of children from 2 to 5 became laden with odious comparisons.

The odious comparisons suggested that children's thinking between the ages of 2 and 5 is a kind of disaster area. Young children have been, and still are, most frequently described in terms of what they can *not* do, rather than what they can do. Here are some widespread descriptions of children from two to five: they are 'egocentric', 'pre-operational', 'non-conservers', 'unable to classify' or to 'put things into orders', they are 'idiosyncratic' and they 'flit' from pillar to post. Most research findings before the 1970s suggested that children under 5 were a cognitive mess. This view existed side by side with a growing mass of evidence on the competence, and the unbelievably systematic behaviour, of infants.

The truth is that young children only seem inadequate when testing, or inappropriate questioning, leads to comparisons with older children. In such situations younger children cannot give the right answers because the questions do not match their level of understanding.

In planning courses for the expected expansion of teacher training it was realized that there was a dearth of positive information on intellectual development of children from 2 to 7.

THE START OF A NEW ERA?

Reading about the proposed planned expansion of early years services, there is a serious mismatch between the rhetoric of politicians and the concerns of informed practitioners: practitioners are exploring the meaning of the term 'pedagogy', whereas politicians are not.

The year 2006 may be a turning point in British early education. If successive governments honour the 10-year pledges that are being made now, the increased quantity of integrated early education and care could find itself in a better position compared with the short-term and fragmented objectives of the past. Most of the expansions of the past were not, of course, presented as short-term solutions at the time.

Most of the mission statements and the resources being made available in some communities are welcomed by most people involved in the early years. Whether policies being discussed under the heading of 'Every child counts' can be translated into practice within 10 years is a moot point because of all the differences that exist at the present time. At a basic level, the Qualifications and Curriculum Authority (QCA) has produced a very long glossary in which initials are translated into the names of organizations involved in 'looking after', 'caring for' or 'educating' children in the early years. The early years are littered with organizations which are involved in custodial care right through to the highest level of 'education'.

There are basic arguments going on at present as to whether the early years should cover ages birth to 5 or birth to 7. Each organization has its own training procedures ranging from a few hours to three- and four-year degrees. Training in different domains differs in length and quality of professional expertise. There are consequent differences in salary structures, conditions of work and so on. Murray states a truth:

> As with most changes in government policies the effects of those policies take root in some places and conditions and not in others. Sure Start Children Centres are (already) to be found in Early Excellence Centres, in neighbourhood nurseries and in other settings (2005).

Winter states a reality that new legislation leads to policies being translated into practice in some places and not in others, depending on many factors (Murray, 2005). This is not the place to examine the 'many factors' but, in spite of the pleas for unity of approach, it is the differences which are likely to predominate for some time to come.

The previous incumbent of a relatively new position in government called Minister for Children recently addressed a conference of 1,000 Sure Start workers on the implications of the Green Paper *Every Child Matters*. She said:

> I sometimes genuinely have to pinch myself because I cannot believe our luck. After years and years and years of endless campaigning for good services for children and their families, our time has finally come. We have now moved from an era when children and families were barely at the fringes of politicians' concerns to a time when childcare is really at the heart of the modern welfare state. It is a time when not just the Secretary of State for Education, but the Chancellor, the Prime Minister,

and the Leader of the Opposition are all vying to get into the headlines to demon-strate their commitment to this [new legislation] (www.everychildmatters.gov.uk/publications).

This is true, and it is worth looking at the reasons for such a general acceptance in the face of all the difficulties in implementing such a large-scale reform.

EVERY CHILD MATTERS

The most recent legislation involved in the policy document 'Every Child Matters' (Green Paper, 2003; www.everychildmatters.gov.uk/publications) talked about by the Minister for Children above was, alas, motivated by several tragedies involving young children. These led to widespread condemnation and recrimination of existing forms of organization involved in relation to the early years. All services had failed to spot the terrible plight of Victoria Climbié, who suffered appalling abuse from members of her family who were supposed to be caring for her. They followed a bizarre religious cult which they seemed to think justified their harsh treatment of Victoria. Her death led to an inquiry headed by Lord Laming, who proposed a range of measures leading to the Green Paper 'Every Child Matters'. This can be downloaded online at www.dfes.gov.uk/everychildmatters.

Past inquiries into other deaths had established common threads which led to a failure to intervene early enough to save the children, namely poor co-ordina-tion between services such as Social Services, National Health Service providers and the police; a failure to share information between services; the absence of anyone with a strong sense of accountability; a shortage of workers struggling to cope with an ever-increasing volume of work; poor management; and a lack of effective training. On 12 occasions, over 10 months, opportunities to save Victoria's life were not taken.

It was the lack of co-ordination between disparate services, with terrible conse-quences, that has led to a large reform package called 'Every Child Matters'. It is hoped that existing fragmentation will make way for a unification of services which will make it less likely that children in need will slip through the net. The policies set out in the Green Paper initiates a framework for services that cover children and young people from birth to 19 living in England. The proposed policies are aimed mainly at reducing society's ills by strong-armed measures against a range of deficits in society. There are no references to anything resem-bling quality of mind. There is no use of the term 'pedagogy' by politicians. The features that are being expressed by people in power are their hopes that the new legislation will reduce the numbers of children who experience educational fail-ure, engage in offending or anti-social behaviour, suffer from ill health, or become teenage parents. Once again, as in the 1960s and before, it is hoped that school (now called 'unified early years centres') will be able to compensate for a wide range of ills of society.

The Green Paper contains hopes of improvement using recent terminology on education. Hopes are for an increase in key stage standards. It is hoped there will be a reduction in poverty as a result of low income measures. It is hoped there will be a reduction in young offenders and unintended pregnancies in those under 18.

It is acknowledged that the UK had a low starting point in the telling sentence 'We need to do more to catch up with other countries' (Green Paper, p. 2). 'Every Child Counts' appears to be a good thing, but the language used shows that it is, once again, a response to crisis at a basic level. Sure Start is part of a Foundation Stage which, in turn, is part of 'Every Child Counts'.

Overall, England is still a country where life chances are unequal. The main mission statement of 'Every Child Counts' is to ensure that every child has the chance to fulfil his or her potential by reducing levels of educational failure, ill health, substance misuse, teenage pregnancy, abuse and neglect, crime and anti-social behaviour among children and young people. The main aim is to reduce negatives rather than increase positives.

A theme repeated over and over again is that everybody must reach their full potential because too many people do not. Who knows what a person's full potential is? Are people born with a potential that is either realized or not? This would amount to an acceptance of a fixed IQ under another name 'full potential'. This is a poor concept for practitioners who are supposed to bring about a change for the better. There is a strong possibility that potential is created. In the Froebel Project, potential was created in parents and children through the nature of what was being investigated. 'Change, for the better' itself was being studied and evaluated. Most people know that, even at the adult level, or in relation to self, very few people are able to do their job as successfully in the first year as subsequently. People tend to become good or better at what they spend their time doing.

The Government has set out to improve 'outcomes' through Sure Start, and through raising school standards in the Foundation stage of education. Sure start children's Centres are to be created in each of the country's 20 per cent most deprived neighbourhoods. The new legislation amounts to substantial 'positive discrimination' in favour of (so-called) deprived people in deprived neighbourhoods. These centres will combine nursery education, family support, employment advice and childcare and health services on one site. There will be provision of full service, extended schools which will be open beyond school hours to provide breakfast clubs and after-school clubs, and childcare. Health and social care support will also be provided on site.

SUPPORTING PARENTS AND CARERS

The government intends to put supporting parents and carers at the heart of its approach to improving children's lives, where support is needed or wanted; £25 million pounds has been made available for this purpose.

There will be targeted and specialist support to parents of children requiring additional support. There will be compulsory action through Parenting Orders as a last resort, where parents are condoning a child's truancy, anti-social behaviour or offending. The direction here would appear to be 'from support to force'.

ADOPTION AND FOSTERING

Through the adoption modernization programme, local authorities are already delivering significant increases in adoption of 'looked-after' children. This Green Paper (see www.everychildmatters.gov.uk/publications) consults on measures to tackle the recruitment and retention challenges in foster care, and to ensure that foster carers have the skills and support they need to care for vulnerable children. The government is seeking suggestions for radical and imaginative ways of encouraging people to become foster carers and ensuring they are valued and recognized.

EARLY INTERVENTION AND EFFECTIVE PROTECTION

Some children will always require extra help because of the particular disadvantages they face. The key to the new legislation is to ensure that children receive services at the first onset of problems to prevent any children slipping through the net. There will be improved information sharing between agencies. This will ensure all local authorities have a list of children in their area, a record of the services each child has had contact with, and the contact details of the relevant professionals who work with them. There will be a single unique identity number, and common data standards on the recording of information.

LEADING OFFICIALS

Every local authority must identify a leading official with responsibility for ensuring that information is collected and shared. This will help towards the development of a common assessment framework across services for children, covering special educational needs, Connexions, and youth offending teams, health and social services. The aim is for basic information to follow the child. One of the main aims of the leading official will be to reduce duplication.

YOUNG PEOPLE'S FUND

There will be the creation of a Young People's Fund with an initial budget of £200 million. This budget will be used for staff and activities for children out of school.

CHILDMINDERS

It has been stated that the decline in childminders has been halted and a competent childminder workforce is not yet trained.

RECENT GAINS

There is evidence that gains have been made recently which increase children's life chances. Babies are healthier through the reduction in parents' smoking. Parents are becoming more confident with fewer mothers suffering from postnatal depression. More breastfeeding helps with early bonding. There are better 'reading' outcomes for children with programmes like Book Start; this is now funded nationally, and there are more children using libraries.

IS SURE START A ONE-STOP-SHOP?

Sure Start is praised as a one-stop-shop where many issues to do with daily lives can be tackled. The Minister for Children said that there was a lot to celebrate: 'In particular,' she suggested, 'let us celebrate the fact that we do now have free part-time nursery education available for every 3- and 4-year-old right across the country' (free at the point of delivery). This amounts to a redistribution of wealth and means that the recommendations of the Plowden Report published 40 years ago in 1967 have, at last, been realized.

Integration between all the services is new, and means and methods of bringing about integration are already being worked out by early years professionals (mainly experienced and highly competent women) who will be able to provide models of improvement unless they are replaced by teams of inexperienced management who will, as has already been seen in hospitals, hold things back.

The Minister for Children stated that Sure Start has developed into a long-term national programme. It is now so popular and so successful that unlike every other targeted programme, which often become stigmatized as they develop, this is one which by popular demand every family in every community wants – although this is a bit of an exaggeration as some families are already protesting that they were not consulted on either the supply or the substance of Sure Start.

THE PRINCIPLES OF SURE START

The Sure Start principles which underpin the programme will hold good as centres mushroom from 500 up to 3,500, but what are those principles? There is the principle about building services around the needs of a child, bringing closer together health, care, education and family support. Education and health are already key partners in the endeavour to building relevant services around the needs of children and the family.

Another principle which has served Sure Start so well is that parents should have a very strong voice, not just a voice that is heard after services are delivered.

Sure Start centres should be managed to ensure that deprived areas have a more generous funding package than those in more advantaged areas where the need is less and the ability for parents to pay some of the services is greater. It is true that privileged families can pay for services at the point of delivery but, as the Froebel Project found out, the needs of privileged parents are not less, just different; advertisements for nannies abound in *Nursery World* and the *Lady*. What was not recognized in the planning of the Froebel Project was the strong desire of privileged parents to join in with the fundamental research aim of the Project. Some privileged parents began to 'search for schemas'. One of the comparison group mothers, who was an architect, greeted the present writer on a second visit with a copy of Piaget's book on space concepts which she had read and was eager to discuss. Her 4-year-old had a large room full of non-cost building materials. Another privileged mother, the wife of an MP, arrived at the project one morning demanding to participate. A project parent immediately handed a microphone over to her – she did have an air of authority which the project parents were just learning to acquire.

QUALIFICATIONS

How can the value and esteem of the professionals who work with children in their early years be advanced? A short answer is through qualifications, stronger career opportunities and more pay. There is a need for continuous professional development. More radically, it requires reformed thinking about what is meant by an 'early years professional'.

Janet Moyles (2006) has already criticized the Direction of Travel (DoT) document as failing to come up with the scale of training that will be required. She warns that 'The vast differentiation in training and background of early years practitioners means that something as potentially huge as EYFS (Early Years Foundation Stage) could prove potentially divisive if someone (or some group) is put in charge who does not understand the current staffing context' (Moyles, 2006, p. 11).

Many problems arise from the new legislation to do with staffing, training and qualifications. However, as Ted Wragg used to say, 'We must not let Mr, Mrs, Miss, Ms or Dr "Ah-but" prevent gains that can be made at this time.' Our goal must be to make working with children an attractive, high-status career, and to develop a more skilled and flexible workforce.

3

Research in Quality Education and Pedagogy

Many studies have shown that early education increases children's later achievements in specifiable ways. This evidence is mainly statistical. However, quality, as inferred from external and quantifiable facts, such as the number of encounters between adult and child, is seldom satisfactory because 'encounters' are not usually examined for any aspect of quality.

Most British studies reveal a conceptual weakness that permeates accounts of education at all levels. Not enough attention is paid to how children learn most effectively and consequently how teachers can teach most effectively. There is plenty of material on an offered curriculum, but hardly anything on how the offered curriculum is received by individual learners. Although there are exhortations from many people outside teaching for teachers to improve the quality of the education they offer, there is an anomalous accompanying denigration of the role of educational theory.

An erroneous idea is constantly being perpetrated, that standards in education can be increased without a concomitant increase in teachers' understanding of the learning process as it occurs in individual learners. Professional advancement necessarily requires the development of a well thought-out pedagogy. Pedagogy is for the teacher what medical knowledge is to the doctor. The problem in Britain is not an absence of excellence in early or primary education; what is lacking is a professional vocabulary that can clearly articulate the nature of excellence. Descriptions of quality must precede attempts to measure it. Measurement without description and conceptual understanding can capture only the organizational, surface or trivial features of situations. Sutton-Smith (1970) suggested that an illuminative theory provides the conceptual cement in which trivial observations can be placed. The co-ordination of trivial examples from children set within an illuminative theory provides useful explanations. It is the power to explain that makes pedagogy so important.

Illuminative educational writing must contain information on the details of learning as well as teaching. Detailed accounts of observation, interpretation, curriculum experimentation and evaluation are badly needed. More teachers could take on the role of teacher/researcher because daily classroom events provide an ongoing source of data that can be professionally interpreted and shared with other teachers. What is needed is more information on the patterns of cognition that children bring to educational situations. What is also needed is more evidence on how children receive or do not receive offered curriculum content. Questions on the nature of 'learning', 'knowing', 'understanding' and 'experiencing' are psychological and pedagogical rather than political, and are of central concern to teachers. They are also of interest to many parents during the years of child rearing.

Bruner (1980) described the ties between conventional psychological research and teaching practice as tenuous and fragile. He wrote that a chasm exists between research findings and classroom observations. He found that research findings arrived at via laboratory experiments had little or no relevance to the classroom. This conclusion points to the desirability of developing more illuminative research with grass-roots in the classroom.

When the researchers in the Oxford study (Bruner 1980) found they could not interpret, to any degree of usefulness, the worthwhileness of what the children were doing, they brought in 'experts' to read transcripts of observed play episodes and to assess them as being either 'complex' or 'simple'. These are external and very general categories of evaluation with little explanatory value. They offer no advance on the evaluations of Susan Isaacs half a century earlier. Susan Isaacs always amalgamated theory, however tenuous, with her observations of young children. By co-ordinating theory and observation, she began to develop a pedagogy of the early years that was not continued because of a general shift in research methodology. Social scientists envied the 'hard-nosed' approach of the so-called 'objective' sciences.

Many writers and researchers, mainly non-British, have pleaded for greater attention to be paid to theoretical notions that inform observation, practice and evaluation.

EVALUATING COGNITIVE GAIN IN EARLY EDUCATION

'The end product of education or schooling is someone who has been improved by what has happened to that person' (Moore, 1982, p. 87). Any general theory of education must start with how improvement might be brought about and how it might be assessed. Educational inquiry does not yet have the status of a science in which clear postulates can be tested for support or refutation. Therefore there is, as yet, no obvious and uncontroversial way of plotting the process of improvement of individuals throughout schooling, particularly in relation to different areas of the curriculum.

Awareness of this problem is dawning. In discussions on accountability and appraisal, teachers and head teachers are asking important questions on the degree to which they can guarantee that individual children, who have been in a class for a year or a primary school for six or eight years, are 'on the inside' of essential or desirable knowledge in relation to the many areas of the curriculum. Although general levels of knowledge can be measured by comparing children with each other on tests, the process of diagnosing the development of conceptual knowledge in individual learners is in its infancy. Finding ways of assessing individual learners could be one of the most exciting aspects of professional development in the years ahead (see Arnold, 2002 and 2003, who has picked up from where the baby biographers such as Darwin and Preyer and many others left off: Darwin, 1877; Preyer, 1882).

From infancy, there are basically two ways in which improvement can be monitored:

- *Summative evaluation* consists of tests given before and after educational programmes. The best-known and most controversial form of summative evaluation is the standardized intelligence test (IQ test). The IQ test was designed within a psychometric rather than a pedagogical framework.

- *Formative evaluations* are descriptions of cognitive advances recorded regularly and usually as an accompaniment to a programme. Formative evaluation requires professional skill in diagnosing concepts or skills in the process of being formed in the learner. The most effective evaluations are where both go on side by side.

Darwin's theories embraced both an heredity and an environmental explanation of intelligence. The environmental aspect has been incorporated into Piaget's theory of the 'functional invariants', which assumes that 'intelligence is adaptation to environmental circumstances' (Elkind, 1969, p. 319). This concept is of particular interest to teachers and will be explored in more detail in Chapter 7. However, it is worth stating that 'intelligence as adaptation to environmental events' may be what the educational process is about, but it is difficult to record the process, much less to evaluate it.

The heredity aspect is of particular interest to testers and to people who would like to gain social control over populations. Standardized tests give a measure of a general standard of a given population. By definition, given the procedures of testing, one section of the population will be below the general standard and one section will be above. This can easily be understood in terms of potatoes on a market stall. Unless buying is highly selective, most potatoes will be around an average size – some will be small, some very small, some large and some very large. However, tiny potatoes are not branded as failures. Whereas on standardized intelligence and attainment tests, children below the norm *are* branded as failures. The very description 'not up to standard' is pejorative.

Standardized tests have items arranged in a hierarchy of difficulty: a child's test results will show where that child is in relation to other testees. For instance, the test results of a group of 6-year-olds may show that some individuals have a mental age above the 6-year-old level and some below. Most of the 6-year-olds in an unbiased sample will produce scores at that level, which is established by 6-year-old's responses to certain test questions. These responses become established as being at a 6-year-old level.

This cross-classificatory view tends to obscure individual improvements. For instance, all children of a given age might be given a standardized reading test two years running. It could be the case that all children tested made a healthy gain in their reading scores between the first and second test. Some children, and frequently the same children, will still be below the average of the total group even though they have improved significantly on their own previous performance. The fundamental tenet of standardized testing is that populations can be categorized in relation to established test norms. Although 'below average' is simply a function of test construction, real causes are sought to account for low scores.

There are two very well-known candidates for blame: the environment and assumed genetic potential. Blaming the environment includes parents as well as the general effects of poverty, such as poor food, poor housing and so on. For many years the aim of a large number of early-education programmes was to educate parents so that they would better educate their children. More recently, teachers have been blamed for low standards. Standards in measurable aspects of the curriculum, as in limited aspects of reading and arithmetic, are rising but a case can be made that they are not rising fast enough for successful competition in world markets.

Historically, tests have been used primarily for selection rather than educational illumination. The original social purpose of standardized tests was to select children on stable and 'measurable' performance criteria for scarce educational resources.

Psychometric and pedagogical concerns have always sat uneasily side by side. IQ tests can be used to measure the starting and end points of different educational treatments, and the treatment that leads to higher scores can be deemed to be a success. Explanations for success, however, can only be at the level of informed hunches because changes in measured scores are only statistics. The researcher who gives reasons for improvement, or lack of it, is expressing informed hunches. The hunches may be true, but they need not be.

Oddly enough, Binet, the inventor of the original standardized intelligence test, the Stanford-Binet Intelligence Scale (Terman and Merrill, 1976), was more sceptical of the value of such tests than many present-day professionals and politicians. He wrote in 1908: 'Our examination of intelligence cannot take account of all those qualities ... attention, will, popularity, perseverance, teachableness and courage which play so important a part in school work, and also in after life; for life is not so much a conflict of intelligence as a struggle between characters' (cited in Brierley, 1987, p. 108).

STABILITY AND CHANGE IN TEST SCORES AND EARLY DEVELOPMENT

In everyday parlance, the definition of the word 'stable' implies a positive judgment. Psychometricians certainly perceive stability of test scores over time as desirable. While scores vary with chronological age, IQ, the measure derived from scores and age should (within the tenets of psychometrics) remain stable. As already mentioned, 'stability' from a tester's point of view means that tests will be highly predictive of future performance. Long-term educational planning would be facilitated if future educational resources could be reliably predicted from the test scores of young children.

However, professional educators, particularly those directing remedial programmes, should not aim at producing stability of test scores. On the contrary, the central aim of education is to bring about cognitive improvement in individual learners. It is incongruous that educational programmes aimed at improvement use intelligence tests that have a built-in bias against change. Test items that produce unwanted variations are discarded. Tests have achieved stability in that IQ does not change much for the majority from the age of 7 or 8. After 10 it is pretty well stable. However, stability of scores is found where there is stability, or no change, in environment.

Education, particularly life-long education, can have a transforming effect on individuals at different stages of their lives. Most evidence of increases in test scores have been as a result of environmental enrichment before the age of 5. However, Bayley and Jones (1937) discovered many years ago that cultural and socio-economic differences are not reflected in baby tests. This may mean that baby tests are not sufficiently refined to detect environmental differences, or it may mean that most babies are potentially sound until privilege or poverty brings about the differences reflected in later test scores. Ordinal scales of infant development based on Piaget's six stages of sensorimotor behaviours have been found to be more sensitive to environmental variation than other standardized baby tests (Uzgiris and Hunt, 1975). Unfortunately, these tests have not been extended beyond infancy and, therefore, they lack the continuity of cross-classificatory IQ tests.

The use of IQ tests is still widespread because formative evaluation of improvement arising from enrichment programmes is more problematical than cross-classificatory testing. A persistent research problem in programmes designed to improve cognitive functioning in young children is how to describe ongoing aspects of improvement. What cannot be measured by tests are fundamental cognitive shifts from early motor and sensory behaviours to later symbolic functioning. The important developmental shift from action to thought is still being worked out at a descriptive level.

Evidence of the effects of environment on early brain development comes from modern biology. There is a 'critical period' which extends for at least the first few years of life (Rose and Chalmers, 1971, p. 247). During this critical period aspects of cognitive functioning, related to experience and symbolic functioning, can be enhanced. It is also likely that the brain will turn out to be a lot more robust than it is made out to be at the moment. Certain functions in the brain can, if injured, be taken over by other parts with no long-lasting bad effects.

Professionals working in early education have a particularly important part to play in the search for pupil understanding between the ages of 2 and 5. These are the ages at which basic concepts are formed. Professional knowledge of 'continuity of learning' cannot fail to be furthered by knowledge of patterns of cognition in children under 5 in that knowledge of early learning illuminates later learning.

RESEARCH AND COMPENSATORY EDUCATION

If someone from another planet were to study research literature on earth in order to find out about early education, they might well conclude that compensatory education of the underprivileged was one sort of human endeavour, and that educational research aimed at finding out more about young children was another, and that the twain never met. This would be largely true. Most compensatory education programmes have consisted solely of ameliorative action that has not illuminated learning or advanced pedagogy.

Twentieth-century research and development has echoes of Owen and Wilderspin (Whitbread, 1975). Very little useful information on high-quality teaching or the processes of children's learning (Owen's concerns) has arisen from compensatory programmes. Modern compensatory programmes share Wilderspin's motivation, summed up in the first line of a chapel hymn: 'Rescue the perishing'. Concomitant with the rescue motive in education is political expediency and social control.

In the 1960s, the purpose of many Headstart and Urban Aid programmes was to compensate for supposed defects in homes. The 'rescue' motive was still apparent, but the children were rescued from inadequate homes and parenting rather than the streets. It was generally accepted that IQ gain as a result of these programmes would provide the best form of evidence for the environmentalists' cause. However, as a result of the over-hastily produced evaluations of these programmes of the past, professionals learnt not to rely too much on standardized test results and IQ is no longer the sole criterion of improvement.

Some educationalists think that improved IQ scores, or scores of any description, should not be an important criterion at all when considering the provision of early education. Blackstone (1971), for instance, argues that early education provision should be related to the needs of parents and children. She argues that this is socially and politically safer than the criteria used for both the selection of disadvantaged populations and the evaluations by which compensatory programmes are judged.

Debates on the proportion of intelligence that is innate or the results of environment have been found to be arid and socially divisive. A truce exists at present in that both are acknowledged to be important. Where children are 'under-functioning', professionals and parents working together can facilitate the growth of intelligence during a period of maximum plasticity.

PIAGET AND ISAACS: THEIR CONTRIBUTION TO PEDAGOGY

Piaget's writings had the most influence on educational research during the last century. Almost all his studies were directed towards detecting a match or mismatch between levels of understanding in children and concepts from different areas of the curriculum. The greatest progress has been made in 'matching' curriculum content with cognitive form in mathematics and science. Constructivist research into early literacy has also produced new information on young children's understanding of language.

As an epistemologist, Piaget asked questions central to education, such as 'What is knowledge?' and 'How do we come to know?'. Unfortunately, Piaget abandoned the research method he used so successfully while studying infancy. Initially he searched for the invariant features of child thought rather than for individual differences. He interpreted detailed and continuing observations of infants within available theory, mainly his own. By adopting this method he was able to document patterns of thought in infants from birth to 2 and, later, in children from 6 to 11. He did not, however, trace even an elementary map of invariant forms of thought in children aged 2 to 5. One reason for this is that he shifted from formative evaluation, which consisted of systematic and ongoing observations of individuals, to cross-classificatory test situations where groups of children of different ages were asked the same questions. Consequently, young children were persistently asked questions that were too difficult, and their answers were at an earlier level than those deemed to be correct (Elkind and Flavell, 1969, p. 43).

Asking children from 2 to 5 'concrete-operational' test questions produced evidence that they could not conserve, categorize or put things in order. The large databank of wrong answers or, more accurately, partial answers, led to the idea that young children are cognitively incompetent. Deficit descriptions were applied to young children, which have persisted. It is said that they are egocentric, idiosyncratic, exhibit static or pre-operational thinking and 'flit from pillar to post'. In literature interpreting Piaget, such deficit descriptions are presented as characteristic of young children's thinking. The degree to which this view persists can be seen, via Google or other search engines, of the general description of 'pre-operational' still applied to young children. Most American universities are still teaching teachers about the deficits of young children. Teachers are not helped by such descriptions in that the process of 'matching' suitable curriculum content to forms of thought requires knowledge of what children know rather than what they do not know (Wynne Harlen's *Match and Mismatch*, 1977, is still the most advanced publications on this theme). Interestingly enough, having established the positive characteristics of children's thinking from the age of 6 or 7, somewhat at the expense of younger children, almost all Piaget's later studies were concerned with match or mismatch in key areas of the curriculum. Current national curriculum documents reflect both the substance and the importance of his findings.

Susan Isaacs was the first researcher to challenge the usefulness of Piaget's deficit view of cognition in young children. In the 1920s, she used theories derived from many sources in order to analyse children's thinking in the Malting House School. She co-ordinated observation of children with psychological theory and subsequently introduced the children to worthwhile curriculum content. This was followed by analyses of the children's responses. The success of this approach of co-ordinating observation, theory, teaching and evaluation can be measured by the continuing demand for Susan Isaacs' books over half a century.

Isaacs and Piaget had great respect for each other. They visited each other's schools and were creatively critical of each other's ideas. Although they both observed young children closely, they drew different conclusions on early cognitive competence as they adopted different viewing positions. Put briefly, when assessment is carried out from a top-down point of view, negative conclusions arise because younger children are seen as less competent than older children. A bottom-up perspective, taken and retained by Susan Isaacs, is founded on initial positive descriptions of cognitive competence in young children. When the more advanced thinking of older children is analysed, cognitive advances are apparent, but the advances do not detract from earlier competence.

The bottom-up, or prospective, approach to assessment is appropriate for teachers in that it leads to the identification of the positive aspects of thought at different ages and stages as they appear during development. As these are identified, steps can be taken to enrich or extend through education. The top-down, or retrospective, view identifies the positive characteristics of older children by reference to earlier deficits. This issue is of considerable interest to present-day teachers, given the current emphasis on assessing children's achievements at different ages.

Recently, some researchers have challenged the view that young children cannot 'decentre', that is, that they cannot understand situations from points of view other than their own. Where test situations have been designed to relate to the concerns and experiences of young children, it has been found that they can decentre (Donaldson, 1978; Light, 1979). In other words, in familiar situations, the young child may not be as 'egocentric' as he or she appears to be when confronted, for instance, with abstract spatial relationships between mountains seen from various points of view (Piaget and Inhelder, 1956, pp. 209–45).

The findings of these studies, while important, mainly serve to push back the age at which there is evidence of concrete-operational thinking as opposed to pre-operational thinking. What seems to be lacking is evidence of systematic behaviours that characterize the positive thinking of children between the ages of 2 and 5. This search requires a 'natural history' approach of observation and interpretation. Although this was bypassed for a long time in favour of the 'cross-sectional' approach, there is now a return to 'illuminative research' (Dockrell and Hamilton, 1980).

TEACHER AS RESEARCHER

A teacher of young children stands as much chance of detecting new knowledge as a researcher who is not a teacher; however, the teacher must have an explanatory theory within which his or her observations can be interpreted.

Traditionally, teachers have been placed in a passive position in relation to research. They are frequently studied as objects rather than treated as active participants in research projects. They are also expected to apply in the classroom research solutions engendered elsewhere. This situation need not be accepted because educational research problems are those encountered by teachers in classrooms inhabited by children, and there is no reason why teachers should not play a more active role in furthering professional knowledge. A more immediate reason for the teacher becoming teacher/researcher is the present lack of resources for fundamental research. Do-it-yourself in the home and garden is a booming business. Do-it-yourself in school could generate a new dynamism, particularly in the light of the proposed expansion of early years provision.

As already suggested, some forms of research have valid purposes and methods but are not particularly useful for teachers working, as they do, within particular constraints of time, space and circumstances. Research problems likely to sharpen professional concepts are those to do with pedagogy, the curriculum and timing. Timing governs whether there is a match or mismatch between an offered curriculum and understanding in the learner. Teachers need to advance their own theory and to become their own experts for various reasons:

1 To increase professional knowledge of children.

2 To assist the process of accountability that requires an articulate rather than an intuitive professional knowledge.

3 In order to communicate more effectively with parents who now want to know more than hitherto about what their children are being taught, how they are being taught and whether their children are working at an appropriate level. These three parental concerns embrace pedagogy, the curriculum and timing – the very issues listed by teachers as being the most important issues to be investigated in future research (Cane and Schroeder, 1970).

The national curriculum clearly defines what is meant by a broad, balanced and differentiated curriculum to which all children will be entitled. This means that teachers can spend less time inventing a curriculum and more time than hitherto on 'fleshing-out' broad areas of study with appropriate content (this is pursued further in Chapter 7).

More attention can now be given to 'how' the curriculum can best be delivered. 'Delivery' is different from the 'delineation' of curriculum areas, which is different again from 'displaying' what is on offer. Display, for the illumination of parents and governors, for instance, will probably involve the selection and co-ordination of programmes, the organization of school time, class time and pupil time. The delineation of programmes of study is now out of the teacher's hands. Display will require a logical or sequential organization of subject-matter. The delivery of the curriculum and formative evaluation of what children have actually received from what is offered will remain the central concerns of the teacher. A more conscious and articulated pedagogy can be expected to help teachers to be more aware of how to extend children's thinking with worthwhile curriculum content and how to evaluate outcomes.

Over the last 30 years there has been a shift in emphasis in parent–professional relationships. Early studies documented the psychological benefits to parent or child as a result of involvement in early education. In the 1980s, in the UK, parents were given considerable political power within the educational system, which still exists today.

4

Towards a Constructivist Pedagogy

PEDAGOGICAL MODELS

As with most words, the term 'pedagogy' has shifted over the years. In ancient Greece it was originally used to describe an adult (usually a slave) taking a young master to school. More recently it has been given the bland meaning of 'the art and science of teaching'. More specifically it has referred to *how* children are taught. The curriculum has determined what is taught. As Clark points out, 'today the term "pedagogy" has taken on new meaning. Now, with many schools using active inquiry techniques, the term "pedagogy" is not just used in relation to passive methods' (1999, www.nwlink.com/~donclark/hrd/history/history.html).

By 'passive methods' he means 'programmed' teaching and learning, to be discussed later in this chapter.

The focus in this book is towards the development of constructivist pedagogy as it can be applied in early education. Constructivism embraces all the features of Earwaker's (1973, pp. 39–59) most complete definition of education, and contains an elaborate system of concepts on how children learn and, therefore, how teachers might best teach. The word 'pedagogy' is not as widely used in the UK as it is throughout Europe. Stukat (1976), reviewing European research into pre-school, concluded that Continental researchers are more influenced by educational theory than their British counterparts, in that reference is usually made to the psychological and educational theories that have guided the choice of the contents and methods of the programmes.

All teachers have pedagogy or, more accurately, a cluster of pedagogical notions. These may be held consciously or unconsciously. During the course of a school day, different pedagogical approaches are required. Crowd control in the playground requires one approach, an individual tutorial requires another. Some school situations may merely require a custodial role or a managerial role.

A teacher's pedagogy permeates his or her thinking on practically every educational issue, from the most general to the most specific.

Weikart, in his High/Scope Perry Project (1972), evaluated three pedagogical models by outcome and process. From a purely measurement point of view, leaving out values, he found that 'different kinds of treatment ... provide little or no evidence that one kind is better than another as long as age and duration of treatment is held constant' (Brown, 1978, p. 33). The three pedagogies investigated by Weikart correspond to Earwaker's (1973) analysis of different levels of education:

1 Child-centred (Earwaker's concept B).

2 Programmed (Earwaker's concept C).

3 The open-framework (Earwaker's concept D) and Weikart's implementation in Ypsilanti correspond to a 'cognitive-developmental' or 'constructivist pedagogy' as it had developed up to that time.

Weikart admits to backing the cognitive-developmental, open framework model. He, along with many others, thought that constructivism must be the way ahead. By criteria other than the standardized measurement of end-products, this probably remains the case. As already mentioned, 'intelligence as adaptation' is at the heart of constructivism as well as life in general, but intelligence as an IQ score is what can most easily be measured (Elkind, 1969). As most important aspects of human functioning elude measurement, the choice between pedagogies is between systems of values rather than measured outcomes.

Earwaker and Weikart both agree that custodial care (concept A) is inappropriate for any endeavour that aspires to be educational. Weikart suggests that in such programmes adults act as caretakers; their responsibility is to 'mind' or 'look after' or 'take care of' children for their own good as the adult sees it, and such programmes have minimal educational value.

Having disposed of custodial care as a candidate for serious consideration, Weikart divides functionally retarded children of 3 and 4 years of age among the other three programmes: child-centred, programmed and constructivist. Two teachers were assigned by their own choice and preference to each programme. The children were taught as a group every morning and a tutorial was given to each child in his own home for 90 minutes every other week in the same style as the school programme.

CHILD-CENTRED PEDAGOGY

This model, according to Stukat (1976), is the pedagogy most widespread in Europe and the UK. It may also be the most widespread in the USA, but it is difficult to find evidence on this. Weikart sums up this approach as 'child initiates, teacher responds'. Within this model, teachers focus on social and emotional growth. Aims are vague, intuitive and very broad. There are many references to 'the development of the whole child'. Weikart points out that these aims reflect positive values in society such as independence, creativity, self-discipline and good peer relations.

A 'child-centred' pedagogy has its roots in a progressive movement that views the pupil with respect and that regards him or her as a unique individual to be kept happy and interested. It is assumed, without being very explicit, that the pupil's stage of development entitles him or her to certain treatments that correspond with his or her development. The aims of 'child-centredness' can be implemented, but it is difficult to evaluate improvements or outcomes resulting from this pedagogical approach.

PROGRAMMED PEDAGOGY

This consists of teacher-centred pedagogy where 'teacher initiates and child responds'. Weikart is particularly critical of this type of programme. He writes: 'The program developers show little respect for traditional education at any level ... these curricula tend to be rigidly structured, with the teacher dominating the child and with a heavy emphasis on convergent thinking' (1972, p. 32). The child is expected to give correct answers in the right manner and to learn through repetition and drill.

WEIKART'S EVALUATION OF DIFFERENT PEDAGOGIES

In the constructivist programme (Earwaker's concept D), the programme is worked out by the teacher, not by a programmer. Because it is assumed that learning comes about through the direct action and personal experience of the child, the teacher attempts to focus on underlying processes of thinking or cognition. 'Her task ... is to find ways in which to help children to get to know things better ... to diagnose which knowledge, or form of knowledge, will most immediately help in the structuring of children's experiences' (Wilson, 1969, p. 114).

Weikart (1972, p. 35) describes the main characteristics of the constructivist approach as follows:

These curricula [pedagogy and curriculum content] are based upon a theory of child development, the most popular is that of Piaget ... The learning process, structured by the teacher ... is usually paced by the child with the teacher attempting to 'match' provision and stimuli to the child's needs and interests. In general, provision and interactions are organized to accomplish cognitive and language development based on a coherent theory of intellectual development. An open framework is provided by the teacher as a context within which she develops a specific program for the children in her classroom.

At the end of the first year of the Weikart experiment, all three programmes showed substantial IQ gains which were uniformly sustained at the end of the second year. This led Weikart to conclude that it did not seem to matter from a measurement point of view which pedagogy was employed, as long as staff motivation was high. Staff knew they were taking part in a research venture and each, presumably, wanted the children in their programme to do well.

THE CHILD-CENTRED PROGRAMME

At the end of the third year there was a drop in the IQs of the child-centred group. This 'wash-out' effect, found in other studies, has led to criticisms of this pedagogical approach. Perhaps there was too much concentration on 'process' and not enough on 'content'. In a compellingly interesting account, Weikart (1972) re-examines some background features of the child-centred programme and highlights issues that beset most real-life experiments but which are seldom reported.

In the middle of the first year, the child-centred class had to move from their building and were relocated near the constructivists. This arrangement interfered with their programme but, more disturbingly, they realized how many visitors the constructivists were receiving. The child-centred team suspected that they were merely a control group. They became depressed; staff began to arrive late and were frequently ill. These motivational factors rather than the difference in pedagogy could have accounted for the third-year losses in test scores.

PROGRAMMED LEARNING

The teachers in this programme also had problems. Weikart described them as working hard and diligently but they worked separately, they did not consult with the director and they were too detached from the children. Both teachers became extremely involved with the content of the programme because this was what they were concentrating on.

THE CONSTRUCTIVIST PROGRAMME

The problems of the constructivist team are the most interesting of all from the point of view of advancing pedagogy. One of the teachers was described as 'brand new' and 'confident'. She was warm and concerned for the children and appeared to pick up the basic ideas of the programme very quickly. The other teacher had been very successful in a different setting but, although willing, was finding difficulties with the constructivist model.

Although both worked hard, they remained too rigid in the implementation of plans. Being new to Piagetian theory would account for their rigidity, in that knowledge has to be assimilated before it can be applied successfully: 'Insecurity in knowledge leads to rigidity in teaching' (DES, 1983). They had not taken their knowledge 'beyond competence to fun'.

GENERAL RESULTS OF THE WEIKART EXPERIMENT

The pedagogical implications of the final results are not clear. They all worked, if a short-term increase in IQ is the main criterion. The long-term results of all of the children showed that when they were aged 15 and then 21 they were ahead of control children in a variety of important ways. The programmes were deemed to be cost-effective, in that fewer children who had early education needed expensive remedial help later. They stayed at school longer and therefore achieved useful qualifications which increased their earning power. They became contributing members of society (Schweinhart and Weikart, 1981).

The Weikart experiment is best thought of as a striking and instructive social experiment where an attempt was made to apply different pedagogies and to record results. Beilin (1972) suggests that it is not a scientific experiment in the true sense because in a real-life educational enterprise it would not be possible to control crucial variables. Weikart himself reflects a dilemma: he remains critical of programmed learning on the grounds of values in spite of IQ gains; he retains constructivist hopes even though the objective results were equivocal and problematical.

ILLUMINATIVE RESEARCH HELD BACK BY DEFICIT THEORY

As there is very little evidence of a deepening professional understanding in the Sylva et al. (1986) report, particularly on the 'plan, do, review' aspects, it will be useful to examine the comprehensive manual for teachers arising from the famous High/Scope project in Ypsilanti (Hohmann et al., 1979). It is presumed that the manual is used in High/Scope training to 'flesh-out' details of children's learning. The manual is useful and informative in many ways. It is clear that the High/Scope teachers are experienced in that they suggest useful curriculum extensions following observations. However, there is a discrepancy between their accounts of children's behaviour and the explanations they abstract from existing deficit theory. The manual demonstrates that much existing theory is holding back rather than enabling advancements in early education. For example, 'Tania put wheels on a stick and spun them round. Mike stuck sticks into every hole on a wheel and called it a "flower"' (Hohmann et al., 1979, p. 244).

Following this type of example, familiar to many teachers and parents, Hohmann and colleagues searched for illumination from the literature, which gave information on 'pre-operational' thinking where the focus is on what children do not know or understand. Having presented the 'party line' on deficits, the authors make skilled and practical suggestions on how children can transform materials by performing different actions on them. This positive aspect of constructivism could have been developed within the High/Scope programme, but urgencies developed because of time passing and because of the Westinghouse Corporation threatening to switch funds to 'genetic determination'.

The Froebel Project findings given in Chapters 5 and 6 illustrate an interesting difference between Tania's spinning wheel and Mike's flower. The diagnoses of schematic differences lead to differentiated and meaningful curriculum extensions. Tania's 'spinning' wheel would appear to be a working model of something that *rotates*, and rotators have different functional effects. Mike's 'flower' is an expression of a different type of schema, in that it has a fixed configuration. Different curriculum extensions, therefore, can be usefully geared to different concepts which are being explored by children. These different concepts (or schemas) are revealed in the differential use of materials. The relationship between action and the effects of action is a central concept of constructivism.

In the High/Scope manual, teachers endeavoured to increase children's consciousness of the transformations they had made on materials. They did this by talking with the children about what they were doing. For instance, one teacher said: 'Oh, I see, you're taking a straight pipe cleaner and bending it into a circle and then you are twisting the ends together'. Here, as Forman and Fosnot point out, 'both the initial and final states are labeled as well as the procedure of transformation' (1982, p. 207). This intervention is positive in that it elaborates verbally on what the child is doing; it is employing the principle of helping the child to become more conscious of the 'doing'.

In Piaget's writings on space are suggestions that the child with the pipe-cleaner might be interested in transforming a line into a closed, two-dimensional curve. If this is so, there are specific curriculum implications stemming from such observations.

In the High/Scope manual, levels of understanding are diagnosed accurately, but only where the characteristics of thought are already known, as in 'concrete-operational' thinking. New patterns of positive thought are not identified. This results in an over-emphasis on acceleration towards later and recognizable cognitions. More detailed information is needed on the positive aspects of thought in children under 5, so that these can be extended.

TOWARDS THE DEVELOPMENT OF CONSTRUCTIVISM

CONSTRUCTIVISM AND CHILD-CENTREDNESS

There is a close relationship between well-run child-centred and constructivist programmes. It could be said that constructivists are child-centred teachers who are trying to become more conscious and more theoretically aware of what is involved in the process of 'coming to know'. Constructivists are interested in the processes by which children construct their own knowledge.

Unreflective child-centredness has led to the false belief that every child requires a unique educational programme. Constructivist teachers know that many children share similar cognitive concerns. Teachers who have taught 6-year-olds, for instance, will know that it is not unusual for over half the class to have reading to an adult at the top of their agenda. During this period of maximum motivation many aspects of reading can be discussed with groups as well as with individuals. In programmes where the focus is on a one-way transmission of information, teachers find it difficult to advance their knowledge of child development because so much time is taken up with the content to be transmitted. It is easier for child-centred teachers to make theoretical advances because listening to children is central to their pedagogy. Stukat (1976) characterized child-centred pedagogy as follows:

1 Staff had broad objectives that were not explicitly formulated and which emphasized general personality development rather than training in narrow skills.

2 The curriculum embraced free play, social events, creativity and activity linked with interest. Adaptation of tasks to the child's maturational level was stressed.

3 Certain recurring features gave a regular rhythm to the day. The first hour was usually devoted to free play or some optional activity, such as drawing, modelling and handicraft or doll play. This was followed by discussion in groups, story-telling, singing and acting. Discussion was usually on a topic of current interest, for instance, Christmas, traffic, food or being ill. A typical pre-school programme included frequent study trips (1976, pp. 22–3). This general description applies to most nursery schools and classes in the UK.

Bruce (1987) shows how research evidence from Bruner, Kellmer-Pringle, Piaget and Vygotsky supports what have been traditions in early childhood. She suggests that the way ahead is for teachers in early education to have a 'better conceptual articulation of what good early childhood education is, with appropriate assessment and evaluation which does not cut across its valuable traditions' (1987, p. 182).

A constructivist knows that experience of teaching is necessary but not sufficient for professional advancement. There is a great difference between 'know-how' and consciousness of 'know-why'. Volpe (1981, pp. 41–51) suggests that an ideal teacher is one who combines practical 'know-how' with the conceptual understanding which can come only from study and reflection. There are indications that, in spite of the politically motivated, anti-theoretical *Zeitgeist* of the present time, many teachers of young children wish to evolve from intuitive knowledge towards a more articulate system of professional understandings. Conferences designed to advance pedagogical skills are as packed as those designed to give practical help without pedagogical underpinning.

THE CONSTRUCTIVIST TEACHER

Within constructivist pedagogy, the teacher seriously considers what the child brings to the learning situation as well as what he or she wishes to transmit. Because the teacher observes children closely and attempts to evaluate their valid contributions to the negotiation of meaning, the teacher is able to accumulate deep understanding of stage levels of cognition in children as well as other aspects of development. There are other advantages for the constructivist teacher. Within limits determined by values and theoretical notions, each teacher creates his or her unique programme, which engenders commitment because it is self-generated. Teachers who are intrinsically motivated generate considerable enthusiasm.

To a constructivist, the process of learning consists of an active construction of knowledge. The teacher, therefore, must arrange things so that knowledge is actively constructed and not simply copied. One problem arising from an open-framework form of organization is that it may be 'invisible' to a casual observer (Bernstein, 1974b). For instance, to the uninformed observer, early writing may appear to be mere scribble or a mass of mistakes. Research into children's writing development, however, shows that children as young as 3 are systematically testing out hypotheses on the nature of print and the process of writing (Ferreiro and Teberosky, 1982; Worthington and Carruthers, 2003). Because the teacher plans according to observed developmental levels of children, procedures can be used effectively with children of varying abilities and from diverse ethnic and socio-economic backgrounds.

Children's achievements also need to be construed conceptually, not simply perceived. Parents who find it difficult to understand what is going on in school during brief visits need information and explanation. In a stimulus–response situation, for instance, children may be copying the teacher's writing from the blackboard. The educational value may be minimal, but the product will be visible and will appear to be correct. Parents who are not informed of the research basis for certain approaches to teaching may find the appearance of correctness desirable.

Teachers of young children who are working with parents need refined professional constructs. The concepts of constructivist theory, such as 'action', 'schema', 'assimilation', 'accommodation', 'stages', 'match' and so on, can be thought of as working hypotheses which can illuminate the learning of young children during the process of 'coming to know'.

GENETIC EPISTEMOLOGY: THE SOURCE OF CONSTRUCTIVISM

Piaget developed the discipline 'genetic epistemology'. This deals with the development of knowledge. Constructivism concerns itself with the processes by which knowledge evolves in the learner. Piaget's work has illuminated cognitive structures in children from the age of 5 or 6 and in infants. Most professionals are familiar with terms such as 'permanence of the object', 'classification', 'seriation', 'conservation of length, area, volume, weight' and so on. Little is known about the course of cognitive development in children from 2 to 5; there must be stages from lesser knowledge to more complete and effective knowledge that are not yet known. Teachers in early education have a great opportunity to embark on a 'do-it-yourself' identification exercise, on how the children they teach construct knowledge.

Piaget (1969) claims that, at every stage, a child assimilates perceived content to cognitive structures. Cognitive structures should not be thought of as empty baskets labelled with the names of particular structures such as *one-to-one correspondence*. Neither should particular content be thought of as having the cognitive characteristics of the cognitive structure. For instance, 'six eggs and six egg cups' may be assimilated into a *one-to-one relationship* at a certain stage, but at an earlier stage, given the opportunity, these objects would be systematically dropped in order to inspect the trajectory and point of arrival. Later, the cost of free-range versus battery eggs might be assimilated to still other concepts and values. External objects do not have cognitive structure. Cognitive structure is a feature of mind. Environmental content either can or cannot be assimilated into developing cognitive structures. To the constructivist, the description 'structuring the environment' is a misnomer. Environments can and must be organized to enhance learning, but 'structuring' is essentially a biological/psychological feature of mind.

All the constructivist ideas introduced in this chapter are discussed in depth in Piaget's work. They are introduced briefly here because they were the conceptual tools used by the professionals in the Froebel Project. Meanings will be elaborated and illustrated within specific situations in Chapters 4, 5 and 6.

ACTION

Piaget approved of 'new methods of education', by which he meant constructivist pedagogy as opposed to traditional methods. He noted that almost all the great theoreticians in the history of pedagogy have 'caught a glimpse' of the central feature of successful learning that is 'the active participation of the learner'. What William James, Dewey, Baldwin, Bergson and many others have in common with Piaget is the idea of action: 'The life of the mind is a dynamic reality and intelligence, a real and constructive activity' (Piaget, 1971b, pp. 139–46).[1]

The associated notion (at the heart of Piaget's theories) that 'thought' is 'internalized action' has been slow to be adopted as a research hypothesis, probably because it is difficult to test.[2] Although a start has been made in mapping out the relationships between action and thought in controlled experiments, the progression has not yet been explored within an early-education setting (see Chapter 6 for evidence of the developmental route 'from action to dynamic thought').

STAGES

Most writers who describe Piaget's theories give a great deal of space to the 'sensorimotor' stage of development, which lasts from birth to approximately 18 months. This detailed account is usually followed by a very short section on the deficits of children's thinking from the age of 2 to 6 – the so-called preoperational stage of development. This is typically followed by a detailed description of the positive characteristics of the concrete-operational stage of development, which lasts from approximately 6 to 11 years. The unequal attention given in the literature to these three broad stages of cognitive development reflects the paucity of existing knowledge of children from 2 to 5. Schwebel and Raph summarize this situation:

> Between two years and seven years is the stage of pre-operational thought during which the change from sensorimotor to operational thought is gradually prepared. The pre-operational period is usually negatively characterized by lack of reversibility, a lack of decentration and the absence of stable, quantitative constants. (1974, p. 46)

Opinions vary about when the so-called pre-operational stage begins and ends. Most writers, particularly mathematicians, regard the emergence of 'one-to-one correspondence' as the beginning of a cognitive renaissance after the dark ages of pre-operationalism. The positive characteristics of thought between 2 and 5 have been discussed in general terms in the literature. However, detailed documentation is lacking of developmental increments in thinking and behaviour typical of studies on infants from birth to 18 months.

The end of the sensorimotor stage is heralded by 'symbolic functioning', although sensorimotor behaviour persists to some degree right through life, particularly while new skills, such as learning to drive a car or to ski, are being acquired. Many skills begin with sensorimotor action, although internalization of action is speeded up by verbal (symbolic) instruction.

During its first months, a child has certain elementary motor behaviours such as sucking, banging, looking, smelling, waving and so on. Each of these behaviours, when applied to objects, brings sensory feedback. Banging on the table produces an interesting sound similar to banging on a chair and different from banging on a cushion. A child's understanding of the relationship between his or her motor actions and the sensory or perceptual feedback that follows is central to the constructivist view of learning.

At the stage of symbolic functioning, it is not just the relationship between motor action and effects that give information. 'Internalized actions' lead to transformations on material and persons. Feedback from action assisted by 'thought' suggests that the thinking is either sufficient or that it needs to be modified. For instance, at a sensorimotor level a child may fit together 10 hollow bricks in a size series. Because the action consists of fitting one thing inside another with only a dawning notion of 'size seriation', the series may need 30 or 40 fitting-together actions. The actions of fitting together with follow-up perceptions of success (good fit) gradually become internalized and more efficient. Actions become speeded up and redundancies are eliminated. This leads to a more economical success and the series is constructed in fewer moves.

'Operational' thinking takes place when the child evolves from the relationship of action to effect and 'knows' that there is an invariant correspondence between certain kinds of actions (operations) and certain kinds of effects (transformations).

The most important aspects of constructivism, examined by Forman and Fosnot (1982), are the relationships between transformations and static states. All the 'conservation' experiments illustrate that 'knowledge is the coordination of correspondences and transformations' and what is required for 'operational' thinking is the ability to relate a transformation to a 'state' (1982, pp. 93–135). For instance, for the pre-operational child, the initial 'state' of water in a jar is perceived to lack correspondence with the final 'state' of water in a differently shaped jar (the amounts look different). 'Conservation' is achieved when the apparent transformation of the two different 'states' is compensated for by the understanding that the action of pouring is equivalent and, therefore, the quantity of water must be equivalent in spite of apparent figurative differences. The pouring action did not include *adding* or *subtracting* action, and therefore the two 'states' must represent conceptual equivalence.

Presumably the so-called pre-operational stage is where actions are being developed, increased, practised and internalized, and where differentiated actions are being associated with various kinds of sensory and perceptual effects. What is needed is a documentation of the actions.

Forman and Fosnot (1982, p. 197) propose a new unit of knowledge or a new professional concept for early education that is 'the co-ordination of correspondences and transformations'. The pedagogical implication of this is that the young child would be encouraged to know 'not only what is [the effect] but also the procedure by which it became that way and, equally important, the procedures that can bring about this or that correspondence' (1982, p. 209).

SCHEMAS

There are many different definitions of 'schema', and there is no single definition with which all will agree.[3] In Piaget's early work he uses 'schema' to mean 'general cognitive structures in children under the age of 5'. Later, while exploring the mechanisms of perception (1969), he began to differentiate between 'schema' and 'scheme'. He states: 'The terms "scheme" and "schema" correspond to quite distinct realities, the one operative (a scheme of action in the sense of an instrument of generalization) and the other figurative' (1969, p. ix). From that time, when he used the term 'schema' he meant 'figural thought', and when he used 'scheme' he was referring to 'operational thought'.

If the problem is to discover how early sensorimotor systems develop into symbolic systems, a conceptual teasing-out of 'scheme' and 'schema' would seem to be necessary prior to carrying out an actual investigation. However, most of Piaget's writing of greatest use in the study of young children was written before he differentiated between the two terms. The task of re-interpreting the early work, even if possible would be a major undertaking. It will be convenient therefore to start with a generalized meaning of the term 'schema', and to see whether a further differentiation is possible or useful.

Bartlett (1932), while discussing 'schemas' or 'schemata', pointed out that motor actions have consequences that lead to adjustments (accommodations). A tennis player, for instance, will adjust his or her stroke if the ball does not take the route intended. Skilled actions, therefore, become modified and linked with each other. As Neisser puts it, 'A schema is a pattern of action as well as a pattern for action' (1976, p. 56).

'Pattern' can be defined as any sequence of events in time and space. In other words, 'pattern' can apply to dynamic sequences of action as well as static configurations. Patterns of either type in the brain can correspond with, or be discrepant with, dynamic or configurational patterns in the environment. Aspects of environment provide either a 'match' or a 'mismatch' with inner patterns.

All organisms exhibit behaviour that implies inner structure. Animals go round actively searching for things to see and they 'see' mainly what they expect to see. This is because they have 'plans' or 'schemas' that function as built-in hypotheses as to how things are. At a very simple level, fish that swim in caves or moles that live underground will interpret light as something to turn away from. Certain stimuli are approached and other stimuli are avoided (Young, 1978, pp. 117–20).

Cells are sensitive to certain aspects of environment and allow stimuli in the environment to be coded and to be given meaning at some level. Functioning improves with use. Where biologically determined cell assemblies are prevented from functioning, the coding and interpretive functions of these cells disappear (1978, p. 126). Kittens, for instance, have specific cells at the back of the eyes that become activated at critical periods. Features in the natural environment of kittens 'feed' these cells. Where the kittens are artificially deprived of the correct stimuli, for instance, horizontal stimuli, both the perceptions and action patterns of the kittens are damaged. They can no longer jump onto horizontal surfaces. They are permanently damaged (Hubel and Wiesel, 1962).

In humans, the patterns in the brain that are compared with patterns in the environment are complex and developmental and are affected by experience. A general feature of 'plans for action' or 'schematic action' is that schemas are 'dynamic, active, information-seeking structures' (Neisser, 1976, p. 111). In humans, schemas (or cognitive structures) acquire content from experience that modifies hypotheses. There is a strong motivational and affective aspect in both the search for meaning and in the confirmation or disconfirmation of hypotheses.

Piaget's definition of a 'schema' is anchored in the definitions given so far, but his particular contribution was to tackle the developmental route of schematic behaviour from birth right through to the advanced cognitive structures of the adolescent. He describes the general features of schemas and concepts as:

> Cognitive structures contain within them elements of 'perception', 'memories', 'concepts' and 'operations'. These are linked together in various types of connections. The connections may be spatial, temporal, causal or implicatory. Structures can be organic, as in very early behaviour, or static or dynamic. (Piaget, 1971b, p. 139)

The function of a schema is to enable generalizations to be made about objects and events in the environment to which a schema is applied (Piaget and Inhelder, 1973, p. 382).

The most easily understood meaning of 'schema' is: 'Schemas of action [are] co-ordinated systems of movements and perceptions, which constitute any elementary behaviour capable of being repeated and applied to new situations, e.g., *grasping, moving, shaking* an object' (Piaget, 1962, p. 274). Schemas are patterns of repeatable actions that lead to early categories and then to logical classifications. As a result of applying a range of action schemas to objects, infants arrive at the generalizations that objects are 'throwable', 'suckable' and 'bangable'. An infant may perform one schema on a range of objects, or a wide variety of schemas on one object (Foss, 1974, pp. 208–9).

Like most of the constructs within constructivism, schema must be understood in relation to other notions within the system. What enables a schema to function in a satisfactory way depends on its history. If early schemas are applied to a diversity of events in the environment, then the schemas will have assimilated many contents (Piaget, 1953, p. 384). Piaget suggests that the extension of schemas, like the extension of action itself, consists of all the objects or contents to which the schema has been applied.

As Hunt puts it, 'At each age and level the environmental circumstances must supply encounters for the child which permit him to use the repertoire of schemas that he has already developed' (1961, p. 279). Experience is thus assimilated to cognitive structures, and this is how knowledge is acquired. This would appear to be a useful hypothesis in the study of under-functioning children. Increase experiences, and schemas will be enriched. A schema, therefore, is a pattern of repeatable behaviour into which experiences are assimilated and that are gradually co-ordinated. Co-ordinations lead to higher-level and more powerful schemas.

Two early schemas are *tracking* objects and *gazing* at objects. Gazing leads to knowledge of configuration. Tracking leads to knowledge of the movement aspects of objects, including self and other persons. Initially, gazing and tracking are two separate forms of behaviour. If an experimenter makes a stationary object move, a very young infant will continue to gaze at the blank space. Similarly, if a moving object is stopped, the infant will continue to track. One of the first great accommodations takes place when infants realize that objects can be stationary or that they can move (Bower, 1974, 1977a).

CO-ORDINATION OF SCHEMAS

Co-ordination of sensorimotor schemas is the practical equivalents of concepts and relations (Piaget, 1969, p. 357). At a later point in development, a toddler moving between points *a* and *b* is co-ordinating, at a motor level, *points of departure* and *points of arrival*. He or she will not be able to 'imagine' this *group of displacements* because sensorimotor co-ordinations consist of successive perceptions and successive overt movements and there is no all-embracing representation. Sensorimotor intelligence has been likened to a slow-motion film in which all the pictures are seen in succession but without fusion.

A 5-year-old may be able to co-ordinate, at a representational or 'thought' level, the distance between *a* and *b* with the distance between *b* and *a* and arrive at equivalence. As schemas are co-ordinated into more and more complex amalgamations, the environment is comprehended at higher levels by the child.

Probably the most important accommodations, or steps forward in knowledge, are where there is a new co-ordination between two separate aspects of knowing. Some of these are dramatic and give rise to exclamations such as 'Oh, yes!', 'Eureka!', 'The penny dropped!', 'I suddenly saw the light!', 'I put two and two together!'. Such co-ordinations have an agreeable affective or emotional component. What is 'known' leads to what becomes 'better known'. It would be useful from the point of view of assessing incremental learning if the component parts of co-ordinations could be described.

STRUGGLE, PRACTICE AND PLAY

Each important advance in cognition is synonymous either with learning something new or realizing something for the first time. Sometimes an advance follows the cognitive discomfort that accompanies an unsolved problem. Piaget's theoretical model of the 'functional invariants', consisting of the processes of accommodation and assimilation, explains the mechanisms involved in cognitive advance. Each aspect of functioning has its affective component. Functioning ranges from struggle through practice to play.

The relationship between stage-level characteristics and different kinds of functioning can be illustrated from a typical behaviour of the first year. *Permanence of the object* (Oates, 1979, section 3) develops from 'out of sight, out of mind' to 'absence makes the heart grows fonder'. Before *permanence of the object* is well established, the child will be distressed if a toy is hidden. There is a conflict (or a struggle) between permanence and impermanence. When permanence is sufficiently established, through practice, *permanence of the object* enters its play form – best seen in the 'peek-a-boo' game. The form of the cognition is: 'now you see it, now you don't, but you know it is still there'. The child knows something so well (that objects are permanent) that he or she can even play with it (Chukovsky, 1966). Similarly, it is only when staying upright has reached a high degree of competence that the game of 'Ring-a-ring o' roses' can be enjoyed. When toddlers fall down they are usually furious because falling down means failure to stand up. Having fun with pretend falling down signifies real competence in staying upright.

Theoretically, cognitive competence could be studied by reference to the affective accompaniments of behaviour. Struggle would indicate new knowledge or skill; playfulness would indicate the well assimilated. Cognition in infants is frequently assessed in relation to their affective responses.

STAGES OF PERCEPTION

Bower (1977a) describes six stages in the perception of configuration during the first seven months of life (see Figure 4.1). His stimuli resemble the human face represented in different degrees of complexity from a few simple lines to a

Simple dots or angles.	 • ∨	Under 6 weeks
Eye section alone; under portion of face unnecessary.		10 weeks
Eye section still suffices, but under half of face must be present even though mouth movements only fleetingly noticed; motion facilitates.		12 weeks
Eye section still suffices, with wide individual differences. Mouth gradually noticed. its movements particularly effective. Wide mouth best. Plastic model of adult effective.		20 weeks
Effectiveness of eyes lessens; mouth movements generally necessary, especially widely drawn mouth. Still no differentiation of individual faces.		24 weeks
Attention to face as such lessens; recognition of facial expression begins, interest in other children. Progressive differentiation of individual faces.		30 weeks

Figure 4.1 Six stages in the perception of configuration during the first seven months of life.

Source: from *A Primer of Infant Development* by T.G.R. Bower. Copyright © 1977 by W.H. Freeman and Company. Reprinted by permission.

complex representation of two faces (1977a, p. 79, Figure 2.1). If the configuration of a stimulus is too simple, the infant will opt out and doze (habituation). If it is too complex, there is also an opting out (too much struggle). The level of stimulus must 'match' the stage level of the child for absorption, interest or delight to be shown. In infant studies 'playfulness' is used as an index of something well understood.

Piaget (1962, p. 91) gives an example from one of his children that shows the child's active attempts to increase the interest of a perceptual feedback by varying action. The child was 2 months old (sensorimotor 2) and had developed the ability to throw his head back in order to look at familiar objects from a new position. Piaget describes this:

> He repeated this movement with ever increasing enjoyment and ever decreasing interest in the external result. He brought his head back to the upright position and then threw it back again time after time laughing loudly. This behaviour ceased to be 'serious' or 'instructive' and became a game. (1962, p. 91)

The child was generating his own experience in that he was varying his motor actions in order to vary the perceptual effects of those actions.

SYMBOLIC FUNCTIONING AND SYMBOLIC REPRESENTATION

The stage of cognition from approximately 2 to 5 years can be described positively as the stage of symbolic functioning in that children become able to represent known events symbolically. Representation can remain internal, as in representational thought, or it can be made manifest in drawings, symbolic play or speech. At this stage, children symbolically 're-present' objects and events that have been experienced. Representation means being able to 're-play' in the mind the 'look' of objects or the movement patterns of objects or other features of objects that have been experienced. Action or movement 're-play' can be seen when the child uses some simple object (such as a stick) to represent objects moving, such as an aeroplane or a car. Action images are most clearly recognizable in symbolic play.

Action images are based on the perception of the movement aspects of objects. Iconic, or figurative, images are based on the perception of the figurative aspects of objects. Speech representations can signify all known motor behaviours, how things look, how things feel and a range of motivations – provided the child has learned the words necessary for expressing experiences and desires.

Different writers refer to these three forms of representation by different names. Bruner (1974) describes the three modes of representation as 'enactive', 'iconic' and 'symbolic' (speech). Piaget differentiates between 'operational', which has a basis in action, and 'figurative', which is based on perception. He refers to speech as a system of signs.

Processes involved in representation are not easy to understand. Forman and Fosnot describe representation as follows:

> Constructivism assumes that we have no direct accessibility to an external world. We therefore have to construct representations that have more to do with acts

of knowing than they do with the external object per se. To Piaget ... what we represent is our own mental activity and not some static external object. We then externalize this mental activity as if it were a static external object. (1982, p. 186)

The difficulty lies in understanding the constantly changing relationships between our own mental activity and external objects. *Permanence of the object* is a mental activity applied to objects in the first year of life. *One-to-one correspondence* is a mental activity applied to a range of objects at around 5 or 6. The notion of different levels of mental activity can be illustrated by children of different ages playing with pebbles on a beach: a 3-year-old might place the pebbles in a *linear order* because that is a form of order typical of 3-year-olds; a 4- or 5-year-old might place the pebbles in a *one-to-one correspondence*, one pebble next to one shell, for instance; and a 6-year-old might arrange the pebbles into two lots of six, or six lots of two, or three lots of four. Such motor actions are clearly guided by cognition. Piaget showed that actions reflect symbolic thought from the second year, but more recent research has shown that the symbolic process starts earlier (Bower, 1974, 1977a). Symbolic functioning evolves from the sensory and motor stage of development.

Becoming 'operational' means that actions can be carried out intellectually. Operational thought has certain characteristics, such as 'reversibility', which is essential for 'conservation'. For the stable mathematical operation of *addition*, the mental action of grouping together must be able to be cancelled out by reversing the process. For instance:

$$2 + 5 = 7$$

$$7 - 5 = 2$$

$$7 - 2 = 5$$

Subtraction *cancels* addition *and* division *cancels* multiplication.

There is no point in continuing to perform physical actions on stones after the actions have become internalized, operational and permanent. Fundamental learning lasts for life. The process of internalizing action is facilitated by speech, although speech alone cannot generate fundamental learning. (This is discussed further in Chapters 3 and 6.)

Seriation and *classification* have their origins in early actions applied to a wide range of objects and, later, to events. The common-sense world contains sufficient information to feed *seriation structures* such as *size, height, weight, strength, temperature, porosity, number* and so on. Even if children did not go to school they would still make statements such as 'I'm taller than Charlie' or 'I have more marbles than Jenny'. An important role of the teacher is to feed spontaneous structures with content not necessarily found at home, street or playground. In other words, worthwhile curriculum content can be offered that, if received, will extend cognitive structures educationally. Within the highest concept of education, teaching facilitates and 'fleshes-out' spontaneous and natural concepts with worthwhile curriculum content.

A problem in early education is a lack of knowledge of spontaneous concepts that can guide the search for appropriate curriculum content. This is not to say that appropriate curriculum content is not offered in early education, but that evaluation of what has been received is weak. The weakness in diagnosing cognitive structures has led to demands for external structuring. This merely deflects from the need to study mental action as expressed through representation. Mental representation cannot be studied directly, but it can be construed from symbolic play, drawing, brick constructions and the like.

Knowledge consists of internal constructions that have 'form' (schemas and concepts and constructs). The content of experience 'feeds' the forms of thought. Improvements, or modifications in functioning, are brought about by psychological processes such as 'accommodation' and 'assimilation'.

FORM, PROCESS AND CONTENT

Three important aspects of professional knowledge on learning and development are:

1 Cognitive 'form'.

2 The 'content' of experience.

3 The processes by which content can, or cannot, is assimilated to cognitive form at different stages of development.

Because the characteristics of later forms of thought are better known than earlier forms, there is a temptation for teachers of young children to accelerate development towards the known. Teachers who try to respond appropriately to children's existing behaviour have little option but to focus on content.

A focus on content can be illustrated in Lowenfeld's (1957) advice to teachers on how they might extend a child's thought in relation to a drawing. He suggests that if a child draws his or her mother, the teacher might ask questions such as 'Where is your mother?', 'Is she alone?' or 'What is she doing?'. Such questions, suggest the author, are aimed at enlarging the experience of the child in relation to the subject-matter of the drawing. Similarly, if a child draws an aeroplane, he suggests that questions might be asked about its size, where it lands, whether there are people on the plane and so on (1957, p. 67). Such extensions encourage associative rather than conceptual thinking in that the child is encouraged to associate content with content: 'sun' will be associated with 'sky'; 'houses' with 'roads'; 'aeroplane' with 'size'; 'person' with 'place' and so on. The children's attention is drawn only to thematic or proximity relations between 'unlike' things.

Attempts are being made, mainly in mathematics and science, to match worth-while curriculum content to prevailing cognitive structures. These attempts are mainly in relation to children older than 5 because the cognitive structures, such as *seriation*, *classification* and various *conservations*, are known (Harlen et al., 1977).

The search for the relationship between 'form' and 'content' has been going on for a long time. In the following example from Katz and Katz (1936), the difference between 'content' and 'structure' (or 'form') can be illustrated. The 'cognitive form' is *seriation of size*. The 'content' or 'stuff' of thinking is that of natural science, more specifically, 'elephant', 'mouse', 'snail' and 'flea'. Here the child is an intelligent and experienced 5-year-old having a conversation with his father, who is a natural scientist:

Child: The elephant is the biggest animal and the mouse is the smallest.
Father: The mouse isn't the smallest.
Child: No … it's the snail.
Father: There are still smaller ones.
Child: The flea is of course the smallest.
Father: There are still smaller ones, but you don't know them. They live in water.
Child: I know them but I don't know what they are called.

If this conversation took place in class, the teacher might decide to ask questions on where elephants live, how a snail protects itself or what kind of food a mouse eats. These questions may interest the child and they are worth asking, but they have a 'hit-or-miss' quality. The responses the father gave show that he is aware of the prevailing concern of the child, which is *size*. A size continuum is an invariant cognitive structure that links individual objects in the world with each other. Schemas and concepts facilitate a cognitive organization of disparate content.

Sinclair (1974, p. 46) refers to the search for invariants of behaviour, or thought, as the search for 'cognitive constants' – schematic patterns that exist beneath the flux of personally experienced content. Teachers who initiate a 'search for schemas' will subsequently find it easier to select appropriate curriculum content to enrich those schemas. To advance a pedagogy of the early years, more research into schemas (cognitive forms) that are self-generated rather than other-generated is needed (Forman and Fosnot, 1982, p. 194). The identification of fundamental cognitive structures in young children will lead to a greater rationale for a pre-school curriculum.

CONSTRUCTIVISM, EXPERIENCE AND THE CURRICULUM

Central to constructivism is the idea that the teacher should match worthwhile curriculum content to diagnosed cognitive structures. It must be stressed that the aspiration to match is a professional ideal. All teachers who listen to children know that there is many a slip between what is offered and what is received.[4]

The curriculum is a heading under which many issues are discussed, such as the organizing of environment, the provision of concrete materials, managerial matters and curriculum content. Curriculum content is knowledge given educational validity by people 'in the know' and by people in power. The central feature of the curriculum is knowledge. This exists objectively in encyclopedias and so on, and it remains external to the knower until constructed psychologically in the individual. External knowledge, once validated for 'truth', 'worthwhileness', 'relevance', 'usefulness' and 'generalisability', must be discovered, assimilated and mastered by the learner. If knowledge is to be successfully assimilated, it must fit in with the learner's 'lived experience' (Greene, 1971, p. 30). As 'lived experience' is itself, according to Piaget, subservient to the cognitive structures that assimilate experience, then the most important aspect of 'psychologizing' curriculum content is to identify the cognitive structures to which the curriculum content is to be assimilated.

Until recently, individual teachers had too much responsibility for deciding on appropriate curriculum content for their own class. This was wasteful of effort. Reform came with a collective rather than individual effort towards planning and articulating whole-school programmes. There are dangers in the drastic shift from the judgments of individual teachers to the implementation of a national curriculum. Programmers will try to sell curriculum content organized into neat, logical programmes of instruction. Blenkin and Whitehead (1988) have criticized such programmes because they remove control of the learning process from the child. They maintain that the imposition of a subject-based curriculum runs counter to 'developmentalism', which is learner-centred. They suggest (1988, p. 34) that teachers should aim at refining their judgments in action rather than relying on a tight prescription for action.

The idea that the child should be in control of his or her learning does not mean that the child can choose to study content in school that is not 'worthwhile'. Although there is enough information in the common sense world to 'feed' all spontaneous cognitive structures, qualifications for higher education require more specialized knowledge. Each society considers some knowledge to be of particular importance. Sub-groups within society may have different hierarchies of importance. As well as issues of content, there are issues of timing and the means by which agreed content should be introduced to children. In very early development, sensible adults tend to follow the natural proclivities of the child. Adults who try to re-route natural baby behaviours are on a losing wicket. The energy of the infant throwing things out of the pram exceeds that of the exasperated adult.

Unless early education is to remain both static and apart, teachers must try to work out appropriate content for the early years that has some kind of continuity from infancy towards primary education. The chances are that more accommodations of a worthwhile nature will take place in a classroom containing materials from various curriculum areas than in a classroom that simply echoes a common-sense world. From a curriculum and a continuity point of view, the search for patterns of behaviour is simultaneously a search for the foundations and future of both scientific and mathematical thinking (Piaget, 1977, Preface).

Piaget claims that, as experience increases, development itself is provoked because 'New schemas are endlessly constructed by the subject assimilating the content of experience to schemas' (1969, p. 364). The more that is assimilated, the more extensive the schemas and the more coherent are resulting 'networks of schemas'. From an affective point of view, Piaget maintains that the more a person knows, the more he or she wants to know.

NOTES

1 There is considerable empirical evidence for the premise that successful learning depends on the active participation of the learner. Support comes from animal studies (Hubel and Wiesel, 1962; Held and Hein, 1963; Young, 1978) and from studies of children (Bruner, 1971; Bailey and Burton, 1982; Forman, 1982; Newell and Barclay, 1982).

2 This is now being remedied. Forman (1982) has edited a collection of research studies on this theme, called *Action and Thought: From Sensorimotor Schemes to Symbolic Operations*.

3 Oldfield and Zangwill, 1942; Oldfield, 1954; Vernon, 1955; Skemp, 1962, 1971; Neisser, 1976; Anderson et al., 1977; Rummelhart and Norman, 1978.

4 For the most illuminating and entertaining account of 'match' and 'mismatch', see Harlen et al., 1977.

Part II

The Findings of the Froebel Early Education Project

5

From Marks to Meanings: The Language of Lines

> Graphic ability, judged by whatever standard, will not develop unless the individual is in a social and educational setting which places considerable importance on drawing according to that standard.
>
> (Harris, 1963, p. 235)

In Chapter 2 it was suggested that there may be two kinds of cognitive patterning evolving from early action and early perception. When the general findings, given in Chapter 4, were analysed in detail, two kinds of representation corresponding to early action, on the one hand, and early perception on the other were found. Dynamic thought patterns, emerging from action, provide the substance of Chapter 6. Figural representation that appears to have developmental links with early perception are discussed and illustrated in this chapter. The materials of representation include drawing, brick constructions, clay and scrap-material models. The following few examples will help to establish a difference between the figural representations of this chapter and the action representations of Chapter 6.

Lois (4:0:9) made 'a pavement' with square mats and 'an aeroplane' with two pieces of wood stuck together. She would not be parted from a wooden tortoise. Soon afterwards she drew a *core-and-radial* pattern she named 'spider'.

Amanda (4:1:3) made a three-dimensional *grid* and named it 'scaffolding'. Although she described the actions she performed on the scaffolding (to be discussed in the next chapter), the *grid* represented the static configuration of the scaffolding.

Lois (4:1:8) drew *zig-zag lines* she named 'stairs'. She drew *circles* she named 'wheels'. She then drew small *open curves* that were called 'tunnels' and a *rectangle* she named 'This is a window with a curtain across'.

In each of these cases there is a correspondence or an equivalence between a graphic schema (*grid, core-and-radial, zig-zag lines, circles* and *semi-circles*) and experienced environmental content. Amanda's assimilated environmental content consists of 'scaffolding', 'spider', 'stairs', 'tunnels', 'pavement' and 'window'.

Of the 5,333 observations collected during the project, 46 per cent consisted of drawings, paintings and three-dimensional constructions. All observations were included in the analysis except where several drawings were virtually identical. Jock (2:2:1), for instance, produced 30 drawings in one morning when he was struggling to combine a vertical and horizontal line. In such cases only one drawing was included in the analysis. If a child repeatedly used the same graphic form and named them all the same (for instance, ten *grids* all named 'ladder'), only one example would be included. If the same form was used but named differently, all the drawings would be included.

Twenty-four marks were distinguishable from each other. To aid analysis the marks were sub-divided within two criteria – *straight lines* and *curves*. They were also sub-divided into 11 *space orders*, some of which are of more theoretical interest than others.

The three continua (with frequencies of occurrence) that are illustrated and discussed in this chapter are as follows:

Lines		*No.*
1	Vertical scribble (the effects of vertical action of the hand)	254
2	Horizontal scribble	80
3	Continuous horizontal and vertical scribble	97
4	Horizontal and vertical differentiated scribble	70
5	Open-continuous triangle	92
6	Horizontal line	36
7	Vertical line	49
8	Straight parallel lines	42
9	Grid	177
10	Stripes	90
11	Triangle	52
12	Rectangle	205
13	Right angle	45
14	Two right angles	48
Total number of observations		1,337

Curves	*No.*
1 Circular scribble	254
2 Circular enclosure, or core and radial	385
3 Oval	17
4 Enclosed curve with or without corners	75
5 Closed semi-circle	119
6 Open semi-circle	200
7 Helix	19
8 Plane spiral	14
9 Concentric circles	46
10 Multiple loop	17
Total	1,146

The following space orders were categorized in terms of space relations between things represented. If hair was placed *on-top-of* a head in a drawing it would be placed in a category described as *vertical order between elements*.

The following space order schemas, given with their frequency of occurrence, are systematically related to increases in age.

Space orders		*No.*
1	Proximity between marks	1,477
2	Vertical order of elements within figure	155
3	Horizontal order of elements within figure	41
4	Grid order within figure or within enclosure	143
5	Grid order inside and outside discrete figure	202
6	Proximity between figures but no order	114
7	Vertical order between figures	74
8	Horizontal order between figures	135
9	Grid order between figures	39
10	Projective space. Representative of 'in front of' or 'behind'	44
11	Representation of figures in different positions	56
Total		2,480

THE DEVELOPMENT OF DRAWING

As already discussed in Chapter 4, the sequences of representation presented here should not be viewed as scales typical of larger populations because the collection of data was influenced by increasing professional insights. There is little doubt that drawing development is sequential and it may be that the sequences are as listed in *lines*, *curves* and *space orders*. What cannot be generalized are the ages at which schemas appear, because symbolic functioning occurs earlier in conditions of privilege.

A careful study of the literature on drawing shows that there is a lack of firm research evidence on invariant sequences of drawing behaviour. Normative studies on large groups of children have shown that children typically produce marks and shapes at different ages. These are of limited use in the developmental assessment of individual children for the following reasons:

1 The norms are usually given in widely spaced time intervals such as years or half years.

2 In the interests of standardization, norms are usually arrived at by asking children to copy a standard (copying does not reflect spontaneous development).

3 Individual meanings attributed to spontaneous 'mark-making' are not considered in normative studies.

A typical norm is as follows: 'Child (2:6) imitates horizontal and vertical strokes' (Gesell, 1971, p. 330). While of some use in comparing children of very different abilities, norms do not illuminate important features of spontaneous development.

Kellogg (1968, 1969), who studied the drawings of young children from 30 different countries over a period of 18 years, is thought by many to have described a developmental sequence in drawing. She describes (1968, p. l) her own broad findings:

> *Early drawing evolves out of scribbling and proceeds according to a developmental sequence scale. Regardless of ethnic, geographical and cultural influences, young children the world over make identical scribblings between the ages of two and five years. … The various scribbled forms occur in definite sequence, according to maturational levels, and therefore they should be viewed as products of biological behavior, rather than of culturally learned behavior.*

Kellogg was in a powerful position to document the developmental sequence claimed above because she was the first researcher to study thousands of scribblings (starting with 2-year-olds) collected at the Golden Gate Nursery School in San Francisco. As a result of her time-consuming analysis, she identified 20 basic scribbles and demonstrated the universality of basic graphic forms in different cultures and at different times. What she did not show was a developmental sequence in which the 20 basic scribbles emerged. This was because she became increasingly absorbed in pursuing logical rather than developmental complexity; because she was defeated in her attempts to establish a developmental sequence in children's drawing by problems of measurement; and because she did not believe in talking with children about their drawings.

Kellogg is firm with teachers on this last issue: 'No questions need be asked... comments can be restricted to such constructive ones like "very interesting", "nice colors", "I like that", "good work", "a nice scribble", "pretty"', and so on. (Kellogg, 1969, p. 156). Kellogg warned teachers on the dangers of accelerating children out of their biological art stage. Unfortunately these warnings became generally associated with adults talking to children about their art. There is now evidence that children who function well are those who are talked with, and one of the most satisfying topics for young children is what they are doing. This is not simply affectively satisfying, it also facilitates cognition: 'young children enjoy discussing their art work as they are in the process of creation and cognitive growth is assisted by the integration of language and motor processes' (Mann and Taylor, 1973, pp. 36–7).[1] Being interested in the representation of content was frowned upon as much as talking with children. Kellogg hardly considered the content of children's drawings so taken up was she with form.[2]

Lowenfeld (1957) also warns against adult attempts to accelerate graphic representation: He writes (p. 87): 'While a baby is still in the state of disordered scribbling, drawing a picture of something "real" is inconceivable. Such attempts would be similar to trying to teach a babbling baby to pronounce words correctly or to use them in sentences'. Many writers since Stern (1924) have used the analogy between scribbling and babbling. Without talking with children there is little information on whether children are investing their marks with meaning. The shift from 'motor' to 'symbolic' functioning is clearest when children describe the content they are expressing through marks.

What is left out of the scribbling and babbling analogy is extension. Good parents babble back to their infants. This has been found to increase the frequency of babbling (Dodd, 1972). Also, most good parents recognize that babblings have meanings. However, parents do not usually scribble with their children nor do they validate scribbles sufficiently.[3]

Kellogg and Lowenfeld view intervention as pushing a child on towards a future stage of development. They seemed not to consider intervention aimed at extending and enriching an existing stage ('match'). This is the kind of intervention used in the Froebel project and it was quite clear that the children thrived on this kind of adult verbal participation.

CONTENT AND FORM IN CHILDREN'S DRAWING

Eng (1959, first published in 1931) carried out a detailed developmental study of her niece, Margaret. It is interesting to compare her work with Kellogg's in that she paid great attention to 'content' at the expense of 'form'. Margaret drew her first mark, a vertical line, at 10 months but Eng was so influenced by the movement for free and spontaneous art where 'The history of graphic art is hidden in a scribble' (Eng, p. 19) that she attributed no importance to the line and waited for a scribble before she began to record progress systematically.[4]

Because Eng illustrated, wrote about and meticulously recorded background information, the drawings are still valuable to present-day readers. Her interpretations, reflecting the theories of the day, have been superseded but the drawings can be re-interpreted in the light of current theory. Eng was working with theories mainly concerned with individual differences rather than with the search for cognitive constants and, consequently, she did not document similarities of graphic form. She was particularly interested in changes in content, especially where they seemed to be related to emotional or moral issues. For instance, when Margaret draws 'jagged teeth' Eng speculates on why she is feeling aggressive. She does not point out that 'jagged teeth', 'stairs' and many other types of content are drawn with a common zig-zag form. Similarly, she does not point out that several drawings ('family on a sledge', 'a sitting figure' and 'an old fashioned letter F') are ways of using a newly acquired mark that resembles a *semi-circle*.

This is an important issue because focusing on 'content' at the expense of 'form' can lead to the conclusion that young children 'flit' from one theme to another and that they are unsystematic or even idiosyncratic. In fact, Margaret shows systematic experimentation of disparate content that can be expressed within particular forms, particularly as they appear in development.

One of the uncharted areas of early cognitive functioning is children's own search for commonalities. While it is true that children often name a drawing as one thing and then change it to another, it is also true that, more often than not, there is a common form underlying differences in content. In the Froebel project, for instance, it was observed that if a drawing was named 'wheel' at one time, followed by 'flower', it was because the child was representing those, and other objects, with a particular graphic form, such as a *circular enclosure*.

Thus, paying too much attention to content can prevent the perception of similarities of form. One project child, for instance, drew lots of 'apples' and 'clocks'. A teacher, focusing on content, might decide to develop a topic on either apples or clocks. If the teacher perceived, however, that the 'apples' had *radials connected to the outside of the enclosure* and that the 'clocks' had *radials connected to the inside of the enclosure* a different kind of provision might suggest itself, such as objects and creatures with a *core-and-radial* configuration. The extension of form rather than content is not yet widely adopted in early education.

TOPOLOGICAL SPACE NOTIONS

Before presenting the developmental sequences of *lines*, *curves* and *space orders*, we discuss five topological space concepts as early 'mark-making' takes place within these notions. In order to focus on the space aspects, 'content' will be kept constant. Drawings and models of 'faces' will be used to illustrate a topological space sequence. Although these particular space notions have received some attention in the literature they have not been employed in empirical studies.

Drawing and spatial organization appear to be closely related to earlier stages of perception. Goodenough, the originator of the 'draw-a-man' test, suggested, in extremely tentative terms, that 'Possibly in depicting a concept by drawing, the progression is the same as that observed by perception, from undifferentiated whole, to partial differentiation, to more complete differentiation' (cited by Harris, 1963, p. 202).

Most teachers who have taught intellectually impoverished children will know that their drawings are usually poor, stereotyped and undifferentiated. If children of 7 years, for instance, are still representing 'tree' by a lollipop form (core with *one* or *two radials*) it probably means that earlier perception has not been sufficiently well cultivated.

Bower (1977a) has demonstrated clearly defined stages in the development of perception during the first year and has suggested that each stage needs to be 'fed' with appropriate stimuli. He shows that under the age of 3 months infants respond as readily to the parts as to the whole of a stimulus. After this age, infants need a whole pattern. There is evidence that the whole face pattern begins to be perceived at about 3 months. By 5 months a face pattern must include a mouth if a smile is to be elicited. By eight months a baby can respond to subtle indicators of mood on adult faces (Bower, p. 79).

Bower (1977a) cites Ahrens (1954), who illustrates a 'match' between stimulus and response at different stages of perception. These stages are shown in Figure 4.1. It is well known that infants at Ahrens' final stage begin to distinguish between faces sufficiently well to refuse to go to strangers. Six-month-old infants can also discriminate between different geometric forms (Ling, 1941, cited in Ruff, 1978, p. 294).

The representations of the Froebel project children followed a similar sequence to early perception. Individual marks, such as lines and dabs, were drawn within simple spatial organizations before aggregates or combinations of marks appeared. Only from the age of 4 did some children begin to draw two differentiated persons. This corresponds to the last stage of perception in Figure 4.1, where the 30-week-old infant differentiates between individual faces.

Figure 5.1 'Two bears. The polar bear Figure 5.2 'This bear has a happy face.'
in the water has a sad face.'

Lois (4:1:12) drew 'Two bears. The polar bear in the water has a sad face (Figure 5.1). This bear has a happy face' (Figure 5.2). Here the differentiation between two 'face' configurations ('happy' and 'sad') was based on 'good' and 'bad' form. In other words, she knew that her marks inside the enclosure labelled 'sad face' were not correctly ordered topologically. The bear with a happy face has the 'eyes', 'nose' and 'mouth' *spatially ordered within the enclosure* although the whole figure is not yet represented in a vertical position.

After children managed to order features within enclosures and between elements in a drawing they sometimes temporarily lost the order. Lois (3:3:22), for instance, painted 'Mrs Bruce'. Instead of putting 'hair' *on-top-of* the head enclosure, she put it *underneath* so that it looked like a beard (Figure 5.3). Similarly, at 3:7:14, she put hair *on-top-of* instead of *underneath* a hat on a model (Figure 5.4). In both the above instances, on realizing what she had done, she laughed. As she looked at her model she said, 'Oh! His hair is on top of his hat'.

This example highlights a difference between 'perception' and 'representation'. Lois has 'known', on a perceptual level (since infancy), that hair is *on-top-of* the head. Now she is learning this on a representational level. In the above examples the spatial relationship is not quite stable. Bower (1974, pp. 205–8) has pointed out that behaviours recur at different levels of development and that what is learned at one level has to be 're-worked' at higher levels.

Lois differentiated between two people in three dimensions before she did so in drawing. Two early clay models were described as 'The man has a flat head and the lady has a round head'. This, and many other examples, show a growing

Figure 5.3 'Mrs Bruce.'   Figure 5.4 'Oh! His hair is on top of his hat.'

awareness of the use of geometric form in representation. Later, Lois used head-wear stuck *on-top-of* models to differentiate between 'king' and 'queen', 'man' and 'woman', and so on.

TOPOLOGICAL SPACE AND REPRESENTATION

Here we discuss one drawing from a project child to introduce topological space orders. Graphic schemas will be discussed later. Randolph (4:4:2) named his drawing 'Boy's skipping. He's happy. He's sad' (Figure 5.5). The spatial orders he uses are as follows:

- *Proximity*: The features of the face are near each other.

- *Enclosure*: Features of 'faces' are enclosed as are 'buttons' within 'body' shapes.

- *Connection*: The head, arms and legs are connected to the body.

- *Separation*: Different parts of the body are separated from each other.

- *Horizontal and vertical co-ordinates*: The features and all parts of each body are organized within an internalized system of horizontal and vertical co-ordinates.

Graphic schemas used to represent content are as follows: *dabs* (eyes), *circle* (nose and buttons), *horizontal lines* (arms), *vertical lines* (legs), *downward curve* (sad expression, skipping-rope and eyebrows), *upward curve* (smile), *rectangle* (body).

Randolph progressed systematically through marks and spatial orders. He first made *dabs* and *scribbles* and then began to *enclose* them. He advanced to *circular enclosures*, enclosures with *radials attached* and *enclosures* with *ordered marks* within. *Order* became increasingly elaborate. In Figure 5.5, for instance, *rectangular* bodies are placed *underneath circle* faces and *vertical-line* 'legs' are placed *underneath* heads and bodies. His developing repertoire of marks and spatial orders were not confined to the representation of people. Drawings, clay models and scrap-material models included plants, people sitting on chairs, mincers, spectacles, aeroplanes, letters, people at the pictures, and so on.

PROXIMITY

Bower (1977a) has shown that *proximity* is the earliest perceived topological space relationship (first-stage stimuli of dots and angles). Piaget and Inhelder (1956, p. 450) write that 'Proximity is to space what resemblance is to logical classification'. At first, marks are *heaped together* rather like the heaps made by toddlers at the end of *transporting*. Resemblance between things in the heap is 'transportability' or 'I put them there'.

Proximity may be the earliest spatial organization used in representation in that marks and objects are placed *next to* each other at a very early age. However, determining *proximity* in drawing, model-making and brick play is difficult because there is little indication (before 'content' makes it clear) as to whether *nearness* is simply fortuitous. For this reason, *enclosure* was the earliest space order that could be meaningfully classified in the project children's representations.

ENCLOSURE

In Bower's (1977a) experiments, positive affective responses were taken as indices of 'match'. Infants began to respond positively when marks were placed near each other. By 10 months they required a 'mouth' and 'eyebrow' configuration (*horizontal lines*) before showing pleasure. Later positive responses depended on partial and then complete enclosure of marks.

All the topological space notions that provoked interest in infants were featured in project representations. It is an interesting thought that if project infant, Jim, had been one of Bower's babies, he would have been excited by a stimulus of *dabs* and *horizontal lines* inside an *enclosure*, while his brother Alistair (3:1:11) was using those equivalent elements and space orders for representing 'Two eyes and a mouth' (Figure 5.6). In common with other children starting to *enclose*, he has not managed to get the 'mouth' (a pipe-cleaner) *inside* the clay *enclosure*. Similarly in two dimensions, Susan, at a similar age (3:1:6) (Figure 5.7), has not quite managed to get her *horizontal* line 'mouth' *inside* her 'face' *enclosure*. At 3:1:6, however, she has managed to *enclose dabs* in her representation of 'stone' (Figure 5.8).

The failure to *enclose* the 'mouth' is probably due to the fact that 'line' does not yet entail the Euclidean notion of length. The length of line, therefore, would not be judged as equivalent to the breadth of the enclosure.

HORIZONTAL AND VERTICAL CO-ORDINATES

After *proximity* and *enclosure*, the third topological space relationship generating perceptual interest in infants is 'horizontal and vertical co-ordinates'. In order to stimulate a 6-month-old, a 'face' must have two eyes above a nose and a mouth

Figure 5.5 'Boy's skipping. He's happy. He's sad.'

Figure 5.6 'Two eyes and a mouth.'

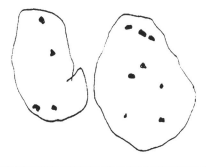

Figure 5.7 'Face.'

Figure 5.8 'Stone.'

below the nose and eyes. In other words, the form must consist of *enclosed dab* and *line-like* configurations in a *horizontal* and *vertical relationship* with each other. The features are *separate* from each other but *connected* within the enclosure by an ordered space relationship.

Earlier, while discussing Lois's drawings of 'sad' and 'happy' faces (Figures 5.1 and 5.2), it was suggested that although her ability to order features spatially within a face enclosure was not quite stable, she could discriminate between her representations in terms of 'good' and 'bad' form.

This level of representation echoes experiments on 4-month-old infants who were found to prefer good face configurations to 'scrambled' faces (Mussen et al., 1969, p. 162). In other words, at a certain stage infants reject or show an antipathy towards faces that lack good spatial order.

Two-year-olds have internalized a sufficiently wide range of faces to recognize familiar adults in photographs (Sheridan, 1975, p. 46). Because their knowledge is stable they show interest in discrepant configurations. They ask questions such as 'Did he fall off a bus?' (Fantz, 1961).

Three- and four-year-old project children rejected 'poor form' in their representations. It was quite common for them to stop brick *enclosure* play when the bricks were out of alignment in order to 'mend the hole'. They became capable of 'topsy-turvying' established orders for fun.

SEPARATION AND CONNECTION

Children sometimes draw parts of an object *separately* before they correctly *connect* and *order* the parts. A staircase, for instance, might be represented outside a house. Luquet has described this as 'synthetic incapacity' (cited in Piaget and Inhelder, 1956, pp. 46–9). Figure 5.9 could be so described but this would miss all the positive features of the representation.

Pete (3:1:5) was excited by being given his first toothbrush and small tube of toothpaste by a dentist visiting the project. Pete cleaned his teeth for a long time. Later he drew 'toothbrush' (an elementary *enclosure*) and 'bristles' (short *horizontal lines*) (Figure 5.9). Deficits are a lack of *connection* and *order*. The following four points describe positives:

1 The drawing represents an exciting first-hand experience.

2 He has two available graphic schemas for representation, *enclosure* and *lines*.

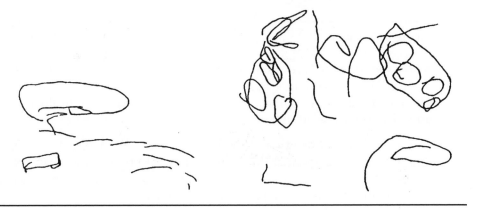

Figure 5.9 'Toothbrush, bristles.'   Figure 5.10

3 He may not be able to *connect* but he can place marks in a *proximity* relationship.

4 He can express the meaning of the representation in speech.

From a teaching point of view, deficit descriptions can only suggest acceleration. Identification of positives can lead to curriculum extensions (this is discussed further in Chapter 9).

The following three drawings show a progression in the evolution of topological space notions. Lois (3:1:19) (Figure 5.10) has started to *enclose* marks. The marks are *near* each other but *separated*. There is no *order*. Lois (3:2:10) (Figure 5.11) draws a face *enclosure*. Hair is not yet *connected* to the head. An *order* is emerging in that the nose is under the eyes and the mouth is further down than nose or eyes.

Lois (3:7:29) (Figure 5.12) draws 'Humpty', which shows a clear advance on Figure 5.11 in that, pupils (*dabs*) are *enclosed* within eyes that are *enclosed* within the face. The circular scribble hair is *connected* to the head. The mouth (*horizontal scribble*) is *ordered* below nose and eyes. The *order* between the features shows an

Figure 5.11 'Face.'

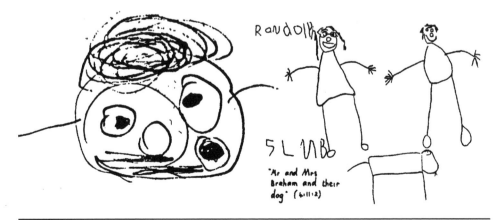

Figure 5.12 'Humpty.'   Figure 5.13 'Mr and Mrs Braham and dog.'

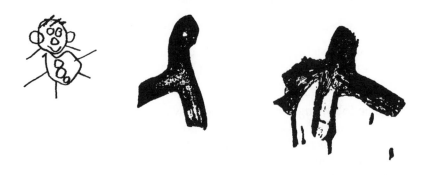

Figure 5.14 'Draw-a-man' test.   Figure 5.15 'Pakistani aeroplane, broken.'

advance on Figure 5.11. *Horizontal* arms are *connected* to the enclosure. Having drawn the two eyes, with pupils for the first time, she held up her drawing and shouted out 'eye'. She then added the third 'eye' out of sheer ebullience.

The final stage of perception in Figure 4.1 shows the complexity level reached by 30 week-old-infants. They can recognize facial expression and differentiate between individual faces.

It has been said that pre-school children cannot distinguish between male and female forms in drawings (Harris, 1963, p. 208). However, in spite of initial selection criteria, several project children were able to represent, as well as to distinguish, differentiated male and female forms. Following a farm visit, Randolph (4:11:2) drew the farmer, who was differentiated from his wife in many ways including the wearing of spectacles: 'Mr and Mrs Braham and dog' (Figure 5.13). The configurational differences between the two heads reflects the differences shown in the most complex stimulus level (Bower, 1977a) for 30-week-old infants (Figure 4.1).

Figure 5.16 'Tiger, stripes.'

There seems little doubt that access to materials, as well as appropriate adult intervention, can facilitate graphic representation. Randolph's 'draw-a-man' test at the age of 3:2:0 was unscorable, which put him in the bottom 2 per cent of the population on which the test was standardized. A later drawing at 3:11:10 (Figure 5.14) placed him among the top 20 per cent. Although tests are known to be unreliable at the earlier levels, this increase was echoed in the 29-point IQ gain he made during the two years of the educational programme.

Figure 5.17 top shows, on the left-hand side, a set of 9 out of 20 'best' drawings by project children. On the bottom right are 9 'best' drawings from children matched for age, sex, ethnic background and neighbourhood during their first week of playgroup. The developmental difference between the two sets of drawings are obvious and give support for the importance of early education in developing representational competence.

LINES

It is not difficult to see how sensorimotor actions acquire symbolic meaning as when a child *moves forward*, imitating 'the movement of an ambulance'. Children's actions become signifiers of things that move. This type of signification is usually called symbolic play and is discussed in the next chapter.

In symbolic play, actions are used as symbols and the actions are carried out in a transient sequence. The products of drawing and model-making are not transient. The visibility of products may serve to deflect from the actions that gave rise to the products.

Piaget and Inhelder (1956) maintain that marks (and three-dimensional constructions) are the figurative effects of sensorimotor movements. These movements or *groups of action displacements* can be seen in a wide range of situations such as when the infant *throws things onto the ground* and the toddler *transports* objects and places them into *heaps*. Mark- and model-making emerge from groups of undifferentiated movements that produce differentiated groups of figurative effects.

In drawing, for instance, the hand moves about on surfaces in *horizontal, vertical* and *circular* movements. Each movement produces a different feedback. As motor actions become more controlled, one set will result in *lines*, another set in *circles, angles, quadrilaterals*, and so on. By co-ordination and differentiation movements become increasingly skilled and the figurative effects reflect this. Mark- and model-making, therefore, are abstractions from the child's own movements. Motor mechanisms and perception are both employed in mark- and model-making in that visual perception 'picks up' the graphic images that result from motor movements.

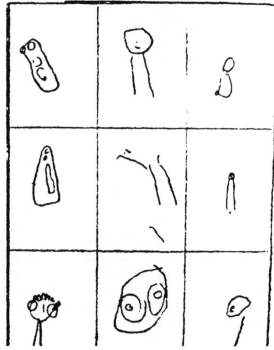

Figure 5.17 'Draw-a-man' comparisons.

From an early stage, pleasure accompanies 'matching' internalized *groups of actions* with their known figurative effects. The pleasure of being able to perceive predictable effects from known actions sustains the activity of mark- and model-making.

Arnheim (1972, p. 35) describes the match between outer stimuli and inner processes as follows: 'The stimulus configuration seems to enter the perceptual process only in the sense that it evokes in the brain a specific pattern of general sensory categories which "stands for" the stimulation'. In other words, a pattern must already be in the brain in order to perceive external configurations that 'match' it. Piaget would maintain that the pattern becomes established in the brain through action and not simply by perception.

Even if the importance of action in drawing were appreciated, which it is not, it is difficult to know how the teacher can facilitate the relationship between skilled action and figural outcomes in individual learners. One possibility is to implement the constructivist idea, already discussed, of focusing simultaneously on the action and end-product, the figural effect, but to place particular emphasis on the action.

Here is an example from the project. Brenda drew a recognizable 'house'. After a short discussion on 'houseness', the project teacher commented on the interesting fact that the day before Brenda had drawn a 'box of chocolates' and the day before that had drawn a 'table' and that Brenda in each case had used a similar shape. Recognition was therefore given to the shape similarity between those objects as well as giving recognition to the recent advance in Brenda's motor skill in producing a *rectangle*. This developed into a discussion on a wide range of content that could now be represented with that group of motor movements. The motor movements were treated as a great source of interest. When an advance was made, as in making a corner with a continuous line, Mrs B commented on the advance.

As each form appeared it was practised spontaneously until a standard was created against which 'good' and 'bad' form was judged. The standards being built up through experiences of mark- and model-making had nothing to do with external 'standards' representing norms.

The following age-related sequence of developing actions is called *'lines'*. Given the opportunity, young children draw *lines*, make *lines* with any objects that can be aligned and run in *linear directions*. They construct *circular enclosures* and run in *circular directions*. They construct and draw *zig-zag configurations* and they run in *zig-zag directions*.

The issue of how one level of marks evolves into another level is considered below, starting with *horizontal, vertical* and *circular scribbles*.

HORIZONTAL, VERTICAL AND CIRCULAR SCRIBBLES

Most early marks are the figurative outcome of bodily movements. Some arm movements knock things down, some produce interesting sounds and some produce marks on a surface. Of 3-year-olds, 80 per cent can copy a vertical line (Stanford-Binet intelligence test – Terman and Merrill, 1976, p. 95). Most 3-year-olds also make lines and towers with bricks. Although building actions (*connecting*) are different from drawing actions, there is a figurative correspondence between outcomes. There is an element of *'connection'* between paper and pencil. Young children obviously need to see the results of their actions because, from the age of 2, scribbling soon stops if no marks appear.

The following sequence of observations from one child cannot illuminate the whole process of how motor actions become signifiers for graphic representations. However, the observations suggest that the transition from action to graphic form does occur spontaneously. Kamal is an Asian child. When these observations were made, he had very little English. Kamal (1:11:28) tipped things onto the floor and *transported* objects from various places in the classroom and grounds to his mother. There is a formal resemblance between this and learning to walk with starting and end-points.

Kamal (2:0:4) placed four cars in a *line* on the slide. He knocked them out of place and then put them back in *line*. He repeated this behaviour with many different objects typically picking up two objects in each hand. Kamal (2:0:12) painted his first *circular scribble*. He followed this by making *circular arm movements*. These gestures seemed to be repetitions of his drawing action.

Kamal (2:0:19) put four trains in a line and moved them along. He held one end of the line with his left hand and the other with his right hand. His hands could be said to be at *end points of the line*. He alternately gazed at the line then moved it along.

It is tempting to think that Kamal is representing the movement of trains because the children had just been on a train journey. However, the observation does not contain sufficient information for such an interpretation.

Kamal (2:1:1), on a three-wheeled vehicle without pedals, followed his brother, Salam, who was on a tricycle with pedals. They moved in a *forward direction*. At a certain point, Salam made a sharp turn on his tricycle and started to ride back over the same route. Kamal lifted his vehicle round and followed him. The two children rode back and forth along the *straight-line trajectory* for some time. Then Salam made a *wide arc*, followed by Kamal. After repeating this several times, Kamal left his vehicle, entered the classroom, painted a clear *arc* and named the product 'My bus'. The arc, coming as it did after his own *arc-like trajectory*, could be a graphic representation of his own movement. Kamal (2:2:23) made a row of bricks. He placed one car at each end of the line. He then built a tower of bricks. He carefully topped the tower with two bricks.

The literature is not very helpful on the significance of such behaviour. Statements are too general. Piaget (1968b, p. 14), for instance, has suggested that, in similar kinds of behaviour, 'objects are co-ordinated with each other and with the child's own body'.

Kamal (2:2:29), *matched a row* of four cars with *a row* of four shops. This could be a case of *one-to-one correspondence* but it is more likely to be an earlier *line-to-line correspondence*. Most of the project children drew *line-to-line correspondences*, the figurative effect being *parallel lines* or 'stripes'. It is of interest to note in passing that the two lines, consisting as they do of 'cars' and 'shops', are early spontaneous groupings based on similarity of configuration but placed in alignment.

For the next few days Kamal's favourite occupation was as follows. He would arrange cars in a long *row*, bunch them into a *heap*, *enclose* the *heap* within his *encircling arms* and then put the cars back into *line*. This may have been an exercise (an assimilatory form of functioning) in making a 'good form' *(a line)*, before 'spoiling' it in order to reconstruct it, or it could be an early co-ordination of two schemas:

■ Making lines

■ Enclosing.

He had been producing *enclosures* in painting. At 2:4:16, he named one *enclosure* 'Balloon' and another 'Face'.

Young children are said to evaluate quantity by two primitive topological notions, *heaping* and *length*, with length defined as an ordinal comparison of *points of arrival*. In a typical test situation, two rows of bricks are placed before the child, one spread out and one with bricks placed close together. Children of a certain stage judge the crowded one to be *more* by the criterion *crowded together*. But they also judge the line to be *more* because the *point of arrival (the end of the line) is further away*.

In the observations on Kamal, given so far, it can be seen that he *transported* and made *heaps*. He then made *lines* with the ends marked out that appeared to have a formal similarity with both toddling and transporting. He then spontaneously experimented with two topological space notions of *crowding* followed by *spreading out* lines. According to Piaget (1968a, p. 977), all of these behaviours provide the basic experiences on which later evaluations of *length* and *distance* are based.

So far, action appears to be related to action representation and also to configuration. Further information became available when Kamal began to talk about what he was doing. Kamal (2:11:2) spent a long time gazing at a caterpillar. His mother asked him what the caterpillar was doing. He said, 'He stretched … he oped' (opened). His perception seemed to be related to schemas, discussed above, of *bunching* and *spreading-out*.

Kamal (2:11:2) painted a thick *horizontal line* with short *radials connected* with the *line*. He named this 'Crocodile'. The next day he painted a row of short *vertical lines*. When the paint began to trickle down he named it 'Raining'. He showed a picture of water spraying out of a watering can to Mrs B. He recognized the short, vertical lines in the picture as graphic signifiers of water. It seems clear that Kamal can interpret static lines as equivalents for something that moves.

One month later, his favourite game was making cars go up and down a slope, using speech such as *going up, going down* and *fallen down*. Several *grid* representations, such as 'aeroplane', followed. It looked as though the figurative aspects were paramount. However, while painting an 'aeroplane' Kamal made engine noises. After another *grid* painting he made cars run down a slope to car sounds. It is possible that, in early representation, configuration and movement are held in the mind simultaneously.

Kamal (3:2:23) drew a common graphic schema consisting of a *horizontal line* with an elementary *circular enclosure at each end*. The drawing was not named but earlier Kamal had been observed finger-tracing worm tracks that were visible through the glass sides of the wormery. Kamal was very absorbed in Mrs B's explanation of the worm tracks (*going through* is discussed in Chapter 6). A *line* may appear as a configuration but it may also represent *a trajectory with a starting- and finishing-point*.

Kamal (3:3:12) drew 'Crisps falling on the bus'. For this he used a *circle scribble*. His speech indicates the *dynamic trajectory* of what is being represented. The project bus driver had been having a vigorous campaign against crisp-eating on the bus and Kamal had received the message. Kamal became more competent in representing static configurations but he continued to represent the movement aspects of objects.

As children get older, configuration becomes more clearly recognizable to adults and dynamic representation in drawings less recognizable. It is possible that too much emphasis on figural resemblance will reduce the number of dynamic representations through lack of validation. This is, no doubt, what Kellogg, Lowenfeld and Bell (discussed earlier) were warning against.

Kamal had an IQ of 109 at the age of 3 after attending the project for one year. This was 10 points higher than his brother at an equivalent age before attending the project. (Kamal's IQ was much higher than his brother's at the end of the project.)

There appears to be a close relationship between mark-making and an increased perception of objects in the environment that have a figural equivalence. Also a great deal of language is used in describing objects that correspond with their available marks. Some of these correspondences are illustrated in the following short sequence. Jock began to draw *circular scribbles* at 1:2:0. At 1:8:28 he watched, at short range, people playing golf. Suddenly he shouted exuberantly,

'Football'. A few days later, on a visit to Teddington Lock, he gazed at a buoy for some time, pointed and shouted, 'Football'. Mrs B explained, 'That's a buoy' – a reaction of disbelief. Two weeks later on a visit to Kew Gardens, he was absorbed by a *circular pattern* on the floor.

When he was 1:9:6 he spent almost the whole morning with his father selecting *spheres* from a range of other shapes. At 1:9:10 he named a *circular scribble* for the first time. He called it 'Football'. On a subsequent visit he spent a lot of time examining *spherical* door-handles. After seven months of absorption with *circles* and *spheres*, Jock had begun naming objects that had a perceptual correspondence with the visual effects of his *circular scribble*.

This sequence can be compared with another sequence from the same child, which suggests that the relationship between mark-making, perception and representation is not random. Jock (2:5:22) drew a *vertical line* and named it 'Crocodile ... a tail that's burning'. One month later he painted a strong *vertical line* he named 'Animal, one leg'. He repeated the *vertical line* the next day and called it 'Leg'.

Jock (2:7:8) painted a thick *horizontal line* with a *vertical line next to it*. He named this 'Aeroplane'. He was dissatisfied with this and struggled through thirty paintings trying to *intersect* a *vertical* with a *horizontal line*. He finally succeeded in producing a perfect *grid*. He became as absorbed with *grid-like* configurations as he had been with *spheres*. At 2:7:9, while on the project bus, Jock shouted to his mother twice on the journey, 'Look'. Once it was 'scaffolding' and once it was 'a fence'. On that same day he rolled out some long pieces of clay and called them 'Spider's legs' and, later, 'stripes'. This is an example of 'fitting' form (*parallel lines*) onto suitable content.

Jock (2:7:14) would not be parted from a tennis racquet. He hugged it and gazed at it alternately. Two days later he pointed to a *grid* configuration and said, 'Windmill'. He followed this with a painting of *four vertical lines* named 'Horsey, Man, Sheep and Tree'. Jock (2:7:28) carefully inspected a hammock. Jock (2:8.0) made a model. He called it 'Tiger', pointed to the nails and called them 'stripes' (Figure 5.16).

These short sequences illustrate that, right from the earliest representations, content had a perceptual equivalence to graphic form and there appeared to be a heightened perception of objects in the environment that also matched existing form. Objects such as 'aeroplanes', 'fences' and 'scaffolding' were not represented with *circular scribble* but with *grids*.

It would seem that different acts of drawing, each with its figurative feedback, engenders interest in objects with similar configurations. Most people who have painted know that this subsequent perception of what has been painted has been transformed.

◾ HORIZONTAL AND VERTICAL LINES CO-ORDINATED: GRIDS AND GRID ORDERS

Subjects, human and animal, respond to the stimulus characteristics of objects that are equivalent to the cognitive structure on the subject (Hubel, 1963). Infants less than 1 month old can perceive stripes that are vertical or horizontal, one-eighth of an inch wide at a distance of ten inches (Fantz, 1961, p. 69). At 6 weeks, infants can see vertical and horizontal stripes better than oblique stripes (Leehey et al., 1975, p. 579).

Again, there are interesting similarities between early perception and later representation. For instance, children can copy *vertical* and *horizontal lines* before they can copy *oblique lines*. Children draw *circles* and *stripes* simultaneously as earlier they perceived *circles* and *stripes* simultaneously.

As with the earliest mark-making, once a good *grid* form has been mastered, then poor form is disliked. Kamal (3:5:29) managed to draw perfect *grids*. The figurative effects suggested to him a variety of content, such as 'kites', 'window' and 'aeroplane'. At 3.5.29, his brush slipped. He named the product 'Pakistani aeroplane, broken' (Figure 5.15). The term 'broken' acknowledged bad form.

The day after this observation Kamal laid out a neat three-dimensional *grid* (a fire) for Mrs B, who intended to demonstrate transformation of matter brought about by burning. He went straight from this to examine the spokes of an umbrella.

When *parallel lines* were 'discovered' they were used in drawing, three-dimensional models and symbolic play. For instance, when a group of children found *parallel lines* painted on the floor of the movement hall, they played chasing games (horses and drivers) within them. They invented their own *parallel lines* in the form of reins. This kind of game had been stimulated previously by the tracks in the snow made by pram wheels.

The main mention of *parallel lines* in the literature is that they are first used to *connect* face *enclosures* to legs. Later they represent 'neck' (Cambell, 1958, cited in Harris, 1963, p. 162). Only one project child, Randolph (3:6:27), represented 'neck' before 'legs'. He drew a row of small *circles* between the *parallel lines* and named his drawing 'Lady with beads' (this was probably a two-dimensional representation of '*going round a boundary*').

The same day, Randolph (3:6:27) asked his mother to write his name, which he then tried to copy (Figure 5.18). As can be seen, he was constrained by his prevailing schemas. Of particular interest is the *core and radial* letter 'p' and the *parallel lines* he used for the lower part of letter 'R'. He was still drawing letter 'R' in this way at 3:7:22 (Figure 5.19). In Figure 5.19, he drew *parallel line* 'lips', 'hairs', 'legs' and upper-case letter 'A'.

Figure 5.18 'My name.'   **Figure 5.19** 'Lips, hairs, legs, letter "A", my name.'

The *rectangle* first appears as a figurative feed-back from *grids*, as can be seen in Joel's (3:8:9) 'Umbrella' (Figure 5.20). *Grid* structures have a great potential for extension. When children acquired the *semi-circle* they represented 'umbrella' with that. After a visit to the park, Adrian (4:5:15) made a flat, oval shape with clay. He drew a *grid* on the surface and said, 'Look... a leaf' (Figure 5.21). Like Randolph in Figure 5.18, he modified the *oblique* veins on the leaf towards *grid*.

At this stage children were particularly interested in comparing *grid-like* objects. For instance, during a visit to Hampton Court, the children were shown the earliest tennis racquets. Jack (5:2:2) said, 'My daddy's racquet doesn't look like this. This one is bigger'. He then asked, 'Is the net bigger?' Later, he showed his mother a knitted shawl. He said, 'This is like a cage but this one has round holes'. He was paying close attention to different *grid-like* configurations and comparing them. He was also paying attention to size. There are probably continuities between earlier schemas and later concepts that are, as yet, undiscovered.

STRAIGHT AND OBLIQUE LINES

There is uncertainty in the literature on when children can identify and when they can represent *oblique lines*.[5] Gesell (1971) did not include 3-year-olds in his test on 'copying a diamond' and this task only appears in the Stanford-Binet scale at the age of 7. Many project children used *oblique lines* from the age of 3.

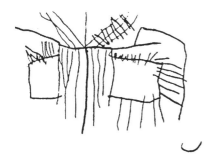

Figure 5.20 'Umbrella.'   **Figure 5.21** 'Look... a leaf.'

Just as the *rectangle* is a figurative effect of drawing *grids*, so '*triangularity*' is a figurative effect of drawing *oblique lines*.

Amanda (3:5:28) began to copy the letter 'A'. Like other children, she modified the 'A' towards *parallelism*, with a curious exception. She reported to Mrs B that 'Linda fell over when she came down the slide'. Outside, Amanda climbed to the top of the ladder (at an *oblique angle*), and shouted to Mrs B, 'You have to come down like this'. She then slid down (also at an *oblique angle*). When she returned to the classroom she drew two upper-case letter 'As'. One was *upright* and one was *on its side*. She laughed and said, 'Look, it's fallen over'. What was curious is that these letters were more *oblique* than many drawn later. It was as though her verbalized sensorimotor actions on the slide had helped her to achieve temporary *oblique* lines.

For several weeks Amanda practised *grids* and *oblique lines* with varying success. She made several static three-dimensional models, each named 'see-saw'. She then produced a working model of a see-saw after using a balance bar. She added weights to both sides and then removed the weights from one end. At first she enjoyed the crash down before making the ends move more slowly.

Amanda (4:6:9) followed this with a model of 'A gun', which could be moved up and down and followed by 'A boat' with a rudder that could be moved back and forth. At 4:7:20, Amanda aimed at getting *weight equivalence* with the balance bar. She made the bar *oblique* and then said, 'That's got to be even'. She then levelled it up. In the following observations, Amanda tried to modify her *straight-line* schemas towards the *oblique*.

At 3:5:28 (Figure 5.22 – 'Mum, Dad, Nichola and me'), her letter 'As' are *grids*, but she also draws a continuous *zig-zag* (a section gives the figurative effect needed for an *oblique* letter 'A'). The next day she managed to draw *oblique lines* (Figure 5.23) but they are all going in the same direction. A *triangle* requires *oblique* lines going in opposite directions. She called this drawing 'Amanda's slide, Mum's slide, Nick's slide', so the action element is still there. As though 'worn out' with her efforts, Amanda followed with a spate of *parallel line* and *grid* drawings of which the following are typical.

Figure 5.22 'Mum, Dad, Nichola and me.'

Figure 5.23 'Amanda's slide, Mum's slide, Nick's slide.'

'Railway line' (Figure 5.24) was drawn with two pens in one hand. Figure 5.25 was named 'This is a chipper for cutting carrots', which introduces *a function* for the *grid*. Formally expressed this would be 'The cutting of carrots [into those shapes] is *functionally dependent* on the *grid* shape of the chipper'. *Function* also comes into Figure 5.26, which she drew at 4:3:26 and is named 'A man and a ladder for climbing up'.

Function was usually defined initially in terms of personal action. Ladders, for instance, were 'for jumping off' as often as 'for climbing up'. Probably for two reasons: ladders were assimilated to dynamic schemas of *up* and *down*; and personal experience of ladders and slides provided the content for the judgment.

Adrian (4:7:18) described Figure 5.27 as 'Noughts and crossed' (not 'noughts and crosses'). 'Crossed' describes the action of making the mark. 'Crosses' would describe the figurative feedback from the mark-making.

Piaget (1971a, p. 139) has suggested that even the most elementary aggregates of behaviour are connected with each other. From an early age, marks are connected spatially. For instance, following a candle-making activity, several children represented 'Candle with a flame on top'. They *connected* marks in a *vertical order*. They placed the flame (*a dab*) *on-top-of* the candle, (*a vertical line*). Several researchers have found a preference for vertically organized objects in early perception, which is echoed in early representation.

Graewe (1935, cited in Harris, 1963, p. 14) found that children move from *vertical* to *horizontal* orientations, particularly in relation to drawings of animals. At first the same general schema serves for both animal and human figures. Later there is an attempt to differentiate the animal from the human by drawing the animal on a *horizontal* plane. An early example of this from a project child is as follows.

Amanda had been using *parallel lines* in a variety of representations. Her mother was a heavy smoker and several representations were of 'Cigarettes on an ashtray'. For this she placed thin, wooden cylinders side by side on a shallow

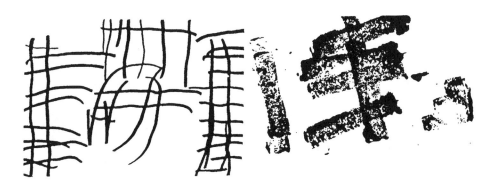

Figure 5.24 'Railway line.'   Figure 5.25 'This is a chipper for cutting carrots.'

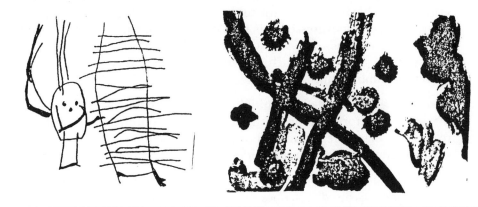

Figure 5.26 'A man and a ladder for climbing up.'

Figure 5.27 'Noughts and crossed.'

container. At 3:4:22 Amanda represented 'Rabbit … long ears' (Figure 5.28). Here she has used *parallel lines* to represent the long ears of 'rabbit' but, for the first time, she has also represented an animal on a *horizontal* plane.

As with the initial placing of marks, it is not always easy to differentiate between intended spatial orderings and orderings that are simply the fortuitous effects of drawing objects on a page. It is easier to see advances in *ordering within figures* than to see developments in *ordering between figures*. For instance, in the following two drawings, the children drew, pointed at and named the parts as though they were working within an internalized *horizontal and vertical Coordinate system*. Brenda (4:7:11) pointed at and named each part of Figure 5.29: 'Police dog, leg, leg, leg, leg, head'. Similarly, Stephen (3:7:28) drew 'Elephant, trunk, eyes, ear, four legs, tail' (Figure 5.30).

Figure 5.28 'Rabbit … long ears.'

Figure 5.29 'Police dog, leg, leg, leg, leg, head.'

The following observation illustrates an earlier stage of spatial organization. It also illustrates the close relationship between cognition and affect. Alistair (3:1:11) painted 'A horse'. The teacher talked to him about it within hearing distance of Stephen, who had just painted Figure 5.30. Alistair said, 'That's the head', pointing with his brush. Stephen saw this and quickly pointed to the opposite end and said, 'That's his tail'. Alistair was furious, pushed him away and said, or rather shouted, 'No, it isn't, that's the legs'. The legs were at an *oblique* angle, half way between *horizontal* and *vertical*. He had not managed to place his marks accurately within a set of *horizontal and vertical co-ordinates*.

When young children squabble they are often described as naughty or socially immature. It came as a relief to parents to realize that children, like adults, might have understandable reasons for being annoyed. In the example just given there was a lack of cognitive match between the two boys in relation to spatial ordering. Interestingly enough, when these two boys first made a positive social contact (Alistair was 2:10:10 and Stephen 3:2:0), it was on the basis of a cognitive match. They were both making *lines* with cars. When they noticed each other's *lines* they made them meet to their mutual satisfaction.

CIRCLES AND ENCLOSED CURVES

Of 3-year-olds, 53 per cent can copy a circle (Stanford-Binet intelligence scale). Such norms of development were made available to project parents but they were not interested. What did interest the parents were examples from the children as shown in this and the next chapter. Some examples, such as the following, generated particular interest.

Meryl (2:3:0) drew an *enclosure* and named it 'Button' (Figure 5.31). Her mother reported, with excitement, that while Meryl was 'helping' to wash curtains she had handled a curtain ring and said, 'Button'. The experience followed by the

Figure 5.30 'Elephant, trunk, eyes, four legs, tail.'

Figure 5.31 'Button.'

representation indicates that a shape generalization has been made. After discussion on extension, Meryl's mother gathered together circular objects and played a 'naming' game, thus helping Meryl to differentiate between objects in the general class of *circular* objects.

During a home visit, after the end of the project, Meryl (5:7:2) drew 'My house' (Figure 5.32). The actual house is on a new, imaginatively planned estate, high on a hill with an attractive view. During the project the family had lived in one damp room in an inner-city area where the atmosphere was polluted by heavy and noisy traffic.

During the project Meryl's scores on intelligence, language and drawing tests went up by about 20 points and, two years after the end of the project, she was one year ahead of her chronological age in reading recognition and comprehension. Teachers will recognize that the drawing of the house is advanced for a 5-year-old.

Salam (2:11:26), following a project visit to a park, drew a *vertical line* and a *circle*. He named the *circle* 'Conker' (Figure 5.33). This was the first English word he had spoken in the project. The drawing may have suggested that he had a 'figurative' mental image except that in the park he had put conkers in one container and twigs into another. The sorting was *classificatory*. To collect objects on the basis of similarity and to differentiate those from others is to *classify*.

Pete (3:1:0) struggled to draw a *discrete enclosure* instead of his habitual *circular scribble*. When he achieved a fairly good form he named it 'Bubble'. Five days later, he used his new form to represent 'Hat'. At that time he could not be parted from a white bowler hat. Mrs B admired the drawing and asked, 'Where is the rim?' Pete looked at his drawing with interest and said, 'Oh!' He drew a *circle*

Figure 5.32 'My house.'   Figure 5.33 'Conker.'

next to the first one and said, 'That's the rim' (Figure 5.34). One week later, in the park, he collected pebbles and placed them in a neat *circle* around a hole.

Pete (3:2:17) selected buttons from a box of odds and ends. He stuck these onto the top of a carton and named it 'Bus and wheels'. At 3:2:30 (in a burst of effort) Pete did six *circular* paintings one after the other. At this point he began to show an obsessive interest in things that *rotate*. The figurative appearance of a circular hat may seem to be in a different category from an interest in *rotation*, except that *rotational actions* produce the figurative effect of *circles*. The widespread representation of 'wheels going round' indicates that children often represent *rotation* with circular action.

At 3:2:30 Pete watched Alistair pulling a toy bird, which made its wings swivel. He said, 'Look, that goes round'. Every day for weeks he borrowed Mrs B's keys and matched up keys with locks throughout the building. His two criteria for success were whether they would *rotate* and whether he could make the lock move. He was exploring a *functional dependency relationship* that, formally expressed, would read 'Opening the lock is *functionally dependent* on *rotating* the key in the lock'. This dynamic aspect of *one-to-one correspondence* has more curriculum potential than more static types of matching.

Pete (3:5:0) suddenly, and atypically, appeared to be both social and cooperative in offering to fetch water for a group of children playing in the sand. Further observation showed that this was a ploy for investigating the *functional dependency relation* between the force of water and the *rotating* tap. He discovered that the sharpened end of a pencil is *functionally dependent* on *rotating* the handle of a pencil sharpener; that he could make a bell ring by *rotating* the hands of a clock; that hinges on the oven door allow the door to *swivel* back and forth; that the *rotation* of a ratchet wheel-handle makes a driver's seat move *backwards* and *forwards*; and that a right or left *rotation* of a driving wheel steers a pedal car in a *right* or *left direction*.

Figure 5.34 'Hat.... That's the rim.'

On a project visit to a museum, Pete accompanied every right and left turn of the bus with an equivalent right and left turn of an imaginary wheel. He also represented the starting and stopping of the bus with a backward and forward movement of an imaginary brake.

Pete was taken into the project in response to a concerned paediatrician. initially he was unstable and unpredictable. His IQ increased from 87 at 2:8:0 to 92 at the age of 4:8:0 and to 100 at the age of 7:1:0. He became much more stable emotionally and his social relationships improved.

Stephen (3:1:26) ran round and round in a *circular direction*, laughing. The next day he told his mother while having breakfast that his plate had two *round lines* on it. He also pointed to a tin and said, 'That has a *stripe* on it'. His mother wrote this information in his 'home book' and he took it to the project. Stephen (3:4:30) drew a *circle*. He called it 'Puddle and snow'. The snow was signified by *dabs*.

Newly emerged graphic forms were usually content-free and small modifications served to differentiate content. For instance, a *circle* with a small *radial* would be called 'apple' but not 'orange'. This route from generalizing assimilation to differentiation also took place with speech, as when Jock (1:8:28) assimilated 'golf ball', 'buoy' and 'beads' to a *spherical* schema, all expressed by 'Football'. Similarly, Meryl assimilated several *circular* objects to a generalized schema called 'Button'.

Much parental help was directed towards naming differences within schematic similarities, as in the following example. Alistair (2:9:1) pointed to a *circular*, numbered dial on a toy petrol-pump and said, 'It's a clock, mummy'. His mother replied, 'It looks like a clock, doesn't it? I wonder why a clock would be among the garage toys?' Together they explored and decided that it was more likely to be a petrol-pump.

Observations discussed so far show that graphic representations are based on schematic form combined with personal experience. Both the form and the content of experience can be extended by adult interest and help.

CORE AND RADIALS

Werner (cited in Harris, 1963) points out that the crudest drawings of 'men' are often just completed closed figures and that this central core soon acquires various radial appendages. There is some disagreement in the literature as to whether children begin to draw and model with global, undifferentiated wholes before adding particularized elements, or whether they begin with individual elements they then build up to wholes. This is probably an artificial problem in that cognitive development is seldom related to 'either/ors'.

The project children represented 'wholes' with simple enclosures, but they also represented 'parts' of an object from an early stage. A single *enclosure*, for

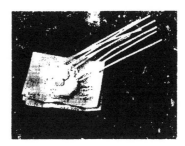

Figure 5.35 'Deer with antlers.'

instance, could represent 'apple', while a single *line* could represent 'stalk'. A single *enclosure* could represent 'brush' but a few unconnected *lines* could represent 'bristles'. The children represented the salient features of objects related to their existing schemas. Whether the prevailing schema was used for the representation of wholes or parts did not seem to matter.

Marks are co-ordinated and the *core and radial* is one result. In many cases, *radials* represent the appendages of main bodies. For instance, after seeing deer in the park, Clare (4:1:22) represented 'Deer with antlers' (Figure 5.35). The 'antlers' consisted of seven *radials* stuck through the boundary of a *core* of clay. Although the form is basic, the 'antlers' are not spread all over the core, they are clustered *near* each other as are actual antlers. Kellogg (1969) found the *core and radial* form to be universal and biologically determined. What is not determined is richness of content that can be assimilated through experience.

Enriching experiences cumulate. Young (1978), while working on nerve cells, found their 'tree-like' forms attractive because programmes in the human brain have a special affinity for such shapes. In the interests of continuity it would be useful to have curriculum materials based on schematic themes.

Much adult help can be received at different cognitive levels, during which children find their own 'match'. For instance, Amanda (3:3:15) drew a straightforward *core and radial* pattern and named it 'Spider on the grass' (Figure 5.36). Spiders, of which there were many in the project, had been examined under magnifying glasses. Amanda's 'spider' had eight 'legs'. Mrs B and Amanda's mother showed enthusiasm over the correspondence between Amanda's radials and the number of actual spider's legs.

It was known that Amanda was unlikely to have represented *eightness* because she was paying almost exclusive attention to *three*. She drew *three* see-saws and *three* letter 'As'. She told Mrs B that there were *three* ways of coming down a slide. She clung to *three* pens and tried to use them simultaneously to make *three* lines, and so on. The adults were validating *one-to-one correspondence* up to *eight* on a 'fingers crossed' basis.

Figure 5.36 'Spider on the grass.'   **Figure 5.37 'It's an animal, it has four legs.'**

The following example illuminates the action basis of *one-to-one correspondence*; it also dashes hopes that the figurative effect of early radials necessarily corresponds with perceived content. Adrian (4:8:19) drew 'It's an animal, it has four legs' (Figure 5.37). At this point it did have four legs. Mrs B admired the drawing and asked how many legs there were. Adrian said, enthusiastically, 'Four... look'. He drew another four strokes saying, 'Look … one, two, three, four'. The counting was a tally of his actions. He disregarded the altered figurative effects. The chances are that he was equally indifferent to the original effect of '*four*' legs. An explanation may lie in the fact that an interest in *radials* is spatial; an interest in *one-to-one correspondence* is logico-mathematical. The two aspects do become co-ordinated but it is an unsolved pedagogical problem as to whether co-ordinations can be helped along by intervention.

As might be expected, conventionalized 'suns' and 'hedgehogs' are common representations with this form. As with other schemas, perception is sensitized to similar things in the environment. For instance, while on a visit to Kew Gardens, Alistair (3:5:17) shouted with excitement when he came across three objects. One was a water sprinkler that *rotated* and produced a dynamic *core-and-radial* spray. One was a besom broom (a bunch of twigs tied round a handle). The third was an open pine cone.

'Intension' to a class (aspects that are common) begins in sensorimotor assimilations. For instance, objects are perceived to be *suckable* or *throwable* (Inhelder and Piaget, 1964, p. 283). Intension, therefore, is truly spontaneous.

'Extension', on the other hand, requires that the subject must be able to define specific members of a given class. Language is crucial to extension. Although some aspects of language are spontaneous, names for specific members of a given class have to be taught. When project adults helped to extend the range of objects that shared a common property, by naming, they were 'fleshing out' form (intension) by extending content.

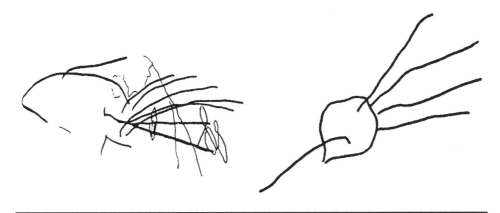

Figure 5.38   Figure 5.39 'Flower.'

The earliest *core-and-radials* were simple and undifferentiated, as in the following. Meryl (2:2:5) stuck pieces of curved pasta into a lump of clay. This seemed to influence her perception as she became fascinated by a bubble pipe and a magnifying glass, both with *a core* and *one radial* configuration. This interest was reflected in her drawings and models. At (2:2:21) she drew an incomplete *enclosure* with *radials* next to it (*juxtaposition* rather than *connection*) (Figure 5.38). Meryl (2:10:8) amalgamated *core* and *radials* and named the result 'Flower' (Figure 5.39). She had been showing a lot of interest in flowers. Like many other children with this schema, she liked representing 'umbrella', using a configuration similar to Figure 5.39.

Jock went through a sequence similar to Meryl. When the schema was at its most powerful he became devoted to a large, soft model (Humpty-Dumpty) made by a mother, consisting of four lozenge-shaped radials sewn onto a *core*. After a few days he represented the model and called it 'Humpty-Dumpty' (Figure 5.40). He was also inseparable from a puppet made for him by a mother. He made his own puppet called 'Animal … one leg' (Figure 5.41).

Figure 5.40 'Humpty-Dumpty.'   Figure 5.41 'Animal... one leg.'

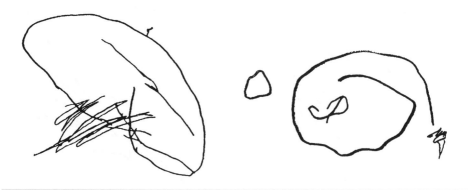

Figure 5.42 'Plant in a pot... a bean plant.'   **Figure 5.43 'Elephant, eye... eye.'**

Figure 5.44 'Elephant ... tortoise.'   **Figure 5.45 'Tortoise.'**

Pete (3:1:5) drew 'Plant in pot' (Figure 5.42). Mrs B asked if he had any kind of plant in mind and he replied, 'A bean plant'. The example of 'Toothbrush, bristles' (Figure 5.9) showed an *unconnected core* with *radials*. In Figure 5.42, Pete has *connected* plant with pot.

Advances in schematic development are frequently lost temporarily. This obscures developmental advances. Usually the first drawings in a sequence have the poorest forms as though the act of drawing needs to 'get into gear'. For instance, Pete (3:2:20) drew Figures 5.43 and 5.44 on the same day. The first was named 'Elephant' and the two small *enclosures* were named 'Eye ... eye'. He seemed quite happy about one eye being *inside* and the other *outside* the main *enclosure*. He went straight on to Figure 5.44, which he first named 'Elephant' and then 'Tortoise' – another example of fitting different but appropriate content on to a particular form. On two criteria, either skilled action or resemblance between mark and depicted content, the second drawing is the most advanced. Advances are developmental but not within a narrow time interval. Alistair's (3:10:1) drawing of 'Tortoise' (Figure 5.45) is similar in form to Pete's.

Clare (4:7:17) focused on a life-belt during a project visit to a lock. She had a long discussion with her mother about a true incident when a little girl, having fallen into a canal, was rescued by a man with a life-belt. This discussion included *functional dependency* relationships based on belt and rope. On returning from the visit, Clare drew 'Life-belt and the rope. A big rope, another rope' (Figure 5.46). Many children could not resist the impulse to add extra *radials* long after they knew how many appendages there were on the object being depicted.

Figures 5.47 and 5.48 show how *radials* gradually become more specific to the content being depicted. In these drawings children were careful to point out individual features, such as 'trunk', 'tail' and 'horns'. *Radials* also became increasingly organized within *a horizontal* and *vertical co-ordinate system*.

Figure 5.49, drawn when Saima was 4:6:12, shows that a complete *core and radial* form has been used for the representation of 'tambourine' but 'tambourine' is

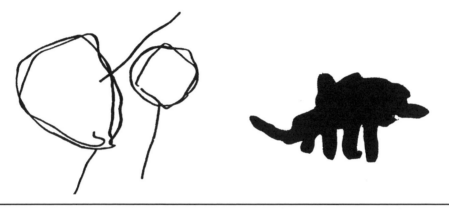

Figure 5.46 'Life-belt and the rope. A big one, another rope.'

Figure 5.47 'Elephant, trunk, tail.'

Figure 5.48 'Rhino, one, two, three, four legs and horns.'

Figure 5.49 'Tambourine, man with one leg.'

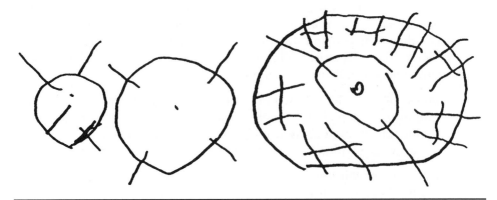

Figure 5.50 'Clock and apple, hand, stalk.'

Figure 5.51 'Saima is going to make a clock, numbers, hands.'

now just one object in the picture. Saima had been dancing, and tapping her fingers against one. The fingers (the *grid connected* with the right arm of the figure) are an important part of her representation.

Figures 5.50 and 5.51 show an interesting differentiation, mentioned earlier. Saima (4:7:5) and (4:7:8) began to draw *radials inside* and *outside enclosures* and to name with content that fitted the configurations. Figure 5.50 was named 'Clock and apple'. The *inside radial* was named 'hand' (the hand of a clock) and the *radial outside* the *enclosure* 'stalk'. Figure 5.51, drawn three days later, was named 'Saima is going to make a clock'. The *grid* shapes are 'numbers' and the *radials* are 'hands'. Within the general form of a schema, young children are able to make many, minute differentiations.

OPEN AND CLOSED ARCS

The use of the *arc* in project drawings appeared after the forms discussed so far. Similarly in early perception, during the first year, infants respond to simpler configurations before they begin to respond to *upward curves* (smiles). This again suggests a developmental link between early perception and later representation.

In common with all the marks discussed so far, the arc was frequently used for representing *trajectories*. Stephen's (3:7:17) 'Aeroplane landing on the runway' (Figure 5.52) is an instance of this. Stephen had painted several similar *trajectories* with expansive motor actions. One was called 'A cloud going down into a path'. The invention (rather than discovery) of content that can be expressed by a schema (in this case, a particular *trajectory*) is called by Piaget 'distorting assimilation' (Piaget, 1962, p. 102).

One of the most familiar and common uses for the *upward arc* is as an equivalent for a smile. Less frequently, a *downward curve* is used to represent a sad expres-

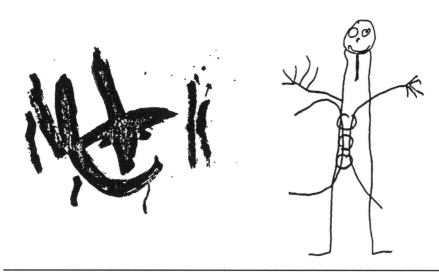

Figure 5.52 'Aeroplane landing
on the runway.'

Figure 5.53 'Man.'

sion. Many investigators have observed this but have floundered on interpretations. For instance, Eng (1959) linked her niece, Margaret's, drawings of 'smiles' with Sully's theory of the emotions. She interpreted content. This is easy to understand because the figurative features of the drawings and Margaret's speech reflect content. For instance, after drawing an *upward arc* for 'mouth' Margaret said, 'That's cheerful isn't it?' (Eng, p. 51).

Researchers are constrained by the richness (or otherwise) of theories. Eng was not informed by theories concerned with commonalities. The theories of her time illuminated individual differences. This is probably why she focused mainly on content. When Margaret (4:9:7) represented 'Man' (Figure 5.53), Eng wondered why she represented a man in a frock-coat. What she is actually doing is trying out a wide range of content with her new form – the *arc*. With this new form she represented 'cheerfulness', 'fingers', 'frock-coat', 'letters' (Figure 5.54), 'trees' (Figures 5.55 and 5.56). She also drew a group of men skiing down a slope. The skiers have curved skis.

Eng categorized individual drawings into groups but again based on content. This failed because the content defied useful categorization. For instance, when Margaret drew 'tulip' and used a *zig-zag* form, this was categorized as the 'tulip formula'. When she drew 'button' using her *circle* schema, Eng called this the 'button formula'. Unfortunately, this led to almost as many categories as the content being represented.

It is doubtful whether 'content' has a developmental sequence because it is subject to individual first-hand experiences. There are, of course, common

Figure 5.54 'Letters.'   **Figure 5.55 'Tree.'**

experiences – being smiled at and smiling are instances. Experience of skiing is not shared by all.

THE USE OF THE ARC IN LETTER FORMATIONS

Before Figure 5.54, Margaret had drawn only *straight line* or *circular* letters as in 'O', 'H', 'L' and 'T'. In other words, she had used earlier graphic schemas. The formation of upper case 'B', 'D' and 'R' in Figure 5.54 is a manifestation of the use of the *arc*.

The relatively late use of the *arc* in letter formations requires a re-think about blaming parents for teaching children upper-case letters. An analysis of project children's drawings shows that there is a direct correspondence between the marks they use in drawing and marks they use for 'writing'. In environments where 'writing' goes on, early writing is as spontaneous as early drawing. Adults do not 'teach' as much as 'validate' with interest and approval.

When project child, Shanaz, was using a *grid* schema for the representation of 'aeroplane', 'dishcloth', 'sieve', 'net curtains', 'window', 'ladders', and so on, she signed her name with marks that had no relationship to letters in her name. She used a small *circle*, a-back-to-front letter 'E' and a small *right angle*. These marks were identical to the marks used by Eng's niece at a similar age. However, when Shanaz began to use an *arc* in her drawing, like other project children whose names began with letter 'S', she produced letter 'S' with two distinct *arcs*, one below the other (Figure 5.57). She also modified her *grid* letter 'H' into a lower-case letter 'h'.

The earliest attempts to co-ordinate *lines* and *arcs* in letter formations consisted of placing *arcs next to* lines but not quite *connected*. For instance, Clare (4:7:17) (Figure 5.58) attempted to write her name from memory. The 'C' and the 'l' present little difficulty. The 'a' requires that the *line* and the *arc* should be the same height and that the *line* and arc should be in a particular right and left order. Clare has not managed this but the sources of both error and achievement are clear.

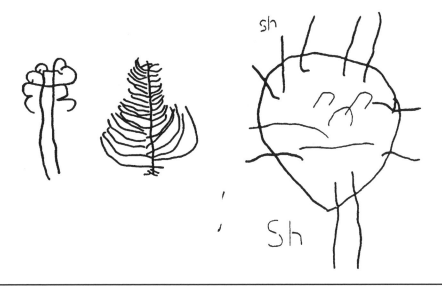

Figure 5.56 'Tree, Christmas tree.'   Figure 5.57

Figure 5.58 'My name.'   Figure 5.59 'Lesley's baby Deborah.'

The project children found it easier to construct 'b' than 'a' because the *vertical line* was drawn first. In letter 'b' the *arc* is easier to place on the right. Having to place the arc on the left of the line in letter 'a' requires a directional back-tracking.

Letter 'e' presents a similar problem. Clare makes the *arc* and *next* to it draws a small horizontal line. The *line* is not tucked inside the *arc*. The letter 'r' does not present this problem because the *arc* follows on directionally from the *vertical line*.

Figure 5.59 shows one of Clare's drawings produced two days before she tried to write her name. The drawing was named 'Lesley's baby Deborah'. Like Figure 5.60 drawn by Shanaz (4:2:8) 'Chicken with eggs in the middle', it is an interesting

Figure 5.60 'Chicken with eggs in the middle.'   **Figure 5.61 'Lips, eyes.'**

example of the representation of *enveloping space*, but it also shows both mother and baby smiling with the aid of the *arc*. There are also *arc* 'fingers' and 'arms'.

At this stage many project children *divided circles* into two halves for various representations. Susan used a whole *circle* of clay to represent 'cake'. She cut this in two and called each piece 'half a cake'. At 4:1:5 she drew a face (Figure 5.61) and represented both 'lips' and 'eyes' with her new schema of *circles divided into halves*. However, she did not manage to use the new schema within a *horizontal* orientation.

Figure 5.20 shows the representation of 'umbrella' with a grid schema. With the *arc* appeared the more conventional *semi-circular* representation of umbrella (Figure 5.63). A similar shift took place from a *grid* 'horse' (Figure 3.1) to a *semi-circular* 'back of a horse' (Figure 3.2).

By 4:4:10, Shanaz could almost write her name but some letters were still being modified by her existing schemas. In figure 5.62, 's' and 'h' are still being constructed by *juxtaposing* separate forms. She cannot yet draw letter 'a' by drawing an *arc* on its side and then adding *a stroke* on the right, and yet she virtually managed this form four months earlier when she drew 'Basket' (Figure 5.64). Also, although she has the form for the representation of 'Z' she has not managed to combine this with the correct orientation. Her attempt resembles an upper-case 'N'.

The following observation illustrates, once again, how schemas lead to *functional dependency* relations. Shanaz (4:0:11) had been using the real but unheated steam iron in the home area. She pointed to the *arc* of small holes round the bottom front of the iron and wanted to know what they were for. Mrs B demonstrated the *function* of the holes by heating and using the iron. She had a rapt audience. Shanaz's mother (who spoke very little English) communicated excitedly in Urdu with another Asian mother.

In order to help both child and parent, Mrs B was particularly clear in her descriptions of what was going on with parents who spoke English as a second language. Another Asian mother had observed her son changing *balls* of clay into *cylindrical* shapes before bending them into *arcs*. Salam had organized the *three arcs* in order of *size* and had expressed great satisfaction. Mrs B wrote about this as follows:

Figure 5.62 'My name.'   **Figure 5.63** 'Umbrella.'

'Salam made balls of clay in different sizes. He rolled out the balls and made them into arcs'. His mother drew a two-dimensional representation of the model.

Salam was so taken with this that it was used to start a book. Each page had a drawing with what he had said about it. The content of the book was very much influenced by his prevailing schema, the arc:

> Roads curve. Petals curve. When people smile their mouths curl up. When people cry their mouths curl down. When we bounce a ball the curves in the air get smaller and smaller [note that the decreasing height of the ball bouncing has been observed as clearly as has the decreasing size of spheres in his model]. The humps on a camel curve. Curly hair has curves, straight hair does not. A tortoise has a curved shell. The scales on a fish curve.

Salam became devoted to his book. Having identified the schema, some content seemed predictable, such as 'arches'. Other content, such as the bouncing ball, took the project adults by surprise.

During a visit to the zoo, Salam talked a great deal about the elephant and resisted leaving the enclosure. The next day he painted 'Elephant' (Figure 5.65). The drawing is an exercise in form (the arc) – the content is the experienced 'elephant', the marks are spatially organized within an internalized grid and the drawing is correctly named.

Shanaz, the Asian child who was so interested in the holes at the front of the iron, discussed with her mother the way in which dolphins and seals leap out of the water. She was interested in elephants' tusks, antelopes' horns and the rhinoceros's horns. On the bus on the way home from the zoo, she conveyed to Mrs B her latest bit of knowledge. She said, 'Do you know the monkey uses its tail for swinging?' (another functional dependency relation).

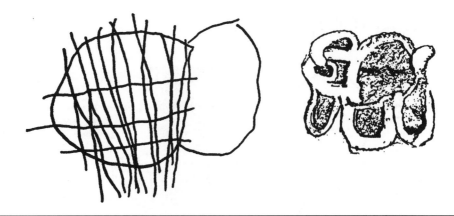

Figure 5.64 'Basket, a ladder.'   Figure 5.65 'Elephant.'

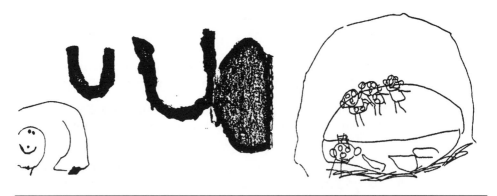

Figure 5.66 'Man, nose, smile, arch.   Figure 5.67 'People on the boat and
That's a man going through the arch.'   the captain smiling and waving.'

Many drawings amalgamated schemas in ways that seemed almost inevitable. For instance, Stephen (3:6:13), mainly exercising the *arc*, drew 'Man, nose, smile, arch' (Figure 5.66). He then said: 'That's a man going through the arch'. A wide range of content, such as arches and tunnels, also include the more dynamic notion of '*going through*'.

Randolph (3:11:20) reached a peak of assimilation in relation to the *open* and *closed arc* in Figure 5.67. He named his drawing 'People on the boat and the captain smiling and waving'. There was a discussion about the boat (*a bisected circle*) and captain's peaked cap (*a small arc connected to a rectangle*). Each of the 'people' has a 'beard' (*small arcs*). The people are 'smiling' (*small arcs*). The 'bridge' that surrounds the drawing is a *large arc*.

The use of the arc in representation comes towards the end of the basic graphic schemas. This position corresponds with the ontogenesis of perception in infants in that signification attached to *arc-like* configuration appears late in infants. Fantz expresses this evolution in relation to 'face' configurations.

Perception culminates in recognition of 'happy or sad, pleased or displeased, friendly or unfriendly' (1961, p. 72).

This growing differentiation can be observed in representations other than the face. For instance, in Randolph's drawing: 'Boy's skipping. He's happy, he's sad' (Figure 5.5) the facial expressions represent 'happy and sad' with the aid of the *arc*. However, the skipping activity is represented by *arc* skipping-ropes.

Randolph first attempted to draw spectacles when he was 4:5:9 (Figure 5.68). The drawing is mainly an exercise in *core* and *radials* but he has discovered the arc and uses one for each side of the spectacles. When he drew 'Mr and Mrs Braham', six months later, there is not only a clear differentiation between the male and female figure but there are also other refinements, such as Mrs Braham wearing spectacles (Figure 5.13). This has been made possible by the coordination of schemas, in this case, *circles*, *arcs* and *projective space*.

Two months later, after a visit from the doctor and a quarrel with another boy for the much-desired stethoscope, he represented the full figure of the doctor together with his stethoscope (Figure 5.69).

OPEN CONTINUOUS TRIANGLE (THE ZIG-ZAG)

It was not easy to see continuity between sensorimotor actions and later *zig-zag* mark-making. The most likely precursor is sensorimotor experience of stairs. Crawling up and down stairs takes place at about 13–14 months (Sheridan, 1975, p. 36). Certainly, 'steps' and 'stairs' are often among the first representations expressed with this schema. Salam (4:6:21) drew 'The boat in Teddington Lock' (Figure 5.70). The 'boat' was the small scribble inside the *enclosure*. The *zig-zag* part of the enclosure was described as 'Steps going down into the lock. The gate goes *up and down*'. The language illuminated the drawing and included a dynamic component.

Salam (3:9:14) placed bricks in a *horizontal zig-zig* formation he called 'Steps'. Mrs B asked him if he could make the steps go in an upward direction but he

Figure 5.68 'The glasses.'   Figure 5.69 'The doctor and that.'

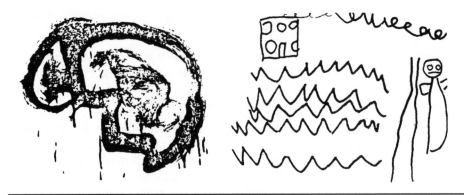

Figure 5.70 'The boat in Teddington Lock.'

Figure 5.71 'Mrs Bruce watching the water. House near the river.'

showed no interest in this. Many children represented 'steps' following visits to the swimming baths.

Clare (4:7:17) used *zig-zag* lines to represent 'water' (Figure 5.71) and a different schema to represent 'smoke'. Her drawing and speech contained two *'proximity'* relations: 'Mrs Bruce watching the water. House near the river'.

Within psycho-analytic theory, the *zig-zag* in drawing has been interpreted as a sign of aggression although this interpretation has been challenged (Sundberg and Ballinger, 1968, p. 983). Eng (1959), applying this theory, reported that Margaret had represented two rows of terrifying canine teeth with *zig-zag* lines. However, an examination of Margaret's other drawings show that her use of the *zig-zag* covers a variety of content difficult to link to aggression.

The schema appeared at 3:8:17 with eight *zig-zag* lines underneath each other. At 4:8:22 she drew *zig-zag* stairs with a figure climbing down (Figure 5.72). She named this 'A little girl climbing up to heaven. Her legs are like that because she's tired'. She followed this with an even longer flight of stairs and called it 'God carrying a soul up to heaven'. It was only at this point that she drew *zig-zag* teeth as well as 'writing' an uppercase letter 'M' for the first time.

A project child, Stephen (3:4:30), after a visit to the Natural History Museum, drew a *zig-zag* line above seven *vertical lines* and named it 'Stegosaurus' (Figure 5.73). From the age of 4 he always picked out the letter 'W' although it was not in his name. His drawings and models became increasingly refined. Figure 5.74 shows a clay model he made of 'stegosaurus' when he was 4:9:25. His advanced representations had a history in earlier ones.

As with other schemas, representation of the figurative did not preclude an 'action' component. For instance, Adrian (3:7:23), after using a saw, represented 'A saw sawing' (Figure 5.75). The saw blade was signified by the *zig-zag* but the action was represented by a *vertical scribble*. Some time later, on a visit to the

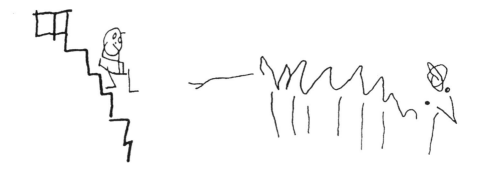

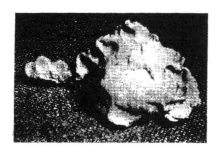

Figure 5.72 'A little girl climbing up to heaven. I've made her legs like that because she's tired'.

Figure 5.73 'Stegosaurus'.

Figure 5.74 'Stegosaurus.'

Figure 5.75 'A saw sawing.'

Science Museum, he was absorbed by a working model of cog-wheels and said to Mrs B, 'Look, it's got teeth'.

The following observation generated a great deal of excitement among project adults. Salam, as early as 3:6:9, had used the *zig-zag* to signify 'king'. When he was 3:11:23, Mrs B found him in the home area placing knives into two heaps. When she expressed great interest in this he showed her the serrated edges on one set of knives. The other set had non-serrated blades. When Salam's mother had this categorization pointed out to her she laughed and said that now she realized why she could never get her pinking shears away from him (she was a home garment-maker).

Discussions on possible curriculum extensions led to the realization that many of the project children had the perceptual ability to identify leaves by three criteria.

1 The arrangement of leaves on a stem (*core and radial* schemas).

2 The edge pattern of leaves (*zig-zag* and other line schemas, such as *continuous curve*).

3 The general shape of leaves (*enclosures*).

The children were not 'operational' in that they could not 'hold on to' the three criteria simultaneously, but they could observe and represent each criterion sequentially. Presumably the ability to hold on to a multiplicity of relations at the late concrete-operational stage of development depends on being able to consider significant criteria separately at an earlier stage.

As with all the other schemas, naming (if viewed from a content point of view) could be taken as instances of 'flitting'. Randolph (3:6:27), for instance, cut out a *zig-zag* pattern to which he attached three different names: 'a bird's wing', 'a fish tail' and 'a fan'. He was 'fitting' different but appropriate content into his latest 'form'.

ANGLES, TRIANGLES AND QUADRILATERALS

There is confusion in the literature between form perception, form-copying and spontaneous form production and the ages at which each is said to appear. Mussen et al. (1969), for instance, referring to Stanford-Binet norms, state that 4-year-old children can discriminate between *squares, circles* and *triangles*. As most 6-month-old infants can discriminate between these shapes (Lovell, 1959, p. 104), they probably mean that 4-year-olds can copy test items of these geometric forms. If so this would not correspond to Gesell's (1971) norms where no 4-year-old could copy a triangle. Forty per cent of 5-year-olds and 95 per cent of 6-year-olds could (Gesell, p. 165). Researchers who have studied children's spontaneous drawings have found that these forms are mastered long before they can be copied in laboratory conditions.[6] Copying should not be confused with recognition because 70 per cent of 2-year-olds can place a *circle, square* and *triangle* in a three-hole form board while doing the Stanford-Binet intelligence test.

Piaget and Inhelder (1956) have suggested reasons why there should be this lag between the production of spontaneous and copied shapes. If, as they suggest, the first abstractions of shape arise from co-ordinated sensorimotor behaviours, then copying the mere percept of an object involves a different process from the production of a drawing as abstraction (1956, p. 25).

McCandless (1970) discusses the experiental origin of the spontaneously drawn *rectangle* and *triangle*. By 10 or 11 months, infants typically *pull themselves up into the upright position and step sideways*, hanging on to the edge of a table. As a 'feedback' from this *trajectory* they have a tactile experience of *edge* and *corner*. If this explanation is valid then the typical form-copying test is testing something other than drawing as reconstruction of action.

Although the route of constructing form from early action is by no means clear, development seems to follow a general route as follows. Infants can track objects moving in *straight-line trajectories* before they can follow objects that change and move in various directions. Similarly, when toddling, the child moves in a *straight-line direction* before he or she can *turn corners* (Sheridan, 1975). Internal images (of action) evolve then become co-ordinated with each other into clusters.

Where a change of direction is made in toddling or running, or as a change of direction at the corner of a table, a sensorimotor *right angle* is experienced. These experiences become clusters of differentiated movement images that, when applied in the activity of drawing, produce a figurative correspondence in different graphic forms.

Inner forms are always in advance of children's abilities to produce forms for the purposes of representation. Therefore, drawing lags behind recognition, which indicates internal images. Leaving aside this time lag, drawing takes a route similar to the route from action to image (Piaget and Inhelder, 1956, p. 46). Children try first of all to reconstruct a *rectangular* form in drawing by employing a *continuous line*. This is probably an effort to preserve the unity of the shape as a whole (1956, pp. 52–68). These early attempts fail because success does not depend initially on how objects look but on a set of co-ordinated actions.

Where co-ordinated actions are not sufficiently skilled, the figurative effects show 'poor' form. A new strategy is, therefore, adopted. Good form is sought and achieved by the use of *horizontal* and *vertical movements*. Of 4-year-olds who managed to copy a *square*, 10 per cent did so by drawing *horizontal and vertical lines* that met at the corners (Gesell, 1971). Eng (1959) recorded that her niece wanted her to draw a flag over and over. Although she was interested in the figurative effects she was mainly interested in how the flag (a rectangle) was produced.

Piaget and Inhelder (1956) give an interesting example of a $3\frac{1}{2}$-year-old child who, having drawn a *triangular* house, explained that she was really trying to produce a *rectangle*. She was able to describe the four movements necessary for success without being able to manage the co-ordination in drawing. There were many similar instances in project children.

Linda (3:4:27) made many attempts to paint *rectangles* but, at first, managed only one good *right angle*. She represented objects such as 'doctor's cabinet', 'house', 'letterbox', 'bed' and 'pillow', while simultaneously paying close attention to *rectangular* objects in the environment.

By 3:11:24, Linda had mastered the *rectangle* and was representing *sub-divisions*. Her names for these products reflected her schematic concerns: 'a house with two doors', 'these are the slide steps' (here *'grid'* has evolved into small, *connected rectangles*), 'the top of the slide is to stand on' (this uses *rectangle* and expresses a *functional dependency relationship*), 'the door is open, it's a cube' (*rectangle*) and 'a door frame, the door is open, a doorstep' (*three rectangles*).

Susan (3:1:6) became excited when she made a *quadrilateral* shape by pulling an elastic band around 3 × 4 nails. She said, 'Look, that's a bed'. Later she drew a man with one *rectangular* 'foot'. The other 'foot' was a failed *rectangle*. She scribbled over this and said, 'It's a broken foot'. There was a four-month gap before she drew another *rectangle*, following a visit, which she named 'The hothouse at Kew'. From then on she began to represent 'legs' with right angles. In most cases her figures looked as though they were running but Susan did not comment on this. She named Figure 5.76 'Two people, smile'.

At 3:9:22 she *connected four* small *squares* that she called 'Seats on the boat'; she cut out a *triangular* 'flag' and stuck it on to a 'flag-pole' she *connected* to the boat. Figure 5.77 (3:11:13) shows how far she has reached in drawing *rectangles*. She named it 'Mrs Bruce house and door'. She discovered the strategy of using an edge of the paper as one side of the *rectangle*.

Two months later, Susan (4:1:5) produced a series of drawings representing actions and ingredients involved in cooking. The *rectangle* was used for representing 'a cooker', 'butter', 'flour' and 'sugar'. 'Sugar' was represented by lots of small *dots* inside the rectangle, and the action of pouring was represented by an *oblique scribble*. 'Eggs' and 'dried fruit' were represented by *circles*. 'Cake in the oven' consisted of a *circle* inside a *rectangle*.

Susan tried to copy the word 'cooker' but failed with the letter 'k' because she could draw a *triangular* shape only in a 'pyramid' orientation, as in the *triangular* skirt in Figure 5.77.

Amanda made many three-dimensional models, using earlier schemas but always incorporating a *rectangle* as in the model 'These are the cigarettes' (Figure 5.78). When she was 4:0:25, after trying unsuccessfully to draw a *rectangle* with *a continuous line*, she folded the edges of a *rectangle* of paper but the last edge defeated her (Figure 5.79). She then tried to draw a *rectangle* with a continuous line but the effect was too rounded. She used 'grid' for the inside and named it 'A crate for milk' (Figure 5.80). The next day she drew her first successful form with four separate strokes, named 'Mouse in a cage' (Figure 5.81).

Figure 5.76 'Two people, smile.'   Figure 5.77 'Mrs Bruce. House and door.'

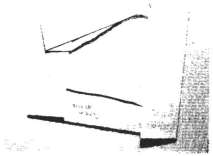

Figure 5.78 'These are the cigarettes.'   **Figure 5.79**

Figure 5.80 'A crate for milk.'   **Figure 5.81** 'Mouse in a cage.'

Amanda began to turn corners without lifting her pencil at 4:3:26 (Figure 5.82). This produced a single *right-angle* 'mouth'. At 4:7:29 she was drawing *rectangles* with *one continuous line*. Figure 5.83 is named 'Lips are for talking'. By 4:7:23 she was drawing 'good' *triangles* and this followed an interest in all things *triangular*. She watched Shanaz cutting a round 'chapatti' into a *grid*. She intervened and said, 'No, you should cut it this way', demonstrating by cutting her 'cake' into quarters.

When she was given a sandwich in a local workers' cafe she announced loudly that she wanted her sandwich cut into *triangles*. In the social circumstances this could have been viewed as annoyingly precocious or as funny. However Amanda's mother was pleased rather than embarrassed.

FROM TOPOLOGICAL TO PROJECTIVE SPACE

We end this chapter with a brief consideration of the shift from *topological* to *projective* space notions used by project children. Project children used projective space mainly in:

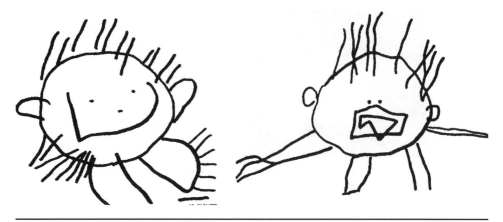

Figure 5.82 'It's my mum.'   **Figure 5.83 'Lips are for talking.'**

- the representation of one object in front of another (44 instances); and

- objects or figures represented from different points of view (45 instances).

Piaget and Inhelder describe the shift as follows: 'From the psychological point of view the essential feature of the shift from topological to projective representation is the introduction of the observer or, the 'point of view', in relation to which the figures are projected' (1956, p. 467).

Randolph (3:11:28) did a rather messy painting but his description indicated that he might have been trying to represent objects relative to each other. He said, 'It's a helicopter and a plane and they are passing each other at the same time'. Four months later he drew himself in bed and in the bath. In both cases he covered up his legs with scribble and explained, 'because you can't see them in the bath or bed'. Randolph (4:10:11) told a story where the theme was the mobility of a mouse in relation to a cat. The idea being explored was that you cannot be seen if you hide (see p. 156 for the full story). Randolph (4:10:14) drew people watching a picture show and represented the backs of the audience. He explained, 'The picture's showing them what it is. It's the backs of their heads' (Figure 5.84).

Randolph (4:10:25) invented a game he played with Mrs B. He asked the question, 'Do you see this?' He showed the object to Mrs B and then placed it somewhere within view. He would then lead Mrs B to a position where the object was out of sight and say, with triumph, 'Now you can't see it, it's disappeared. I'm going to make it come back'. He would go and get the object and say, 'It's here again'. Lois invented a game so similar that it was virtually identical.

It would seem that these children were inventing a version of 'hide-and-seek' evolving from *permanence of the object* acquired during the first year. At the later level it is as if the child were saying, 'I not only know that an object is permanent but I can symbolically represent the hiding and finding of objects and this includes me'.

Figure 5.84 'The picture's showing them what it is. It's the backs of their heads.'

Figure 5.85 'A cow being milked. You can't see its udder, it's inside the pail.'

Lois (4:5:17) drew 'A cow being milked. You can't see its udder, it's inside-the pail' (Figure 5.85). Lois (4:9:3) drew 'Man on a horse. You can't see his other leg because it's on the other side' (Figure 5.86). She followed this with 'Polly the cat. She's lying on her back so she can be tickled' (Figure 5.87).

Lois and Randolph are both able to *rotate* themselves mentally around an object as well as to *rotate* objects in the mind. They can represent the figurative effects of these *rotations* and explain actions and effects in speech.

The few examples given above suggest that, psychologically, the shift from topological to projective space in drawing, and in games, signifies a co-ordination of dynamic and configurational features of action and effect at a particular level of symbolic functioning. At this level, the static configurational aspects of objects can be represented as relative to the points of view of the moving observer.

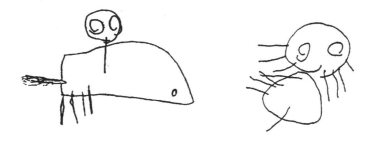

Figure 5.86 'Man on a horse. You can't see his other leg because it's on the other side.'

Figure 5.87 'Polly the cat. She's lying on her back so she can be tickled.'

NOTES

1   Britton also found that children work longer and produce work on a higher developmental level when they communicate with adults (cited in Mann and Taylor, 1973, p. 36–7). The Oxford research project echoes this finding (Bruner, 1980).

2   Clive Bell, 1958, cited in Kellogg (1969), was crushing and dismissive. He wrote (*ibid.* p. 151) that to focus on the representative element in a work of art may or may not be harmful but it is always irrelevant.

3   See Matthews (1984) for a detailed account of the importance of early mark-making.

4   At around 10 months, Froebel project children also drew vertical lines. The line was a graphic effect of making the same gesture with which they threw objects out of their perambulators. The throwing also produced various visual effects.

5   See Rudel and Teuber, 1963; Olson, 1970; Berman et al., 1974.

6   Deutch, 1960, cited in Beadle, 1971, p. 154; Kellogg, 1969, p. 178.

From action to thought

The first aim of the Froebel project was to search for commonalities and continuities ('cognitive constants') in spontaneous thought and behaviour; in other words, to 'search for schemas'. A related aim was to provide developmental sequences of these continuities, or schemas, from early motor behaviour to 'thought'. The project findings show continuity from sensorimotor behaviours, through symbolic representations and functional dependencies, to 'thought'. General findings are given in Chapter 4.

In Chapter 5 the focus was on figural representation and its relationship with early perception. In this chapter the focus is on representation that stems from action. Eight schemas are illustrated and discussed separately at each level, moving from action to thought. Sufficient examples are given to allow the reader to evaluate the categorization of the observations and to consider their usefulness to teachers and parents.

At the end of the chapter, detailed examples of 'thought' illustrate the Piagetian notion that 'thought consists of internalized and co-ordinated action schemas' (Piaget 1959, pp. 357–86). Co-ordination is a feature of operative schemes. Furth (1969, p. 56) has described development itself as 'co-ordinations of co-ordinations of co-ordinations and so on'.

Developmental features of 'knowing' and co-ordinations involved in 'coming to know' have been widely hypothesized but examples are usually developmentally far apart. For instance, the scheme of *the permanent object* is said to be the forerunner of *conservation* (Piaget, 1969, p. 326). Evidence of more detailed increments in development is in short supply.

As discussed in Chapter 2, the gathering of evidence on early learning has not been helped by ambiguity of terms. Rather late in his writings, Piaget began to differentiate between the terms 'scheme' and 'schema'. So far in this book the term 'schema' has been used to describe all patterns of early repeatable behaviours. The illustrated categories in this chapter, 'From action to thought' may be nearer to what Piaget meant by 'scheme' rather than 'schema'. Piaget makes it clear that 'schemes' refer to 'real' operational systems of knowledge and 'schemas' refer to mere 'figurative' knowledge. 'Scheme' is conceptual and 'schema' is mainly configurational. At a 3-year-old level, for example, the figurative aspect of a toy car will be its external appearance. The operative aspect of the toy will reflect 'knowing' rather than perception. The following abstractions signify 'knowing':

1 The car continues to exist when it is not perceived.

2 The toy can be *displaced* from A to B and back to A.

3 Such *displacements* lead to *equivalence of distance between points.*

4 The toy belongs to a *class* of toys.

Although there are conceptual differences between 'operative' and 'figurative', they occur simultaneously in representation just as in infancy knowledge of location and state is built up simultaneously. Many drawings, paintings and models represent both configuration and movement, as in Figure 5.52 where the figurative *grid* schema is used to represent aeroplane and the dynamic *semi-circle* represents 'The plane landing on the runway'.

Another example of the difference between the operational and the figural can be taken from the activity of cooking. It is operational thinking that enables the cook to estimate the *quantity* of ingredients, the *sequence of procedure,* the *length* of cooking time, *degrees of temperature,* and so on. Glancing into the oven after a certain time in order to see whether the cake is brown is simply a figurative check on operational accuracy.

If the differences between 'scheme' and 'schema' reflect fundamental differences between operative and figurative thinking, they are worthy of further study. However, because of the exploratory nature of the Froebel project and the difficulty of clearly differentiating between observations of 'scheme' and 'schema', we will continue to use the word 'schema'. If more were known about the build-up of co-ordinated schemas and concepts, more would be known about how best to teach some of the key concepts of the curriculum right through schooling.

The practical *displacements* that enable a toddler to find his or her way round a garden become the spatial representations that enable him or her to find his or her way to school and later to represent such journeys in the form of a map (Piaget and Inhelder, 1969, pp. 93–4). These early behaviours may well be the precursors of mapping and aspects of mathematics and science. In environmental studies, street furniture might provide figurative cues on where to change direction but it is mainly the *displacements* that develop into internalized cognitive maps. These issues are developed in Chapter 9. In this chapter the developmental route of dynamic and internalized displacements is illustrated.

The sequences illustrate various aspects of 'spatial thought'.

Hayes (1979), in dealing with computer technology, writes about the way science is to do with concepts and clusters of concepts (by which he means 'coordinations') and the way relationships have to be built up in development by observing the minute particulars of events and happenings. He writes about superclusters of concepts, such as systems of measurement of space and time, and notes that these are arrived at via earlier and simpler conceptual clusters, and that these important clusters are built up around such notions as *inside, outside, containment* and *ways through* from one place to another (1979, pp. 242–70).

These concepts are illustrated in this chapter under the headings of *enveloping, containing, going through a boundary,* and so on. Each of these can be found in baby behaviour and each obviously has a healthy future in the primary-school curriculum even though 'matching' developing forms of thought with a progression from an early to a later curriculum has not yet been charted.

Piaget has said that at an elementary level 'form' and 'content' are indissociable because it is acts of assimilation that construct the forms of schemas. This is a difficult concept because, although 'form' can be detected under the surface of content (as is shown in this book) it is not known how much experience is required for a new form to be constructed. If schemas are constructed during the assimilation of content, it is the process of construction that needs to be studied. With existing research tools this is easier said than done.

The project findings, in this and the previous chapter, show clearly that, in symbolic representations, the 'form' of schemes, or schemas, can be distinguished from 'content'. After project visits, for instance, new content was represented within existing schemas. Schemas were thus extended by experience.

Each schema is illustrated at four different stage levels: motor, symbolic representation, functional dependency and 'thought'. This sequence shows differences of stage levels as well as continuity from stage to stage.

SCHEMAS AND STAGES

Of the observations analysed, 2,152 are described as 'action schemas'. These fell into eight clearly distinguishable categories. Each category below is given with the frequency of occurrence. The examples that follow will make the meaning of the labelling clear.

1 Dynamic vertical schemas: 403.

2 Dynamic back and forth, or side to side: 357.

3 Circular direction and rotation: 280.

4 Going over, under or on top of: 204

5 Going round a boundary: 133

6 Enveloping and containing: 351.

7 Going through a boundary: 259.

8 Thought ('internalized data' and 'telling a story'): 163.

Each of the above categories is discussed in this chapter, with the exception of number 8, within the following six sub-divisions:

■ Motor level

■ Symbolic representational level

■ Functional dependency relationship

■ Thought level

■ Discussion

It became clear during the analysis of these observations that actions used instrumentally at a motor level were used as signifiers at the level of symbolic representation. The 'thought' level examples include earlier levels that have been internalized.

DYNAMIC VERTICAL SCHEMAS

From six months, when toys fall from the infant's hand, he or she will watch the fall to the *point of arrival* providing all the action is within the visual field (Sheridan, 1975, p. 30). Infants of 8-11 months are able to monitor *vertical movements* of an object if a stable background is given as a visual frame of reference (Butterworth and Jarret, 1982).

The perceptual effects of objects thrown from 'pram' to ground are closely studied by the infant. Piaget (1969) suggests that, at first, each effect is separate and different, like still pictures. Gradually the child learns that his or her teddy bear retains its identity even though it is *upside-down*. More formally expressed, the child's knowledge of identity results from the co-ordination of changes of states of objects. In the last chapter the shift from topological to projective representation is shown. It is possible that this shift in representation is related to earlier perceptual co-ordinations.

At one year, infants are acquiring more advanced motor experiences of *verticality* when, for instance, they pull themselves upright with the aid of furniture. When 2-year-olds experience a *vertical ascent,* such as climbing, followed by a *vertical descent,* such as jumping, sliding or rolling, they experience asymmetry of effort that is probably why *equivalence* of *vertical distance,* as in the *upward and down-ward trajectory* of a cable car, is understood quite late.

The young children's judgments are influenced by their own internalized muscle effort and these will prevail until an Euclidean framework of fixed endpoints of reference will free them from the error of personal perception (Piaget, 1970, p. 78). Apart from being repeatable, *trajectory* behaviour shows continuity. Motor-level examples are antecedent to symbolic representations that, in turn, are antecedent to later co-ordinations of schemas at a 'thought' level.

MOTOR LEVEL

Jim (0:10:26) spent a lot of time throwing toys out of the 'pram'. Older children returned them with playful attitude. Salam (3:2:2) kept climbing up the ladder and sliding down the slide. His mother pinned appropriate speech on to his movements, such as 'You are climbing right up to the top of the ladder. What can you see from the top? Now you are climbing down. You are coming down back-wards, aren't you?'

Kamal (2:1:3) came down the slide several times, his mother encouraging him with speech accompaniment. Kamal collected a brick from the classroom, put the brick on to the slide and made it slip down the slope. He repeated this several times (there was no verbal exchange in these examples).

SYMBOLIC REPRESENTATIONAL LEVEL

Brenda (3:1:23) dropped toy aeroplanes from a height, saying, 'The aeroplane has fallen down'. Later she played a *falling-down* game, shouting with enthusiasm, 'I've fallen down'. Jock (2:6:6), after visiting police stables where he had observed a policeman mounting and dismounting his horse, pretended to mount a horse by *climbing up and sitting astride* a climbing frame, saying, 'Me, policeman 'orsey'.

Stephen (4:3:25) drew 'Mother whale looking down. Little boy whale looking up' (Figure 6.1). Two different *vertical directions* are now made explicit with speech. Also, arrows signify in which directions the whales are looking. Randolph (4:4:1) drew an aeroplane. He described the drawing as 'The aero-plane over the water ... that's where you pull them down' (Figure 6.2). He was referring to the *vertical movement* of pulling down the blind.

Stephen (4:7:13) drew 'Submarine, periscope, water. The submarine is going up to the top' (Figure 6.3). Lois (4:6:3) sat inside the 'submarine' (a three-dimen-sional brick enclosure) asking, 'Are we near the top yet?' (symbolic representation of the *vertical trajectory* of the submarine).

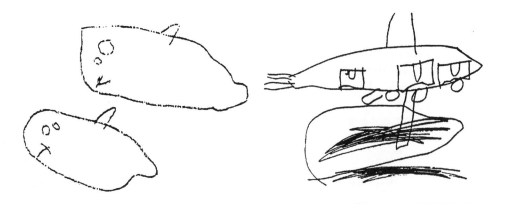

Figure 6.1 'Mother whale looking down. Little boy whale looking up.'

Figure 6.2 'The aeroplane over the water. That's where you pull them down.'

Figure 6.3 'Submarine, periscope, water. The submarine is going up to the top.'

Figure 6.4 'Bang, bang, this man is shooting him. The gun where you hold it.'

Randolph (4:4:1) drew 'Bang, bang, this man is shooting him. The gun where you hold it' (Figure 6.4). For some time he had been able to represent *upright* and *prone* figures but now he was struggling to represent positions half-way between *vertical* and *horizontal*. He explained the *oblique angle* of the figure in his drawing by saying, 'I've done him like that because he's falling out of bed' (Figure 6.5).

Lois (4:7:15) drew an owl. She explained, 'Its wings are down because it's not flying'. After Brenda (4:4:7) had watched one of the gardeners chop down a dead elm, she ran into the classroom shouting, 'Mrs B, the tree is falling down'. Later that morning she made a model by sticking six-pipe cleaners upright into a piece of clay *(core and radial conftguration)*. She made one pipe-cleaner bend over so that it was at an *oblique angle*. She said, 'The tree has fallen down' (Figure 6.6).

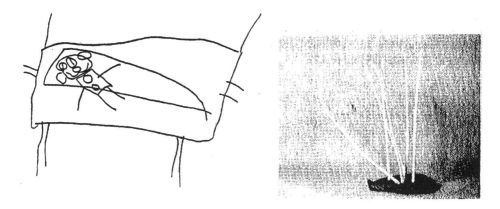

Figure 6.5 'I've done him like that because he's falling out of bed.'

Figure 6.6 'The tree has fallen down.'

FUNCTIONAL DEPENDENCY RELATIONSHIP

The project teacher told an Aesop fable about a clever bird that, not being able to reach water in a dish, dropped stones into it. She demonstrated the story with a dish, water and stones. For several days after the story, Alistair (3:9:22) could not be parted from the materials. He became increasingly excited. When he dropped the stones his mother asked him what happened to the water. After some time he shouted, 'It goes up'.

Alistair (4:0:21) increased his height by standing on a chair in order to peg clothes onto a washing-line. Alistair (4:3:21) placed several blocks on top of each other in order to bring himself up to the equivalent height of the piano stool that was occupied.

Amanda (3:6:6) put water into a balloon. She told the teacher that the balloon filled with water was heavy. Mrs B asked how she knew. Amanda said, demonstrating, 'Look, I can't lift it. I can lift this' (lifting the one filled with air). Susan (4:1:8) attached objects to a hook on a crane. She hauled the objects up by pulling the string vertically.

THOUGHT LEVEL

Stephen (4:5:4) reported on the way home from the swimming baths, 'I jumped in the water from up'. Stephen (4:7:13) drew 'This is Teddington Lock. First level, gate, second level, gate, third level' (Figure 6.7). This was drawn several weeks after a visit but he had been using a simulated lock provided by the teacher.

Amanda (4:1:25) 'You know leaves? They fall off the tree on to the ground [pause] and acorns fall off the tree'. Amanda (4:4:6), after hearing a story, told the teacher, 'There was a mouse and it ran right up the inside of the clock'.

Figure 6.7 'This is Teddington Lock. First level, gate, second level, gate, third level.'

DISCUSSION

When Jock threw things out of his 'pram' he used a *vertical arm movement*. Various objects were given to him, such as drums and cymbals, so that he could experience differential perceptual effects. What excited him most was being given a large brush with paint, with which he made short *vertical lines*. He was held steady by his mother. He was so excited by his marks that he jogged up and down with glee.

Some observations appeared to lie somewhere between motor and symbolic behaviour. In the absence of speech, these were coded at a motor level. However as 'emerging symbolism' is critically important in early development, they provided exciting topics to discuss with parents.

The example of Jock symbolically representing getting on and off a horse ('Me, policeman 'orsey') has already been given as an example of content experienced during a project visit. The example also illustrates the effect on both perception and representation of a prevailing schema. Out of all aspects of the visit, it was the *dynamic vertical aspect* (the policeman mounting) that Jock focused on and represented.

His sister, Lois (4:5:12), had just started to *represent objects from different points of view*. During the same visit she was observed staring at the behind of the horse. Later she painted an *arc* (Figure 10.2). She said, 'This is the back of a horse. He's carrying things on his back'. One year earlier, as already mentioned, following a previous visit to the stables she drew 'Horse with legs'. For this she used her prevailing *'grid'* schema (Figure 10.1, page 200).

The examples of the tree falling, the shot man falling and the person falling out of bed all represent objects in *intermediate positions between the horizontal and vertical*. The project children showed greater mobility of thought than much older children tested in the laboratory.

One of the main sources of evidence that children of 5 and under are 'preoperational' (lacking mobility of thought) is from formal tests with a rotating rod where even 5-year-olds will represent only the *vertical* and *horizontal*. Piaget's explanation of this inadequacy is that young children cannot represent *intermediate positions* mentally and therefore they cannot on paper (Piaget and Inhelder, 1971, pp. 50–84). All the project representations of trees, people and objects falling, birds with wings down, and so on, do not support the theory that the thinking of children under 5 is 'static' and capable of registering only 'configurational' states rather than movement.

In the literature, the terms 'operational' and 'pre-operational' are used to describe various levels of comprehension. Only at the age of 11 (in some experiments) do children fulfil the strictest requirements of *operational horizontality* and *verticality*. It is only then, for instance, that some children can draw the position of a 'mast' on a 'ship' at different inclinations when a jar holding the 'ship' and water is tipped (Piaget and Inhelder, 1956, pp. 381–411).

Piaget (1972b) also uses the term 'representation' in a broad and narrow sense. In a broad sense it means *seriation, classification, spatial metrics* and *projective transformations* (p. 81). Knot-tying involves spatial metrics and projective transformations (Piaget and Inhelder, 1956, pp. 467–8).

'Representation' in the narrow sense allows for the symbolic evocation of absent realities by way of the mental or memory image (Piaget, 1951, p. 67). Absent realities are movable and immovable. The motor *displacement* of objects leads to the internalized *displacement* of objects. This leads to the symbolic representation of those *displacements*. Examples given above indicate that the project children are able to represent symbolically *changes of position* of objects with *dynamic directional trajectories*.

When Alistair was $3\frac{1}{2}$ he had discovered how to lever weights (planks) upwards by hauling them over a wall with a rope. When he was 3:9:22, after much experiment, excitement and struggle, he talked about the water rising as a result of dropping stones into a dish. He cannot be said to have arrived at the concept of *displacement* but he has taken a large step in that direction via a *functional dependency relationship*. If he had been capable of static stage thinking only, he would not have been able to symbolize the *upward displacement* of water.

Stephen's *ordinal* description of the first, second and third levels of Teddington Lock is also more advanced than laboratory results would indicate. Children under 5 are said to think in *cardinal* terms only, such as one, two and three. As well as applying *ordination*, Stephen appears to have internalized the different levels of the lock in *ascending height*.

In order to show continuity of stages in relation to each schema, 'thought-level' examples given at the end of each section are short. Longer examples demonstrate co-ordinations of schemas and consequently would have obscured stage-level continuity. Long examples that demonstrate the complex co-ordinations of schemas are given at the end of this chapter.

DYNAMIC BACK AND FORTH, OR SIDE TO SIDE

Infants pay a great deal of attention to *straight-line trajectories* and this has been well documented. Bower (1974) has shown that 1-week-old infants will show a defensive reaction to an object approaching them from straight ahead. Infants 20 weeks old will continue to track an object back and forth on a *horizontal trajectory* even though the object is made to change in size, shape or colour. Such experiments have shown that the movement aspects of objects are noted before their static configurations. Infants show surprise at movement incongruities before they notice configurational incongruities.

Bower (1974, p. 201) found that *side-to-side* tracking precedes *circular* tracking. At an early motor level, *straight-line* toddling comes before *circular* toddling. In the Froebel project findings, *straight-line trajectory* representations came before *circular trajectory* representations.

Although *circular* and *semi-circular* tracking takes over from *straight-line* tracking, *straight-line* tracking does not disappear from behaviour – it re-appears in a new form at a higher level. Bower *(ibid.,* p. 206) has pointed out the remarkable similarity between 3-month eye tracking and 9-month hand and eye tracking. At 3 months an infant will search with his or her eyes for an object where he or she last saw it. The 9-month-old will also search for the object where he or she last found it.

Piaget (1959) links the absorption of infants with trajectories with the later operational understanding of *lines.* He noted that Laurent, from 9 months, examined the route before and behind him as he was wheeled down a long hall *(ibid.,* p. 203). He interprets this as establishing a *straight-line trajectory between two points.* Towards the end of the first year, Laurent was able to move himself from point A to point B. He was thus able to use himself as a moving object. He was able to toddle the trajectory.

When the youngest project children toddled they simply *displaced* themselves. Later they picked up objects and *displaced* those. At first they dropped the objects anywhere and later at the end of particular trajectories. At this stage the dropped objects formed *heaps.* It is not necessary to wait until objects can be defined logically, in class terms, before 'intensive' properties of those objects are defined. Each schema can lead to the definition of commonalities. If an adult talks to a toddler about what he or she is doing, 'Look, you brought all those things over here, didn't you?' he has a captivated audience. The question, 'What have these things got in common?' can be answered at many different levels: to the young child things can be *banged, thrown, transported, contained, gone through* and *gone round.*

Trajectory schemas have frequently been observed and described as norms without further developmental analysis. In the Stycar sequences, for instance, Sheridan (1975) describes typical absorptions of 1-year-olds just after they have learned to walk. In every case the infant pays prolonged and intent regard to objects that move in a *straight-line trajectory.* Examples are small toys being pulled along, rolling balls, people, animals and cars moving, and so on. The 1-year-old will create *trajectories* and *connection* by bringing two cubes together simultaneously.

When a 2-year-old establishes *starting-points* and *points of arrival* during *transporting* behaviour he or she is presumed, by Piaget, to be experiencing 'physically early *equivalence* of *distance*, *length* and *speed* by traversing A to B on a horizontal plane and then B to A on the same plane. This *displacement of objects* is used symbolically for the representation of events within the child's experience. A 2-year-old, for instance, imitated the coal-man carrying a sack of coal. He walked stiffly from side-to-side with a towel slung round one shoulder (a symbol for the *container* that, in this case, was a coal sack) (Werner and Kaplan, 1967). Both *trajectories* and *containers* had become signifiers for objects and events.

MOTOR LEVEL

Jock (1:5:18) *transports* objects in a straight line from one position to another. He transports two of anything small and makes a *heap* in the telephone kiosk.

Jock (1:9:17) pointed his finger at a moving tractor and moving ducks at Kew Gardens.

SYMBOLIC REPRESENTATIONAL LEVEL

Jock (1:6:22) moved forward making a loud noise: 'Da da da da'. His mother said that whenever he hears an ambulance at home he begins to move forward, making this sound. Jock (2:4:29) transported a black bag around saying 'I'm Dr W' (his own doctor). The day before a doctor had visited the project in his white overall and had brought his black bag with him.

Adrian (3:7:17) lay facing downwards on the floor. He was pretending to swim in a *straight-ahead direction* to rescue his brother who was 'drowning in the water'. Adrian then pretended to climb aboard the ship and to haul his brother up.

Stephen (3:7:27) pushed and pulled a barrel in the garden. When he came inside he said he had made up a dance. He held Mrs B around the waist and moved *backwards and forwards* taking her with him in synchrony. The next day Stephen played 'tug of war' with Adrian. Each boy took hold of an end of a rope and tried to pull the other along. Following this, Stephen painted a *vertical line* with two filled-in *circles* as *end-points* (Figure 6.8). He described the painting as 'This one is pulling that one along'. Randolph (4:3:14) painted 'A dog chased by a cat' (Figure 6.9).

Figure 6.8 'This one is pulling that one along.'

FUNCTIONAL DEPENDENCY RELATIONSHIPS

Alistair (3:6:16) started a conversation with his father about a fishing-rod. He said, 'You know a fishing-rod? When you throw it [he made an enactive gesture of casting the line] the string goes right out'. His mother, who had been working with him the whole morning on wringing out clothes with a mangle, asked, 'What happens when you *reverse* the *rotation* of the handle?' Alistair said, 'The line gets shorter'.

Jock (4:9:3) and Kamal (4:1:14) each had a 'zoom-stick' (a rolled up tube that extends when blown into). This evolved into a game where they estimated how far away they would each have to stand in order for the end of each zoom-stick to just touch the other person.

THOUGHT LEVEL

Adrian (3:9:30) on the bus after visiting the baths: 'I put it over my head [the rubber ring] and I floated backwards and frontwards'.

Stephen (4:5:11), during a conversation with a student on the bus while going to the river, made the following statements:

Stephen:	The bus is going fast … we're nearly there … the people could go over the bridge but not cars … cars go on the road, but not on the bridge.
Student:	How do trains get to the other side of the river?
Stephen:	Railway track.
Student:	Does that go over a bridge?
Stephen:	No! [a pause] Yes it does.

Lois (4:7:7) had a long conversation with a student. During the conversation Lois showed that she was able to organize, on a thought level, familiar movements within three-dimensional space. She was able to talk about her cat moving back and forth and side to side as well as other trajectories.

Figure 6.9 'A dog chased by a cat.'   Figure 6.10 'This is a fan to cool you down.'

DISCUSSION

It is a norm of 2-year-old development that children can walk sideways and backwards (Cratty, 1973, p. 61). Children between 2 and 3 become aware of *front, back* and *side* and children can locate objects relative to these body reference points *(ibid.,* p. 112). When the environment is supportive verbally, children become able to internalize successfully a range of actions. Tania (6:6:0) was able to give an articulate account of her 'bear' dance that contained 22 recalled events.

Jock (1:5:18) was demonstrating a transporting schema. When objects are perceived as equivalent in some way they form a primitive collection. The defining characteristic of the *heap* at the end of the trajectory is *transportability* or 'I brought it here'. The *trajectory* is the forerunner of higher-order notions, such as *distance, length* and *speed.* The *heap* is the forerunner of *classification* (Inhelder and Piaget, 1964; Piaget, 1968a).

When Jock pointed to the *trajectories* of ducks and a tractor he may have been half-way between the perception of moving objects and the representations of those movements. Ambiguous examples are difficult to classify but, as already stated, they generate a great deal of interest in communication with parents.

In the imitation of the ambulance, Jock uses his own movement as a signifier for the movement of the ambulance. Like most graphic representations, the *'chasing'* or action component in Randolph's (4:3:14) painting (Figure 6.9) can go unrecognized because the finished product necessarily takes the form of a static configuration. Adrian's 'rescue' play consisted of co-ordinated *straight-line trajectories.* Each trajectory had different dramatic content assimilated to it. Pushing and pulling can be extended by the provision of wheeled and non-wheeled boxes to be pulled on different types of surfaces. This extends the *moving of mass* into the concept of *friction* (Williams and Shuard, 1980, p. 280).

Although, in early education, children are usually allowed to transport objects about in outdoor space, inside the classroom the managerial interests of the teacher often prevail and the children are discouraged from moving materials. For instance, when children begin to represent the ubiquitous 'picnic', they remove crockery and cutlery from the 'home area' to the *end-point of their journey.* Many teachers scold them for doing so.

If viewed schematically, such behaviours would be extended rather than extinguished. Discussing the route taken on the picnic can lead to concepts of *distance, orienteering, cost* of journeys, and so on. Providing a carefully chosen picnic basket *(an enveloping space)* in which crockery and cutlery can be placed before being transported, is more likely to lead to notions of *volume* and *capacity* than insisting that the objects should remain in the home area.

In the fishing-rod example, Alistair (3:6:16) knew that the *distance* the line was cast was *functionally dependent* on the *rotation* of the handle. He was able to reverse this in his mind. If the *rotation* of the handle was *reversed,* the line would become *shorter.* Here *length* is a function of *rotation.* This example could be given equally under *rotation.* That day Alistair had learnt that water extraction from clothes was *functionally dependent* on the *rotation* of the handle of the mangle.

When children reach the 'thought level', the earlier motor and representational stages, with all the contents of past experience, are 'brought forward' to provide the 'form' and 'stuff' of thinking. As with all schemas, paucity or richness of experience becomes increasingly apparent with age.

CIRCULAR DIRECTION AND ROTATION

Hubel (Hubel and Wiesel, 1971) discovered that where kittens are deprived of specific movement experience during 'critical periods' they are permanently damaged because their brain cells do not become sufficiently activated. After testing for the effects of horizontal and vertical stimulus deprivation, attention was turned to movement in a circular direction. The researcher points out that while thousands of brain cells are activated by the perception of stationary horizontal and vertical configurations, when objects are made to move, each orientation 'triggers' thousands of differentially activated cells. For every different movement there is a particular set of cortical cells that will respond *(ibid.,* p. 131).

Hubel captures the dynamic activity of the brain when *rotation* is perceived. He comments that the number of cell populations responding to a slowly *rotating* propeller can scarcely be imagined.

In humans, where such movements have been widely experienced, simply thinking about them is sufficient to re-activate cells that were activated during initial perceptions. 'Representation', therefore, in the form of mental images, is literally a 're-presentation' of earlier experience. This evidence, and much more, indicates that movement schemas are both activated and nourished by matched stimuli in the environment and that one of the functions of symbolic representation is to re-activate original experiences, thus leading to stability of knowledge. The educational implications of this is that children should have many experiences of the *'movingness'* of objects and they should be given ample opportunities to represent these experiences through symbolic play, creative materials and speech.

The following observations show a developmental sequence from early action and perceptions of circular movement through to action and speech representations. These, in turn, lead to 'functional dependency' relations and 'thought'.

MOTOR LEVEL

Jock (1:10:14) was fascinated by the record going round. After some time he drew a *circular scribble.* Jock (1:10:17) playfully walked round and round in a *circular direction.* Jock (1:10:23) spent a considerable time pulling a big car in a *circular direction.* Jock (1:10:29) connected an engine with a carriage. He then *swivelled round* on his bottom. As a result of this the train moved in a *circular direction.* Jock (1:11:5) ran, with delight, round the Pagoda at Kew Gardens.

Alistair (3:9:8), on a visit to the Science Museum, could not be moved from a mechanical model of a man *rotating* a handle, which turned a large wooden screw in order to winch water up from a well.

SYMBOLIC REPRESENTATIONAL LEVEL

Jock (2:3:30) went on a project visit to a windmill that, unfortunately, was not working. The adults demonstrated the movement of the sail with speech and arm movements. The teacher introduced a working water wheel into the classroom in order to extend the thinking of children who had a powerful *rotation* schema. Jock's mother, after working with him on the wheel for some time, asked Jock what he had seen when he visited the windmill. Jock echoes, 'Imwul [windmill] round and round'. He made his arms go round. The next day he drew a *circle scribble* and described it as 'round and round'.

Jock (2:4:3) drew a *circular scribble* connected with a *grid.* He named it 'Helicopter'. His mother pointed to the *grid* and asked what it was. Jock made an arm go round and replied 'round and round'.

Linda (3:6:28) walked round a fenced enclosure in the park. When she returned to her mother she said, 'The ducks can't get out'. At the project she made a *circular* railway track and made the train go round the track. Thirteen days later she made 'an island' with clay and said, 'Boats go all round an island'.

Shanaz (3:5:13) employed *rotation* movements in making up a dance. She climbed inside a large box and made a lorry and car move in a *circular direction* around the hole in which she was standing. She made her hands *rotate* round each other. She made her whole self *rotate.* She was able to change her *height level* while she *rotated.*

Alistair (3:9:8) made a scrap-material model of 'A train on a track'. He pointed to a bit of the model and said, 'That's where you wait and it goes round'. His mother said teasingly, 'I've never seen a platform go round'. Alistair said firmly, 'Well this one does!'

Alistair followed this by making 'A car with wheels'. He made the wheels go round and said, 'Look, they go round'. He then pointed to square shapes on top (seats) and said, 'And they go round.' He had been absorbed by the typist's chair.

Gary (4:2:16) asked the teacher if he could 'read' to her. After they settled he said, 'Look!' and swivelled a pencil. The teacher expressed interest and said, 'You made that turn round, didn't you? You made it *"rotate"*'. Much later Gary showed the teacher a picture of a cement-mixer in a book. The teacher said, 'That's interesting, you have found something else that goes round, that rotates. Can you think of anything else that *rotates?*' After a pause Gary replied, 'Yes, a candy-floss maker'.

FUNCTIONAL DEPENDENCY RELATIONSHIPS

Brenda (4:7:14) was dancing round the maypole holding one of the ribbons. She kept reversing her direction. After doing this for some time she ran into the classroom and pulled the teacher outside. She was very excited and said, 'When I go round the string gets shorter'. She demonstrated this. She then reversed her direction and shouted, 'It gets longer'.

Jack (4:3:25) pretended to be the captain of a submarine. The children pretended that the enveloping space they had built with bricks was a submarine. Jack put a 'periscope' on top of the 'submarine' and pretended to wind it up and down by rotating an imaginary handle forwards and backwards. The height of the periscope was known to be functionally dependent on rotation.

Alistair (4:9:21), following a visit to the railway, worked with Jack (4:9:21). They made a 'level crossing'. They set up the railway track, intersected with a road (a *grid configuration*). They closed the level-crossing gates by rotating them so that they closed off the road. They formed a queue *(a straight line)* of waiting cars. They made the train go along the tracks. They *rotated* the gates back again and made the cars move across the railway line.

Jock (4:9:13) drew a circle scribble. He said, 'It's a spinner'. Two days later he pushed a short pencil through the hole in a milk bottle top and spun it. His mother made him a spinning-top with variously coloured segments that, when spun, appeared to be white. Although Jock was interested in the transformation of colour his speech indicated that he was more interested in his action of spinning, He kept saying, 'Look, you do it like this'.

Lois (4:9:8) painted over a doily and described the result as 'This is a fan to cool you down' (Figure 6.10). Clare (4:11:19) put one straw through the centre of six other straws and twirled it. She said, 'The wind makes it go round really'.

THOUGHT LEVEL

Jack (4:2:18), when asked what he had done the day before, replied, 'I went round and round on the helter-skelter, it was a spiral'. A few days earlier he had drawn a spiral and called it 'A cowboy ring' (a lasso) (Figure 6.11).

Figure 6.11 'A cowboy ring' – a lasso.

Alistair (3:6:13) noted the effect on wet clothes of turning the handle of a mangle. His mother encouraged him by suggesting he reversed his direction. Alistair's later conversation with his father about the relationship between casting out the line of a fishing-rod and reversing the rotation in order to make the line shorter has already been given.

Nicky (4:4:3) showed his watch to the teacher, who said, 'What do you find most interesting about your watch?'

Nicky:	You can turn the handle.
Teacher:	What does that do?
Nicky:	It turns the hands.
Teacher:	Can you think of anything else that goes round?
Nicky:	Yes, you can put this round your wrist [going *round a boundary*]. Look … you can turn this round [he discovered that the glass cover could move round. He pointed to a small stud on his jeans and said]: That's round and you can turn it round. [He then detached himself from things that were present and said]: A merry-go-round goes round [pause] a ball goes round [pause] a wheel goes round. [He then pointed to a sand wheel and said]: When you pour sand on that it goes round.

DISCUSSION

As with dynamic straight-line schemas, it would appear that objects that move in a circular manner, analogous to a behaviour pattern possessed by a child, have a particular fascination for that child. It is not clear whether Jock's circular scribble was an action representation of the revolving record but it is suggestive in that this was his first circular scribble. As mentioned earlier, these situations excited the parents because they found schematic explanations more interesting and reassuring than thinking of such behaviours as random. Such discussions sharpened adult perceptions in that related examples were then observed. When Stephen (4:2:6), for instance, made a swirl with paint, it might have been considered a mere scribble. His description, however ('That's like water going down a plug hole'), showed his ability to make an analogy between his *rotational* action and the dynamic features of water going down the plug.

It might be said that Jock's action representation of 'windmill' is also ambiguous in that it is not a direct imitation of the sails going round. However, his later action and speech representations, and his representations of the helicopter blades rotating, would indicate that he is sufficiently 'tuned in' to *rotators* to be able to learn from second-hand adult demonstration.

Linda (3:6:28) is showing a simultaneous interest in static configurations (a fenced enclosure and an island) and *circular trajectories* (the action of going round enclosures). This may illustrate Piaget and Inhelder's (1956, p. 25) claim that shape is constructed from action displacements performed on objects. When, for instance, the toddler steps sideways, hanging onto a circular table, he or she is acquiring motor images of circularity. This has more than just academic interest because, at the present time, young children are expected to construct shapes from the static configurations of shapes. Ponds and puddles are common content in young children's drawings and these emerge from active, not simply perceptual, explorations. Linda is also starting to inquire into the function of enclosures. They are: 'to stop ducks getting out'.

The *rotation* dance made up by Shanaz (3:5:13) was followed up by another activity that seemed unconnected with the dance unless viewed schematically. The teacher, in support of rotation schemas, had introduced nuts, bolts, screws of various sizes and tools to go with them. When Shanaz left her dance, she started to use this material. She was so eager to start that she took a screwdriver away from another Asian child, a boy. Her mother, who had been thoroughly approving and proud of the dancing to Asian music, so disapproved that she put this latter activity permanently 'out of bounds' for Shanaz.

It must be admitted that, as far as parents are concerned, to recognize a schema is not necessarily to embrace it. The *rotation* schema may have been behind Shanaz's enthusiasm for the dance and the use of the screwdriver but the dance was viewed as desirable and the other activity as un-ladylike. Pushing an Asian boy was the last straw. There are ethnic constraints against the extension of some schematic behaviours.

There were also sex constraints. An example has been given of Alistair's mother helping to extend functional dependency relationships with the mangle. Although the teacher expediently tried to transform 'mangling' clothes into principles of 'levers, pulleys and cog-wheels', fathers did not fall for it. They simply 'hung about' outside the home area not wanting to get involved in 'sissy' activities.

Ethnic and sex constraints were discussed openly and with good humour in the project. Male-sex stereotypes created quite a bond between mothers from different backgrounds.

The example of Alistair's (3:9:8) revolving train platform is interesting as it seems to illustrate Piaget's theoretical construct of 'distorting assimilation'. He was applying his *'rotation'* schema with abandon. His mother was trying to wean him away from the idea of a *rotating* platform because she viewed it as a wrong idea and, as far as Alistair's intentions were concerned, she was right. When Mrs B and the present writer pointed out that such things existed (the Round House in London used in the past for reversing trains), Alistair was not only absorbed, he was triumphant.

In the level-crossing example, Alistair and Jack were using *rotation* at a *functional dependency* level in that the *forward trajectory* of the cars was *functionally dependent* on the gates being *opened* and the *forward trajectory* of the train *functionally dependent* on the gates being *closed*.

In order to extend *rotation* and *spirality* schemas, it was arranged that all the families would visit a helter-skelter on a very small fairground under a London motorway. (It is worth noting, while these schemas are being discussed, the kindness and complete acceptance of the owner of the helter-skelter to what must have seemed a bizarre-looking and bizarre-acting group of people.) After the visit there was an abundance of representations stemming from the visit. The teacher and parents made three-dimensional curves from plane spirals. The result resembled the helter-skelter. A three-dimensional model of a helter-skelter led to the discovery that marbles moved more easily down the slope than cubes.

GOING OVER, UNDER OR ON TOP OF

Bower (1974, p. 117) has established that 10-month-old-infants can discriminate between an object with a boundary resting *on top of* something else for instance, a book on a table or a box of matches on a book. R. Brown (1973) pointed out that the three young children he studied for speech development seemed to have an absorption with the spatial relationship, *on top of*.

In the analysis of project observations, it was not easy to differentiate between dynamic representations of *going-over* and *going-under* and figurative representations of *on top of* and *underneath*. Some examples of speech accompanied by actions were clearly dynamic when, for instance, cars were moved over and under bridges. Also, some representations were clearly representing the static states of objects when, for instance, cars were described as being *on top of* or *underneath* a bridge.

There were, however, some examples where a child seemed to be aiming for a correct static configuration but that also involved an internalized displacement. Examples involving 'placing hats on heads' may make this clearer.

MOTOR LEVEL

Jim (1:7:2) had an obsession for placing one thing *on top of* another. As a result of his mother giving him the correct language, by the time he was 1:10:0, whenever he performed any kind of 'stacking' action he would say clearly: 'on top'. He developed quite a ritual. He would put on a hat from the dressing-up box and then go round placing objects on top of other things. For instance, he would place a row of toy animals along the top of the painting easel.

SYMBOLIC REPRESENTATIONAL LEVEL

Pete (3:4:6) made a model with clay and named it 'People on top of the boat'. Lois (3:2:10) named her model 'A cake with two candles. That's the flame on top' (Figure 6.12).

Lois (3:4:0) made a model of a slide from a wedge of wood. She placed a circular metal disc at the top of the slope and said, 'It's a slide, me on the slide' (Figure 6.13). Lois (4:4:14) made a model described as 'A house with a chimney on top'. This was followed by another model called 'Snow on a boat'.

Randolph (3:7:22) was shown two rectangular table mats identical in every respect except that one was smaller than the other. He was asked, 'Are these two the same?' He said, 'Yes'. 'In what way?' 'They both go on top of the table.' Randolph (3:8:21) drew 'A man, a hat and a hammer' (Figure 6.14). Randolph (3:10:11) drew 'Me, hat and boots' (Figure 6.15).

Brenda (4:4:2) made lots of hats, each one worn. At 4:4:20 she drew 'Lady' (Figure 6.16), followed by 'People, they've got hats on' (Figure 6.17). Kamal (3:9:20) drew 'This is a mouse on top of the window'. Adrian (4:8:2) drew 'The hill has a lid on top. It's a funny hill with a roof on top. It's a dustbin with a lid on top with all the rubbish inside'.

Stephen (3:5:15) stuck a cake-paper on to a cardboard lid and put a yoghourt carton *on top of* the cake-paper. He then placed a cardboard tube *on top of that.* He described the model as 'That's the baking tray, that's the cake-paper, that's the cake and that's the chocolate on top'. Jack (5:1:2), having built a brick construction said, 'They live on top and we live underneath'.

Figure 6.12 'A cake with two candles. That's the flame on top.'

Figure 6.13 'It's a slide, me on the slide.'

Figure 6.14 'A man, a hat and a hammer.'

Figure 6.15 'Me, hat and boots.'

Figure 6.16 'Lady.'

Figure 6.17 'People, they've got hats on.'

Figure 6.18 'A boat is going under the bridge.'

FUNCTIONAL DEPENDENCY RELATIONSHIPS

Randolph (3:11:14) drew 'A boat is going under the bridge' (Figure 6.18). Jack (3:11:2) pretended to be 'A captain on a boat'. The 'bridge' under which he was moving consisted of planks placed across the bars of a pyramid.

Randolph (3:6:19) hammered three nails into a wooden brick. He then hammered three nails on the other side. He called his model 'Three roots and three shoots'.

THOUGHT LEVEL

Stephen (4:9:1), while playing a game with Alistair, pointed to an empty space and said, 'The soldiers always sleep on that thin bit there' (he was referring to an imaginary bunk bed).

Salam (4:9:13), after returning from Kew Gardens, said, 'On the map you could see the trees, the road and the pagoda'.

DISCUSSION

The representation of *on top of* was aided in three dimensions in that one object, standing for something else, could be physically picked up and placed on another object also used as a symbol. There were many three-dimensional representations, such as 'doll on bed', 'cup on table', 'me on the slide', and so on.

Stephen's (3:5:15) representation of the baking-tray, cake and chocolate followed a cake-making activity. The selection of the lid for the 'baking-tray' did not include the Euclidean notion of relative size, only the topological space notion of *on top of*.

Before Lois (3:3:22) drew 'Mrs Bruce' (Figure 5.3), she had been able to paint hair *on top of* heads in other paintings. However, her two-dimensional space order *on top of* was not quite stable. In Figure 5.3, instead of putting the 'hair' 'on-top-of' the face enclosure she put it underneath. She noticed her mistake while describing the painting and she laughed.

In Figure 6.14, Randolph (3:8:21) has not managed to place the hat *on top of* the head. He is confined to the topological notion of *juxtaposition* or *next to*. By 3:10:11 (Figure 6.15), he is able to place a hat *on top of* a head in a drawing. Comparing these two figures (Figures 6.14 and 6.15), it can be seen that there are many more parts of a person represented and the parts are organized within a more complex set of *horizontal and vertical co-ordinates.*

Brenda (4:4:20) had a similar struggle. First of all she drew 'Lady' (Figure 6.16). She drew the figure first and then the hat to the side *(next to)*. She then began to draw a face *underneath* the hat. She then placed another hat *above* the head *connected* to the figure. Brenda immediately did another drawing (Figure 6.17) she named 'People, they've got hats on'. Note the way in which Randolph's and Brenda's speech matches their stage of spatial ordering.

Opie and Opie (1959, p. 77) give examples of 'playfulness' with the notion that what is under is relative to what is over: 'Riddle me, riddle me, what is that, over the head and under the hat' (from a 12-year-old). Kamal (3:9:20) and Adrian

(4:8:2) are determined to use their *on top of* schema in as many circumstances as possible.

It was difficult to be certain about *functional dependency relationships* in connection with this schema. There were examples such as 'cooking' *functionally dependent* on pots being *on top of* stoves and staying dry *functionally dependent* on having an umbrella above the head. (A 4-year-old intelligence test item asks, 'Show me what we carry when its raining' – Terman and Merrill, 1976, p. 100.)

Trains having to be *on top of* tracks, boats going under bridges and cars going over bridges appear to involve functional dependencies in that 'keeping moving' depends on what vehicles are on and whether they are going over or under. Randolph (3:11:14) painted 'A boat is going under the bridge' (Figure 6.18). Previously he had been talking about the visit, during which he said, 'We went on a boat underneath the bridge'. In speech he is referring to location and state in the same sentence – if, that is, the spatial relationship 'on' can be described as state.

Similarly, Jack (3:11:2) represented 'on' and 'going underneath' in his action and speech representation. These, and many others, seem to be straightforward co-ordinations of *location* (going somewhere) and the state of being *on top of* (the boat). Randolph's (3:6:19) representation of 'Three roots, three shoots' is more than the representation of *on top of* and *underneath*: it includes *one-to-one correspondence, going through a boundary* and the fact that shoots and roots are *connected*.

There is a future for this schema in concepts of *area* and *volume*. *Conservation of area* is achieved when it is understood that the amount of area covered by objects is constant whether the objects are scattered or placed in a cluster. Curriculum objectives designed to bridge the schema of *on top of* with later 'concrete-operational' concepts still need to be worked out.

GOING ROUND A BOUNDARY

Piaget and Inhelder (1956) have described three types of *enclosure*, each defined by a different kind of boundary. In a *three-dimensional enclosure*, such as a hollow cube, each surface is a boundary. *Two-dimensional enclosures*, as in *circles, rectangles* or 'hopscotch' outlines, have lines as boundaries. A *one-dimensional enclosure* has boundaries defined by points, for instance, dots of ink on a piece of thread. In the Froebel project all three types of enclosure were used in symbolic representation. One- and two-dimensional enclosures are discussed in the last chapter, enveloping and containing space in this.

Matthews (1984) has investigated the notion of *going round a boundary* in relation to drawing, painting and symbolic play. He gives some interesting examples from his own children. Ben, at 2 years of age, made a *circular movement* with his brush. He said, 'It's going round the corner, it's going round the corner'. In his symbolic play Ben was absorbed with revolving toy cars in elliptical paths while 'bonding descriptive speech onto their trajectories' (1984, p. 5). Matthews (1984, pp. 17–18) notes that 'the outcome of rotational movement is the closed shape. This is followed by placing dots "inside" and "outside". Once this happens children have started to construct a pictorial space. Lines attain new meanings, new denotational values. The children can now create configurations'.

The notion of *going round* and *going through* are most often discussed in the literature in relation to children learning to tie knots. *Surrounding*, as in the case of putting beads around the neck, an elastic band around nails on a pin-board or placing quoits over a stick, is simpler than co-ordinating the three topological space schemas: *surrounding, enclosure* and *going through* (or going between), necessary for tying a knot (Piaget and Inhelder, 1956, p. 106).

Of 5-year-olds, 69 per cent reach this level of competence in that they can tie a single knot round an adult's finger that will not come undone when the ends of the laces are dropped (Terman and Merrill, 1976, p. 106). Before children can perform the topological feat of tying a knot, which involves making a three-dimensional inter-twinement from a one-dimensional string (Brearley and Hitchfield, 1966), they must be able to move the end-point of the string *in a straight line* (schema two), *in a circular direction* (schema three) and put it *through a boundary* (schema seven).

MOTOR LEVEL

Jim (1:9:18) placed all the toy animals around the bottom of the toy helter-skelter. Jim (1:9:20) covered a plate with aluminium foil *(going round* or *enveloping)*. Jim (2:5:3) picked up a watch and said, 'Put it there', holding out his wrist.

Kamal (2:11:3) made a line of toy cars, which he surrounded with his two arms and brought them forward into a heap. Lois (3:8:4) spent most of the morning putting a collar on a toy dog and dragging it along as though taking it for a walk.

SYMBOLIC REPRESENTATIONAL LEVEL

Stephen (3:1:14) pretended to peel potatoes (balls of clay). Clare (3:2:6) would not be parted from her book called *The Snake that got Tied Up in Knots*. She insisted, like other children with this schema, on tying her cardigan round her waist by the sleeves. Clare (3:2:8) made a 'parcel'. She used a pipe-cleaner as 'string'.

Stephen (3:7:28) put a rope around Alistair. Alistair shouted, 'Look, I'm wrapping it round me, you hold on to it like this'. Alistair ran along in front of Stephen, they were playing 'horse and driver'. Stephen (4:1:4) on a visit to the zoo, looked at an owl and said, 'It has fur [feathers] right round its face'. Stephen (4:2:11) placed a long cylinder of clay around the boundary of a sphere of clay, which he called, 'A face smiling' *(going round* and *connection)*. Stephen (4:3:27) drew 'It's a house. The garden is at the back' (Figure 6.19).

Figure 6.19 'It's a house. The garden is at the back.'

Figure 6.20 'Daddy [later changed to Dick] he's got a belt on.'

Lois (4:7:24) drew 'Daddy [later changed to Dick] he's got **a** belt on' (Figure 6.20).

FUNCTIONAL DEPENDENCY RELATIONSHIPS

Stephen (4:2:11) made 'A basket with a handle'. He put his arm through the handle and carried it about. Stephen (4:3:27) drew 'My sausage dog on a lead' (Figure 6.21). He immediately followed this with 'Sausage dog tied to a post' (Figure 6.22).

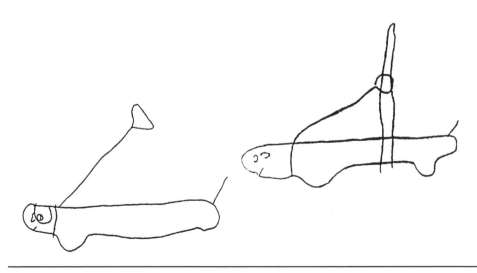

Figure 6.21 'My sausage dog on a lead.'   Figure 6.22 'Sausage dog tied to a post.'

Jack (3:9:2) and Adrian (3:6:20) rolled out clay, which they put round their necks and wrists and called the products 'a necklace' and 'a watch'. The teacher asked them what they did in order to get the clay that shape. Jack demonstrated by rolling out some clay. With questioning Jack arrived at the *functional dependency relationship* between *rolling-out action* and *length*.

THOUGHT LEVEL

Alistair (4:4:11), chatting to the teacher, said, 'I tied a rope round a brick and I pulled it along'.

Stephen (4:7:18) initiated a conversation with the teacher. He said 'I've got a new football shirt at home and it's got blue stripes round here'. He placed his two index fingers where a belt buckle would be and traced round his trunk to the centre point on his back. He continued, 'and its got a blue stripe round my arm like this'. He traced an imaginary line round his upper arm.

DISCUSSION

The day after Stephen (3:1:14) had 'peeled potatoes', one of the youngest Asian girls came to the project with her hair shaved off (in order to increase the growth). Stephen rushed to his mother and said with some distress, 'Her hair came off'. Several times during the morning he was observed feeling his own hair and examining the short, tight ringlets of an African baby. He seemed to have made a frightening and false analogy between hair and potato skin.

Early attempts at *surrounding* were facilitated by pipe-cleaners, milk straws and cardigan sleeves. These allowed the children to perform a kind of slow-motion knot. After a doctor and nurse visited the project, where they demonstrated bandaging, all the dolls and teddy bears were bandaged from head to toe.

Going round, as with *on top of,* was easier with three-dimensional material, as in the 'basket', the 'smiling face' and actually putting a collar round the neck of a toy dog. The difficulty of representing *going round* in two dimensions is illustrated in Figures 6.21 and 6.22. Stephen did not seem to be able to make the collar *go round* the neck of the dog and the lead *go round* the post in the same drawing. Graphically representing *going round* seemed to require a conceptual struggle as did placing hats *on top of* heads. Project children made considerable accommodatory effort while doing these drawings. Again there is a close relationship between speech and schema. In spite of the difficulty of representing the relationship in two dimensions it was understood that *connecting* a dog to a post, or a dog to a lead, is *functionally dependent* on *going round* neck and post.

In Figure 6.19, Stephen represented a house. His description, 'It's a house. The garden is at the back' implies that he is able to make an internalized *trajectory* around to the back of the house. Perception alone cannot reproduce the other side of objects. This example of *going round* suggests *projective* rather than *topological* space. Some children represented the front of a house on one side of the paper and the back on the other side. Mathematically this schema is extended in the primary school in activities such as *measuring* around wrist, waist, ankle and various kinds of perimeters.

Children's comics often contain 'maze' type puzzles where there are *open* and *closed* regions. *Open* regions can be *gone through* in order to reach *inside* regions. *Closed regions* have to be *gone round*. Linda was observing this while walking round the enclosure in the park.

Some games, such as 'rounders', consist of having to *go round boundaries* within a certain time limit determined by how long it takes one side to stop the ball. Many dances, such as 'square' dances, consist of variations on *going round* boundaries.

The notion of *going round*, when co-ordinated with *multiplication*, provides fertile soil for playfulness. When Pooh Bear hunts the Woozle, he is, in fact, tracking his own increasing number of footsteps in a circular direction in the snow.

ENVELOPING AND CONTAINING

Young children are clearly fascinated by spaces that *contain* or *envelop*, and these schemas have received more attention in the literature than the other schemas discussed so far. However, except for research on infants, even this powerful schema is most often noticed by researchers exploring some other issue. Donaldson (1978), for instance, while investigating children's concepts of *all* and *some*, found that her young subjects had such a strong bias towards perceiving the *fullness* or *emptiness* of garages that it interfered with their comprehension of her test questions. The powerfully salient point for the children was whether the garage had a car in it or whether it was empty (1978, p. 67).

Bower (1974) has identified the origin of the notion *inside* as beginning at sensorimotor stage four (from 6 to 12 months). At 5 months affective reactions indicate the dawning notion that one object can be *inside* another. If an infant picks up a cup and sees a toy underneath he or she is so surprised that he or she will gaze steadily at the two objects indicating that, although the event is discrepant with his or her expectations, it is noticeable. Exploration of *envelopment* comes later than the exploration of *trajectories*. In the project children's symbolic representations, *containing* and *enveloping* also came later than the representations of *trajectories*.

Harris (1975) has reviewed the literature on the evolution of the notion of *envelopment* during the first year and reports that it is only at approximately 12 months that an infant knows that object *a* can occupy the same space as object *b* if *a* is *inside b*. The realization that one object can be inside another is linked to the whole area of object permanence. Although these problems are solved at a practical level during the first year, the notion *in* or *inside* is not expressed in speech until around 2 years (Brown, 1973, p. 263).

Brown noted the frequency of the words *in* and *on* in the speech of the three children he studied. He also listed words that were used most often by the children when they were exploring the notion of *inside*. He found that the most frequently used words were related to the schema. They wanted to discuss topics to do with waste-baskets, boxes, pots, and so on.

MOTOR LEVEL

All project observations consisted of children either putting objects into containers or getting inside enveloping spaces – climbing in and out of enveloping spaces by various means, by steps and ladders, by crawling through, by levering themselves downwards into holes, and so on. These behaviours appeared to be extensions of earlier locomotion skills. They also provided the experiental basis for later symbolic representation.

Meryl (1:6:9) began to put small pieces of stone inside a narrow-necked container. Meryl (1:9:4) spent a long time putting toy animals inside and outside a cage. Meryl (2:1:25) placed all the toy cars and then all the toy animals into two enclosures. The teacher asked, 'Where is the horse?' 'Where is the elephant?' and so on. Meryl would pick up the named animal with a great show of pleasure. Her mother continued with this game.

SYMBOLIC REPRESENTATIONAL LEVEL

Brenda (3:1:2) made a model of a car. She placed a small *circle inside,* which she named 'A steering wheel'. Brenda (3:1:14) was dressing her doll. She said, 'This is a big dress to go on the big doll. My baby is dressed'. This example illustrates the way *envelopment* can lead to higher-order concepts, such as *size* and *one-to-one correspondence.*

Brenda (3:1:14) was cooking. The teacher asked her if she knew what an oven was for. Brenda said, 'Yes, it's to put things in'. After a little thought, she said, 'And it's to cook things'. Brenda (3:2:11) was telling her father about the visit of the deaf children to the project. She said, 'They can't hear'. Her father expressed interest. Brenda continued, 'They have plugs in their ears'.

Brenda (3:4:5) made a model called 'The crockery ready to be washed up' (Figure 6.23). This was followed by a drawing of 'Mummy's handbag', which was similar to Shanaz's (4:4:3) painting, 'Handbag' (Figure 6.24). Brenda and Shanaz played together in the home area. The play consisted of 'washing-up', 'drying-up' and 'putting the crockery away in the cupboard'.

Figure 6.23 'The crockery ready to be washed up.'

Figure 6.24 'Handbag.'

Lois (3:5:15) made 'sausages' with clay and wrapped them in tin foil to cook them. Brenda (4:4:12) made 'a house' by placing two shoe boxes on top of each other (Figure 6.25). She described this as 'A house, it's got two storeys. That's upstairs and that's downstairs'.

Alistair (3:9:6) said to Meryl, who was playing with the dolls, 'Look, I'm putting this dolly to bed'. Meryl's reaction was of absorbed interest. Alistair (3:10:14) and Jack (4:7:0) played for most of the morning on the outside climbing frame. Their game consisted of one of them climbing to the top platform, or the bottom, making accompanying remarks, such as, 'I'm just going to pop upstairs now, Jack' or, 'I'm just coming downstairs now, okay?'

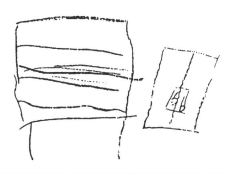

Figure 6.25 'A house, it's got two storeys. That's upstairs and that's downstairs.'

Figure 6.26 'Inside and outside my wardrobe.'

Saima (4:7:8) made a brick model of 'My house'. Her mother talked with her about the various rooms in their house. Randolph (4:6:19) drew 'Inside and outside my wardrobe' (Figure 6.26). He explained how the doors opened (the doors are sub-divided) and he discussed the drawers inside the wardrobe.

Shanaz (3:1:15) drew 'Eyes and mouth' (Figure 6.27). Shanaz (4:2:8) drew 'A chicken with eggs in the middle' (Figure 5.60). Randolph (4:9:25) drew 'Chair and house' (Figure 6.28). Randolph (4:9:25) drew 'Chair in a house' (Figure 6.29). Lois (4:2:20) drew 'It's a fruit bowl with a peach, a banana and an apple'.

FUNCTIONAL DEPENDENCY RELATIONSHIPS

Lois (3:5:13) made a pancake with clay and carefully wrapped it up. She said, 'I've wrapped it up so the children won't burn their hands'. Lois (3:5:14) made a model house. When she finished she stuck sticky paper over the windows and said, 'Now it's dark inside'. Lois (3:5:14) found a worm. She covered it with sand saying, 'You know they live under the sand. At night he'll be asleep'.

Stephen (3:4:13) scribbled over a picture of 'a lady' and said, 'Now I've put her in a dark room' (Figure 6.30). Alistair (4:6:19) drew 'Alistair inside with two legs. I can't do any more children, there's not enough room inside the tent' (Figure 6.31).

Jack (4:3:1) made each toy animal 'walk' into a shed saying, 'It's going in there 'cos it's cold outside'. He drew a rough rectangle and said, 'It's a box of chocolates'. He drew an enclosure round the rectangle and said, 'It's a big, big bag, that's a heavy bag'. A student asked what made it heavy. 'Cos it's got all those things in it'.

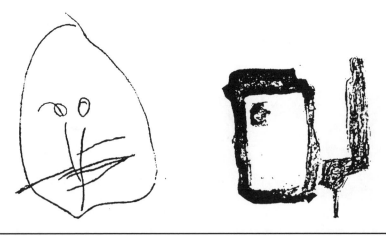

Figure 6.27 'Eyes and mouth.'   Figure 6.28 'Chair and house.'

Figure 6.29 'Chair in a house.'   Figure 6.30 'Now I've put her in a dark room.'

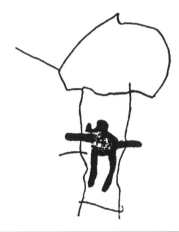

Figure 6.31 'Alistair inside with two legs. I can't do any more children, there's not enough room inside the tent.'

THOUGHT LEVEL

Lois (3:5:15) drew her brother, Jock, in his cot. She covered her whole drawing with a blanket (a square of sticky paper) and said, 'I've covered him up with a blanket'. She then said, 'And I'll put the cot in a cupboard [pause] and I'll put the cupboard in a cave'.

Lois (4:1:9) on the bus on the way back from the Natural History Museum said, 'Tortoises live in cages. I don't think it was real ... was it? It was stuffed. A hippopotamus lives in the water. Sea-lions like dolphins sea-lions do. Sea-lions go in the water like dolphins'.

Brenda (4:5:23) initiated a conversation with the teacher about her nanny (grandmother). She explained, 'Not my nanny F, my nanny S. She's got two front rooms. David [her elder brother] says she's only got one, but she hasn't, she's got two front rooms. We've got one front room and it's the one with the record player in it'.

DISCUSSION

As far as the project findings are concerned, it is clear that early hand and eye investigations of *enveloping* and *containing* reported by Harris (1975) are 'reworked' at a later level when the whole body is used for climbing in and out of enveloping spaces. The sensory and motor knowledge acquired is then translated into symbolic forms, such as symbolic play, model-making, drawing and speech.

When Brenda was 3:7:15, 10 months before her thought-level conversation with the teacher about her nanny's two front rooms, she played a game at home with her mother for as long as her mother was prepared to participate. In this play, Brenda *divided* their sitting room into two parts. She called one part the kitchen and the other part the bedroom. Brenda pretended to knock on a door saying, 'Can I come in?' Her mother had to pretend to let her in. Brenda then *moved through* a pretend door. In other words, the game consisted of *symbolic action displacements within a symbolic sub-division of space.* Her speech reflects the partitioning *of* space, as does Alistair and Jack playing at 'upstairs–downstairs' on the climbing frame and Saima talking with her mother about the rooms in their house.

Almost all the children represented 'darkness', as well as *envelopment* by scribbling over or *covering over,* their drawings. Stephen (3:4:13) scribbled over a sticky paper 'lady' his mother had made for him because she knew he was noticing *triangles.* He said, with considerable satisfaction, 'Now I've put her in a dark room' (Figure 6.30). His mother's feelings were hurt even though she had joined in with discussions on the schema of *covering over.* Teachers tend to disapprove of children scribbling over their drawings, particularly after the drawings have become recognizable equivalents of reality and, therefore, likely to be appreciated by parents. If *covering over* is interpreted as destructive then adult disapproval will follow.

Lois (3:5:15), covering over the drawing of her brother and suggesting that the cot should be put in a cupboard and the cupboard in a cave suggests aggressive 'sibling rivalry' if interpreted within a Freudian framework. However, this explanation could not be applied to the dozens of similar examples that were observed around this time, including the wrapped pancake, the darkened house and the covered-over worm.

Two satisfactory aspects of schematic interpretations is that they embrace a wide range of behaviours, and interpretations are positive. A clear instance of a positive interpretation, instead of attributing naughtiness, is the explanation given by Lois's family when they were late arriving at the project. In spite of having had an inconvenient bus journey with her two children, Lois's mother looked pleased. She said, 'You know that enveloping thing you have been going on about? Well, the reason we are late is because I couldn't find my shoes'. In the end she did, wrapped up in newspaper, in the dustbin. Lois had parcelled them up and posted them. Although inconvenient, Lois's mother found explanations based on schemas more interesting and satisfying than those based on sin.

As with other schemas, it was difficult to diagnose observations that seemed to be to do with *enveloping* but that were accompanied by early telegraphic speech. For instance, Kamal (2:2:29) had been showing his mother how he could climb in and out of a large, hollow cube with five holes. After this he made a model out of an egg box, which he called, 'Two holes'. The egg box could have been a signifier of the cube. The holes in the model could have represented the holes in the cube *(the salience of the circle)*. The representation of *two* was consistent with his prevailing *two* schema. It was not known whether he was representing his actions of climbing in and out, although earlier he had represented himself going down the slide. Many early representations appear to be static but it is likely that they signify action not expressed in speech. Symbolic play reveals action more directly than drawing or model-making.

When Meryl (1:6:9) began to put pieces of stone inside a plastic bottle she was imitating only one aspect of an activity. Some of the older children had discovered that the creation of different sounds was functionally dependent on putting different material *inside* different *containers* (shakers). The teacher was extending this discovery in various ways. Meryl was not interested in making sounds, only in putting stones in the container.

The relationship between schema and affect can be illustrated by Meryl reacting differently to two situations. Susan silently 'took over' her play, which involved putting the doll in and out of a bed. Meryl complained loudly. Alistair (3:9:6) observed this. Later, when she had calmed down, he approached her and said, 'Look, I'm putting this dolly in the bed'. Meryl was absorbed by this. She became very excited when the teacher, while dressing her, said, 'You go inside a coat, don't you?' Meryl shouted, 'Inside a coat'.

As Meryl put animals *inside* and *outside* an open-topped cage, following a visit to the zoo, it was tempting to think that she was representing her first-hand experience that animals move between the inside and outside of cages. However, as she tended to perform the same schema on a wide range of other objects, it would seem that this was simply a general application of a schema.

Alistair (2:9:1) was more than willing to help clear up by putting all the dolls in the dolls' house. When he had finished he said to his mother, 'Now let's take them all out again'.

When Meryl was 2:1:25, she *sorted* toys into two groups of cars and animals and placed those *inside* different *enclosures*. Although her motivation may have been simply to *surround* two groups of objects, the possibilities for extension were greater in that there are particular *containers* and *enclosures* – for animals on the one hand and cars on the other. The teacher made two charts to support this level of *sorting* and *surrounding*. One chart contained pictures of animals seen at the zoo and the other animals seen in Richmond Park.

As already explained, it was not possible to quantify co-ordinations of schemas although these are probably of critical importance in the build-up of systems of thought. The schemas *going through, enveloping, containing* and *going round* were closely related and it was sometimes difficult to differentiate between them. For instance, Lois *wrapped round* the pancake in order *to envelop* it. She understood that this *envelopment* had a *function*. Similarly, Lois (3:5:15) *wrapped round* sausages in order to envelop. This envelopment had a function. A stage in the concept of *size* and *one-to-one correspondence* can stem from *enveloping*, as when Brenda (3:1:9) followed 'dressing' her doll with the comment, 'This is the big dress to go on the big doll'. *Scribbling over* and *folding over* both appear to be variations on the *enveloping* schema. Children frequently represented 'darkness' by scribbling over what they had drawn, as in Figure 6.30.

Brenda (3:5:14), in common with several other children, began to fold 'letters' and to fit them into 'envelopes'. As Brenda posted her letter she tapped the top of the post-box and said playfully, 'And that's a "toppy"'. Although schemas have the important function of enabling similarities between objects to be understood, discrimination is furthered by the naming of differences with similarities. The 'toppy' of a car is different from the 'toppy' of a post-box.

Brenda (3:1:14) 'knows' that an oven is to put things in and, after a slight hesitation, arrives at its function. However, she has not arrived at the function of hearing-aids, which is to magnify sound. She used an earlier level of understanding, to insert or to *go through* is to block. The concept that 'hearing' is functionally dependent on a hearing-aid is too much 'beyond the information given' for a 3-year-old (Bruner, 1974).

She did, however, make other discriminations. When Brenda was 3:8:5 she informed her mother that 'Ovens cook things and fridges make things cold'. Brenda (4:0:20) painted thick vertical lines that looked like a return to an earlier schema. However, they represented 'The lines inside a bulb'. Most of the children represented bags of various kinds wben they had *containing* or *enveloping* schemas. A great deal of time was given to putting things in and out of bags while using dressing-up clothes.

Before Alistair (4:6:19) drew the tent (Figure 6.31) and said that there wasn't enough room inside for more children, he had systematically explored the tent in order to extend the schema of *envelopment*. He would make the guy ropes taut by adjusting the toggle and then crawl into the tent, lie on his back and look at the inside; he would then make the ropes slack and repeat the inspection. His comment reveals a dawning awareness of the *volume* taken up by his own body in relation to the *capacity* of the tent. Also, he knows that the *capacity* of the tent is *functionally dependent* on the tension of the guy ropes. This example, and the example of Jock (4:3:1) bringing in *heaviness* as a function of lots of things in a big bag, again illustrates the way in which schemas, with appropriate experiences, are further differentiated into higher-order concepts.

Prior to the 'thought level' observation, where Lois (4:1:19) thought aloud about stuffed animals, she had spent a great deal of time stuffing nylon stockings with soft paper. She called each product 'A snake'. She later described a gerbil as 'It's an animal and it has fur all over him [pause] so has a mouse'. When Shanaz (4:4:3) painted 'Handbag' she co-ordinated four schemas in her representation. She *connected* a *rectangle* with a *semi-circle* in order to signify *an enveloping space*.

The representation of *enveloping* space evolves into the representation of *subdivided* space, as with the model of the two-storey house, the *inside* and *outside* of the wardrobe and the outside play of pretending to go upstairs and downstairs. Alistair followed this by putting a willing friend 'Down below in the prison'.

When Stephen (4:0:27) saw half a car in the Science Museum he would not look at anything else. He was able to re-create mentally the fact that it had half missing. Soon afterwards he drew 'A boat, broken in half'. As *sub-divisions of space* became more precise they were described in the language of *fractions*.

Saima (4:7:8) *sub-divided* the enveloping space of 'her house' into the bedroom, kitchen, bathroom, and so on. When she was 6 years old and at primary school, she wrote a long account of the layout of a Roman bath and accompanied this with a two-dimensional plan of the various parts of the bath. It is important to note that the motor-level exploration of spaces is followed by symbolic representations of those spaces, which are then sub-divided. Higher-order representations in writing, maps and plans follow from earlier, more direct representations.

As with the notion *on top of* discussed in the last section, there were two levels of difficulty in representing *inside*. It was easier to *enclose* marks, in a face enclosure, than it was to represent a three-dimensional relationship of *inside* in two dimensions. Shanaz (3:1:15), for instance, managed to place marks inside a face enclosure at a very young age (Figure 6.27). She called this 'Eyes and mouth'. She did not manage to represent objects inside three-dimensional space, in two dimensions, until a year later. In Figure 5.60, when she was 4:2:8, she was able to represent 'A chicken with eggs in the middle'.

It is of interest that she did not use the word '*in*' when she talked about the face, perhaps because faces are representations of configurations. 'Eggs inside a chicken', on the other hand, represents the concept of '*inside*'. Similarly, when Randolph (4:9:25) drew 'Chair and house' (Figure 6.28), both drawing and speech represent the spatial notion of *juxtaposition*. Randolph struggled with the problem of how to represent *inside* and at last managed to draw and name 'Chair in house' (Figure 6.29).

On first consideration it seemed odd that the children could not use the same technique or convention for representing *inside* they used in representing *enclosure* (eyes within a face). However, although the figurative effect of 'chair in house' is perceptually equivalent to 'eyes in face', the conceptual processes necessary for the two representations are not equivalent. 'Eyes in face' seems to be the figurative representation of a percept. 'Chair in house' is the operative representation of a *displacement*.

This time lag between two levels of representation is consistent with Bower's (1977a) finding that, during the first year, an 'eye' configuration within a 'face' enclosure is perceived much earlier than is the understanding of the relationship *inside*. The example has been given of Lois *covering over* her brother and putting him into a cupboard and then putting the cupboard in a cave. Shanaz, similarly, followed 'A chicken with eggs in the middle' with a story of a little girl who was hiding in the cupboard. He (the boy chasing her) looked in the cupboard. He saw the cupboard in a cave. The assimilatory exercise that starts with *A* inside *B* and *B* inside *C*, and so on, leads to various play forms based on *inclusion*, such as 'In a dark, dark wood, there was a dark, dark house. And in that dark, dark house, there was a dark, dark room. And in that dark, dark room, there was a dark, dark cupboard', and so on (Opie and Opie, 1959, p. 36).

GOING THROUGH A BOUNDARY

Surrounding and *going through a surround or boundary* are elementary topological space notions. If a person is in a room, they are surrounded by walls. If they want to move from inside to outside, they will move through a discontinuity in the boundary (such as a door). They will move from a point inside the boundary to a point outside. According to Piaget and Inhelder (1956, p. 104) the trajectory of *going through the boundary* defines the topological space notions of *boundary*, *discontinuity* and *between*.

Young children spend much time exploring these topological space notions, initially at a motor level when, for instance, they push their fingers through clay. Most young children are interested in events such as water going through the boundary of a hose pipe and funnel, trains and cars going through tunnels, and so on.

Piaget (1953) gives some interesting examples of young children discovering that one object can go through another. Lucienne (1:1:0), for instance, in attempting to replace a stick through a ring simply presses the stick against the ring. She behaves as though encirclement can be brought about by mere contact (1953, p. 320).

From 1:2 to 1:3, Lucienne systematically puts grass, earth, pebbles, and so on, into all the hollow objects within reach. At 1:3, her finger explores the surface of a space and discovers that the metal handle is hollow. She puts her finger inside and immediately looks for grass to put in the opening (Piaget, 1959, p. 193). By the time she is 1:3:0 she has learnt the relationship *going through* by way of the relationship between the *container* and the *contained*.

In an earlier observation, Lucienne has passed a hoop over her head down to her shoulders, which looked as though she had understood the notion of *going through.* However, she then tried to perform the same operation with a lid. She put that on top of her head and tried to pull it down. She was surprised when it would not. She obviously had no idea that the bottom of the lid stopped her head from going through (1959, p. 200).

In *The Origins of Intelligence in the Child* (observations 162 to 166) Piaget (1953, p. 320) describes, in great detail, what he calls 'the long apprenticeship' needed before Jacqueline managed to get objects through the bars of her playpen. She finally found, by rotating objects, that she could get the narrow side of the toy through the narrow space of the bars. The project children systematically explored the notion of going through at four levels of increasing complexity.

MOTOR LEVEL

Jim (2:1:22) laughed as he passed a hoop over his head. Jim (2:2:5) kept putting his finger in the dead whiting's mouth.

Many motor examples of *going through* consisted of the children experimenting with pushing one thing through another, for instance, pushing nails through clay. This produced a core-and-radial configuration that, from an early age, was given symbolic significance. For instance, Jim at 2:2:20 was absorbed by nails and screws pushed into a ball of clay. He asked, 'What's this, mummy?' When he was 2:4:11 he pushed four nails into a ball of clay and named it 'Spider, that's his legs'.

SYMBOLIC REPRESENTATIONAL LEVEL

Lois (4:1:25) painted 'A Lady sunbathing and the tree and the sun. The sun is shining through the trees'. Lois (4:2:16) cut a tin-foil cake container in two. In doing so she accidentally made a small hole in one half. She called the result 'A sofa with a hole in it'.

Just after this, Lois carefully made a small hole right through her 'home book'. Her mother found her looking through the hole, examining things.

The project teacher saw Susan (4:1:8) struggling inside a box.

Teacher:	What are you doing, Susan?
Susan:	Going through.
Teacher:	You're going through what?
Susan:	This box.
Teacher:	You are going through the hole in the box are you?
Susan:	I can jump out again.
Teacher:	Can you? How do you do it? What do you do with your feet?
Susan:	I dropped in again.
Teacher:	Are you going to get into the next hole?

Susan: That's another hole. That's downstairs. [struggling to get through the top hole again]: I can't get up.

Later in the day Susan was watching some children climbing through the home-area window. She said to Mrs B, 'Look, they're going through that window'.

Teacher: You are interested in holes, aren't you? A window is a hole isn't it? Do you know what windows are for?
Susan: I'm going to jump out [meaning that she was going to jump through the window like the other children].

Susan (4:2:27) spent a great deal of time blowing through a recorder, looking through a kaleidoscope and threading beads. She made clear statements about what she was doing, such as 'I'm looking through the kaleidoscope'. She frequently followed this kind of activity with drawings. One consisted of a flat rectangle with a line going through the middle. This was called 'Looking through the kaleidoscope'.

FUNCTIONAL DEPENDENCY RELATIONSHIPS

While painting or making houses, many children left a small gap they described as 'The way in' or 'That's the way you get into the house'. A more formal way of expressing this is to say *'Getting on the inside is functionally dependent on going through a boundary'*.

Amanda (4:1:14) drew 'A house'. She cut out two rectilinear holes, stood the drawing against a wall and said, 'Look, a house, these are windows'. She brought the drawing forward, looked behind it and said, 'That's inside'. Amanda (4:1:2) pushed her finger through the gill and out of the mouth of the whiting and said, 'That's where it breathes'.

Stephen (3:6:13), after pumping water out of a simulated lock, drew a picture which he called 'A pump with water going through' (Figure 6.32). Stephen (4:3:29) painted a kettle (Figure 6.33). He told his mother, 'This is a kettle and this is the spout. The water goes in the spout' (the kettle was filled via the spout). Stephen (4:4:1) pointed out a red pipe that ran round the wall of the kitchen. He told his mother, 'The hot water goes through there'.

Jock (3:9:2) drew two drawings. One was called 'A cage with a lot of birds inside'. The second was called 'These are doors where people can come through'.

THOUGHT LEVEL

After members of the institute's Movement Department had been working with the parents and children in the movement hall, Amanda (3:6:16) made a model of the climbing frame from tooth-paste boxes. She told her mother about all the actions she had performed on the frame in the hall.

Figure 6.32 'A pump with water going through.'

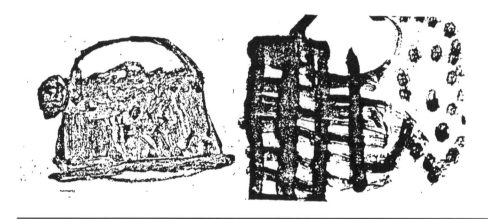

Figure 6.33 'This is a kettle and this is the spout. The water goes in the spout.'

Figure 6.34 'That's a cage and that's rain. The cage is for people to go into when it's raining.'

Joel (3:9:12) drew 'That's a cage and that's rain. The cage is for people to go into when it's raining' (Figure 6.34). The teacher said, 'I didn't quite hear what you said, Joel. Did you say "cage" or "cave"?' Nicky (3:6:28), who was standing by, said, 'But you can see it's a cage. Caves have got stalagmites and stalagtites, they go up and down. A cage has got bars over the front. That's got bars over the front, a cave hasn't got bars over the front'.

The teacher said, 'But, Joel, if it's a cage, and people go into it when it's raining, won't they get wet?' Joel looking very pleased: 'Yes'. Teacher: 'But if they get wet won't they catch cold and have to go to the doctor?' After a polite smile Joel walked away.

DISCUSSION

Amanda's initial exploration of the gill and mouth of the whiting resembled the motor explorations of the 2-year-olds but her speech showed that she was investigating on a higher level. She knew that breathing, in a fish, is functionally dependent on gills. Amanda knew a great deal about animals because her father bought and sold animals and she often accompanied him to markets.

The reader will have observed that the teacher's conversation with Susan (4:1:8) about the motor actions involved in climbing through the holes in a box was less complex than the teacher's conversation with Nicky (3:6:28) about the differences between a cage and a cave. There are various reasons for this. Susan was accepted into the project because her family circumstances were not propitious. She had four older siblings, two of them young adults, all kept by an unsupported mother. The educational standards of the whole family were very low. Her sister, older by four years, had not spoken for the whole of her first year at primary school. The school staff were anxious for Susan to attend the project. At the end of Susan's first two years in primary school, at the age of 7, she was 33 IQ points ahead of her sister and 36 percentile points ahead on the English Picture Intelligence Test. On the Neale Analysis of Reading Ability, Susan was three months ahead of her chronological age while her sister was three years behind.

Nicky (3:6:28), on the other hand, was in the kindergarten comparison group and had an IQ of 146. His reasoning is approaching *transitivity* in that he is able to reason that if caves have x and cages have y and the drawing has y then the drawing must be of a cage.

Joel's description of his painting, on first hearing, sounds like nonsense – which is why the kindergarten teacher asked for clarification as to whether he said 'cage' or 'cave'. A cave would be a logical place for people to go into when it was raining. However, the ensuing discussion made it clear that Joel meant 'cage'. It also became clear that he was exploring the notion of *'a' going through 'b'*, in this case, rain going through the bars of a cage.

The two kindergarten children were well nourished with rich experiences and precise language as were all the kindergarten children. The teacher was therefore able to communicate at a level far above chronological age. Although her particular question in this case, about people catching cold, illustrates a lack of 'match', the organization of her classroom allowed the children to make polite departures. Most teachers in early education will admit that 'matching' questions and comments with diagnosed schemas is as yet relatively unexplored.

As with all the other schemas discussed in this chapter, the schema of *going through* evolved from simple early behaviour to more complex understandings that required co-ordination with other notions. Two examples are given to illustrate this progression. The first example suggests that *going through* (in this case *looking through)* develops from a fixed point of view to a decentred point of view.

Stephen (3:7:19), while in the bath, playfully put a clothes basket with a plastic weave over his head. He looked through the holes and told his mother, 'I'm in my house, looking out of my window'. A few days later he drew a rectangle within which he placed a line of dots. He named this 'This is a coach and these are people looking out'. Although he had had much experience of looking out of the project-bus window, it seems unlikely that he would have been able to represent this in two dimensions without the requisite cognitive ability to decentre. His ability to represent people on the *inside* of a bus, *looking out*, implies some degree of decentration. In other words, a shift to reversibility is implied. There were many drawings of people looking out of windows, particularly from children in the kindergarten group. Most children were able to say quite clearly what the person would be seeing from the window.

Six-year-olds frequently represent animals looking through the bars of cages or people looking out of buses, cars and trains. If these drawings do indicate decentration it could be an important indication to the teacher that the children are beginning to understand spatial relativity, in that objects that are seen are relative to the point of view of the observer. They are shifting from *topological* to *projective* viewpoints.

The second example shows an evolution from *going through* to *time* measured by *going through*. At one point Salam (4:4:15) was pouring water through a very narrow-necked funnel and began to count as a measure of how long water took to go through.

THOUGHT: (INTERNALIZED ACTION)

In this chapter we have selected examples that illustrate different stages in the development of specific schemas. However, in everyday cognitive functioning, particularly as children become more mature and acquire more experience, 'thought' reflects clusters of schemas that contain a wide range of content. In brief, schemas become co-ordinated with each other and develop into systems of thought.

Unfortunately co-ordinations of schemas and richness and variety of content can only be illustrated and described rather than measured. Specific schemas have been used to show the sequential and systematic progression from motor behaviour to 'thought'. The 'thought' level examples have been detached from longer initial observations.

A complete conversation between Lois (4:7:7) and Mariam, a student, illustrates co-ordinated schemas, all of which have been discussed individually in this chapter. Lois was talking about her cat. When 'thought' level observations are looked at in their entirety they show that the children are able to recall and anticipate in imagination the displacements of objects and people within a three-dimensional world. When this stage of internalization is reached, representation can consist of soldiers hiding from imaginary pursuers. The pursued move from point to point, sometimes from one covered position to another. Trees are climbed in imagination in order to escape from the dogs of the enemy. Imaginary submarines are boarded and then submerged. Imaginary aeroplanes are boarded and flown. The children pretend to parachute down, swim away from sinking ships, hide in caves while the enemy marches over the top, and so on.

Action, graphic and speech representations that convey dynamic space notions set within a three-dimensional world have their earlier equivalents at the sensorimotor stage. This route was predicted by Piaget (1959) but only the sensorimotor stage was documented in detail. After discussing the origins of *'space as a container'* and early *rotation* behaviour, Piaget (1959, p. 196) describes and gives one complex illustration of what he calls 'the last essential acquisition' (by this he means internalized action or 'thought'). This is where the child establishes relations of positions and displacements among objects and simultaneously gains awareness of his or her own movements as displacements.

The example Piaget gives is of Laurent (1:2:0) who makes sufficiently complex trajectories to indicate that he has a *mental map*, albeit rudimentary, of his surroundings. He can, for instance, take a detour around a sofa in order to fetch a ball that has rolled under it. He has learnt that two different routes can have the same starting-point and the same finishing-point, He knows how to reach a gate by toddling in a straight line or by another route where he first passes some bushes. When he goes via the bushes he takes a right-angle route. He discovers this itinerary by chance. When he reaches the gate he can reverse his action back to his various starting-points. Piaget traces Laurent's displacements in relation to ten different points in the garden. He shows how a child forms a *group of displacements* and thus acquires a *cognitive map*.

Piaget describes (1959, p. 199) the end of the sensorimotor stage as follows: 'The objective groups discovered during this stage [sensorimotor stage six] remain limited to the displacements directly perceived and do not yet include any displacement simply imagined'. Piaget did not follow through these *groups of displacements* to the symbolic or imaginary level.

The following observations from the Froebel project children show that they have some kind of *cognitive map* and they have assimilated sufficient environmental content to represent imagined situations. However, as will also be seen, Stephen's cognitive map is not sufficiently stable to share with more than one other child.

The 'game' or 'play', shared by Stephen (4:9:1) and Alistair (4:3:2) illustrates 'thought' in that certain spaces are given symbolic significance but the symbolism does not depend on concrete objects acting as signifiers. The two children are attempting to understand each other's point of view, that is, each other's construction of spaces that are purely imaginary.

When two other children joined the game it became too difficult and Stephen complained to Mrs B about their behaviour. The crux of the complaint is that the two who joined them were not playing the game that Stephen and, to a lesser extent, Alistair, had in mind. It was difficult enough for Stephen and Alistair to share their fragile thoughts with each other, without the well-intentioned intrusion of the other two.

IMAGINED LOCATIONS

A game started with Alistair and Stephen agreeing on an imaginary bed position for where soldiers sleep. The soldiers were making an imaginary tar road next to a river. When these locations became established with some difficulty, Pete joined in and lay down on what had been designated as a soldier's bed space. Alistair was the soldier.

Alistair: Pete, you don't sit there. I sit there you sleep there [pointing to an empty space].

Stephen: [pointing to the same space] They always sleep on that thin bit there [it was not clear who 'they' were].

Alistair: [checking with Stephen on one of their agreed upon locations] This is the river, eh?

Amanda was doing something to what she called the road but that was a space demarcated by Stephen and Alistair as the river. After Stephen had expressed his annoyance with Amanda, he decided to change the location of the river.

Stephen: The water's over here now. It's gonna be the water, Amanda was doing it and l told them off [Pete and Amanda]. l don't want them to do it.

Mrs B: What is it that you are doing?

Stephen: Alistair filled this up, this hole [an imaginary hole in the ground] so that Pete don't do it again [Pete doesn't need to do it again].

Mrs B: You know you said you were road men. What are you putting on the road?

Stephen: Tar.

Alistair (not realizing that Stephen had changed the location of the road to where the river used to be, in the light of Amanda digging there) said, 'It's a river'. Stephen got annoyed again: 'No, I want the tar over there'.

Mrs B, trying very hard to follow Stephen's changed cognitive map of the location of the river in relation to the road, asked: 'So this bit can be the river, can it?' Stephen: 'No! This is the tar, over there is the car. I've done the tar here. We're not playing with him any more' (meaning Pete).

■ DISCUSSION

At this stage of social play, Stephen's affective response towards people who fail to follow his imagined locations is one of extreme annoyance. This could be dismissed as cognitive egocentricity but it is just as likely to be based on a cognitive ability to imagine without the requisite speech to convey the imaginings to others.

This example draws attention to the difficulties involved in communicating a subjective system of symbolic locations without the aid of socially shared public speech. Stephen's cognitive map is not private in the sense of being incommunicable because Alistair had already understood where things were located in their play. It was a cognitive achievement for Stephen and Alistair to be able to communicate sufficiently well for them to agree on imagined events taking place in imagined places.

The dissatisfaction and complaints expressed by Stephen indicate that he had the desire to be clear about features of the game but not yet the verbal capacity to negotiate his meanings with more than one friend.

THOUGHT: TELLING A STORY

When Randolph was 4:10:11, he spontaneously told a story to the project teacher, Mrs B. The narrative aspect of the story is not particularly coherent but what is clear is that he is verbally expressing a set of dynamic space notions, each of which had been explored by him, at earlier levels, during the previous year. The story is as follows:

Randolph: One day the lion went down seeing if the rabbit is here. So he was peeping and he was looking and he point to the cat. One night he was hiding near the cupboard, where we can't see him. The little mouse was peeping and he was turning round not looking. One night the cat was looking round and so one night he stuck his head in the clock. And one night he was rolling down and he couldn't hear what is making a noise and so he was behind the cat and the thing still on his head and so one night he was trying to take it off. The night he said he was going to help him and he said, 'I am not your friend' so he run away. I telling a story. Whew!

Mrs B: Thank you, Randolph, I enjoyed that very much. It was a lovely story.

■ DISCUSSION

Internalized trajectories, expressed in the story, are as follows: *lion went down, he point to the cat, he ran away*. The *trajectories* are described in terms of *purpose: the lion went down to find a rabbit* (it could even be said that finding a rabbit was *functionally dependent on going down)*. The sentence, 'He was near the cupboard', expresses a *proximity* relation. He makes his characters *rotate* for the purpose of looking round: 'the mouse was not looking round and the cat was looking round'. One of his characters is hiding therefore he cannot be seen *relative to the point of view of the observer:* 'the cat was hiding where we can't see him'. A character can put *part of himself inside an enveloping space:* 'a head in a clock'. A character can 'roll down the hill' *(dynamic rotation)*. In speech he can express a projective space notion: 'he was *behind* the cat'. He expresses the spatial notion of *on top of:* 'he was trying to take off the thing on his head'.

It cannot be said that this story reflects thought that is static. Randolph is able to describe actions – to evoke the past in the absence of objects originally acted upon. His actions are replaced by words. This is the point of departure for thought (Piaget, 1968b, p. 22).

Part III

Continuities from Earlier to Later Patterns of Thought

7

Continuities in Form and Meanings

One of the problems of working without a clearly defined pedagogy is that nothing is discussed about what goes on inside the learner. Behaviourists (or empiricists) only concern themselves with situations which are external. It would appear at the moment that everything that can be externalized is. Teachers now have to work through miles of print dealing with bland generalizations of what ought to be 'delivered' to learners. In the food industry people are, at last, asking whether what is being delivered is good for the customer.

The central principle of the 1988 Education Reform Act (ERA) was that every pupil should have a balanced, relevant and broadly-based curriculum. Very few people would argue against this sort of mission statement. However, it was also stated that 'It is not enough for such a curriculum to be offered by the school: it must be fully taken up by each individual pupil' (DES, 1989a, para. 2.1). Here is an invitation for school staff to ask whether the learner has learned what has been offered.

In the really old days, as in the 1950s, most primary teachers made up their own curriculum, like Miss Jean Brodie. Half the year was wasted. Mothering Sunday brought its card-making obligations. Easter chicks followed Santa Claus. Halloween witches followed hot on Guy Fawkes and so on.

Now, schools are not short of materials which support programmes of study for particular purposes. A 'whole-school' approach, for instance, can delineate which teachers will tackle which topic and when. Large pictures of 'Spring' or 'animals' or 'flowers' are no longer draped over windows in classroom doors creating private spaces which are now rightly public. Sequences of what is on offer to children in different subject areas, at different stages, can be displayed for the illumination of parents. During the 1960s, many schools had implemented a more systematic and coherent organization of what was on offer to children of different ages and stages from the beginning to the end of schooling. A whole-school approach to the organization of curriculum content into concepts, topics or themes was a considerable improvement on individual teachers organizing and delivering their own curriculum.

In the literature, even today, 'continuity' is mainly discussed in relation to what is on offer and what will be delivered. In the DES publication, 1985 the section headed 'Better schools' states: 'The 5–16 curriculum needs to be constructed and delivered as a continuous and coherent whole, in which the primary phase pre-pares for the secondary phase and the latter builds on the former' (DES, 1985, para. 63). 'Continuity' is advocated but not illustrated.

It will be a long time before secondary teachers know what is being offered in their subject to children from 5 to 11 and before primary teachers know how the various concepts they are presenting have evolved from early education and how they will be developed at the secondary level. British teachers do not think in terms of 'lifelong learning' in spite of all the rhetoric surrounding the issue.

The DES publication also stated: 'To deal adequately with pupils within one phase of education requires a thorough understanding of the educational needs of children in that age range and a view of how a particular phase relates to the whole process' (DES, 1985, paras. 5 and 18). This ideal has never been realized; there has been no help given to teachers to recognize what is going on inside local individual learners, much less learners in general.

Again, DES states: 'Teaching and learning experiences should be ordered so as to facilitate pupils' progress, with each successive element making appropriate demands and leading to better performance' (1985, para. 124). It has been long known that the greatest difficulty in evaluating pupil progress is diagnosing a suc-cessful 'match' between the learning of individual pupils and the offered curriculum content. This requires a high degree of professional understanding of the processes of incremental learning. The more the teacher learns about individu-als, the more effectively he or she will be able to select appropriate curriculum content for both individuals and groups.

As discussed in Chapter 1, viewing any level of education retrospectively high-lights cognitive deficits rather than competence. Continuity is best studied by documenting the developmental links between successful early learning and later learning.

Curtis (1986) gives examples of 'discontinuity' between early and primary edu-cation that are immediately and distressingly recognizable. Children in early education may be learning about real fundamental notions while using sand and water. In the reception class the sand and water tray may be 'somewhere to go when 'work' is finished' (1986, p. 159). 'Fundamental notions' and explo-rations, as discussed throughout this book, are thus trivialized. As suggested in Chapter 4, the concepts of 'work' and 'play' need to be linked more clearly with fundamentals of the learning process.

In effect, we still have a long way to go, but the time might be right for teachers to turn their backs on the miles of platitudes published by different official departments and start seeking evidence from children that there has been a match between what is on offer and what has been assimilated. All teachers will know that this prescription for successful 'continuity in learning' is more easily declared than demonstrated.

In Chapters 5 and 6, continuity between cognition in infants and the Froebel Project children from 2 to 5 is discussed and illustrated in relation to particular schemas. In this and the following chapters an attempt will be made to illustrate how children build conceptually on what has gone before. What links all the examples is how schematic development and curriculum extensions before the age of 5 have direct links with concept development and curriculum extension in children between the ages of 5 and 11.

CONTINUITY IN LANGUAGE AND THOUGHT

Before discussing the findings of the Froebel Project on language and thought with implications for the primary curriculum, it is necessary (because of the rapidly developing links between constructivism and the study of early language) to give a short summary of recent research.

For many years research into language development was dominated by linguists who had been influenced by Chomsky's theory that infants come into the world with an innate language acquisition device. Chomsky (1980) said, 'I consider that there is strong evidence that particular aspects of language are innately determined' (cited in Piattelli-Palmarini, 1980, p. 173). Even more controversially he said that '"Human language" is a "mental organ" having an innate structure as specific as that of the eye or the heart' (1980, p. 276).

In academic debate, Chomsky's position has been contrasted with constructivist theory, Piaget being the main protagonist. Piaget's position on knowledge in general is that it can be constructed only through interaction between certain inborn modes of processing and the actual characteristics of physical objects and events. Although Piaget denies that infants are born with innate cognitive structures, he agrees that cognitive structures are present from birth. He maintains that functioning; assimilation and accommodation, immediately create schemas or cognitive structures, and structuring is brought about through an organization of successive actions performed on objects (Piaget, 1980, p. 23).

In debate both Piaget and Chomsky have shifted from their initial, rather extreme positions. Chomsky (1980) agreed that there were interactions between innate mechanisms and aspects of the external world and that, therefore, experience had some effect. However, he diminished the importance of environment by saying that 'Certain kinds of interactions with the external world serve as a triggering function only for the acquisition of language' (1980, p. 172). There is a conceptual difference between Piaget's claims that 'assimilation feeds' early cognitive structures, and that Chomsky's 'triggering' merely actualizes what is already there. This difference is important, but not from a teacher's point of view.

For teachers, the middle ground between extreme innatism and extreme environmentalism provides the fertile soil for facilitating language and thought in children. Cognitive structures are clearly of importance in relation to children's understanding, while environmental content provides 'food' for the thought structures.

Vygotsky maintained that thought and language have different genetic roots, in that the two functions develop along different lines and are independent of each other. However, he suggested that there is a close correspondence between thought and speech (1962, p. 41). His views correspond to Chomsky's statement: 'I take it for granted that thinking is a domain that is quite different from language, even though language is used for the expression of thought' (Piattelli-Palmarini, 1980, p. 173).

Fodor (1980) illustrated the essential semantic relationship between languages and thought when he pointed out that people are unlikely to learn words that express concepts they do not have: 'Nobody would learn the word "cat" unless he knows what a cat is' (Piattelli-Palmarini, 1980, p. 173). Here, Fodor draws attention to the meaning aspect of language as opposed to linguistic form. An important educational issue is to ascertain that a match exists between existing forms of thought and appropriate speech.

FORM AND MEANING

Since Chomsky, linguists have sought clarification on the structures of language, whereas psychologists and educationalists have been more interested in children and the processes by which they acquire language. Research findings on early language, and thought can be separated into information on the 'form' of utterances and the 'meaning' of utterances. Studies edited by Snow and Ferguson (1977: reported in Lock and Fisher, 1984) have found that the main aim of mother–child dialogue is the construction of conversational meaning and that this aim over-rides syntactic considerations (reported in Lock and Fisher, 1984). Of particular interest is research on meanings intended by speakers.

Although Piaget consistently maintained that sensorimotor actions are inextricably bound up with early speech, he has never produced evidence from children in support of this claim. Recently, however, there has been evidence that infants use early speech (verbal signs or signals) for expressing satisfaction or lack of satisfaction with the outcomes of intended schematic action.

Although debate on what is 'innate' versus social encounters within the environment remains inconclusive, research generated within the debate has led to the realization that all children, whatever their ethnic or cultural background, acquire 'forms of utterances' in broadly the same sequence. A few instances of 'form' will pave the way for a differentiation between 'form' and 'meaning', as well as a closer examination of the 'meaning' aspect of language.

There are nine known major periods of the forms of language acquisition, starting with *cooing*. This *includes speech sound discriminations*, such as 'ba/pa', which lead eventually to an advanced concern with the 'graphic representations' of language, such as the alphabet, writing, signs and isolated words in texts. This sequence applies to children all over the world (Slobin, 1973, discussed in Lock and Fisher, 1984, p. 8). *Cooing* precedes *babbling*, which leads to first words. First words include *discrimination of word pairs*, such as 'bat/pat'. Although it is accepted that two-word utterances contain semantic relations, it is now becoming clear that one-word utterances, such as *up*, *no* and *more*, also include meaning.

Several researchers have recorded that most young children use words such as *gone*, *there*, *oh dear* and *no more* in their early language use. There is also general use of locative expressions such as *down*, *up*, *in*, *out*, *on* and *off*. The Froebel Project findings show that location words are used in a very wide range of situations. These are discussed in detail in Chapter 6.

As mentioned earlier, it is not difficult to record children's behaviour or use of words. What is difficult is to conceptualize the meaning of the raw data of observation in ways that are useful for some purpose or other. Gopnic (1984) observed children's use of certain words within contexts and used constructivist theory to explain what children appeared to have in mind in their early use of speech. Her conclusions may help to illuminate what Piaget had in mind when he insisted that both knowledge and speech proceed from action. Gopnic (1984, pp. 83–101) used the term 'plan' rather than 'schema', but her definition of 'plan' is similar to that of schema.

Gopnic recorded language in children from the age of 1 to 2 and observed that certain words were used within certain contexts. She hypothesized that early words were intended to encode perceptual features, sensorimotor schemes, actions, events or relationships (see Lock and Fisher, 1984). She assumed, as was also assumed in the Froebel Project, that if a child always says *down* when objects move downwards, the child has some general concept of *downward movement* and that this concept was being encoded by the use of the word *down*. All of the nine children she studied used *down*, *up*, *in*, *out*, *on* and *off* 573 times in locative contexts. In some contexts, the children commented on the movements of objects, but in 401 (70 per cent) contexts the children made, or tried to make, an object move in a particular direction.

Words such as *no, oh dear, in, out* and *there* used within contexts signified success or failure, and the criterion of success or failure, from the infant's point of view, is of particular interest. The words expressed satisfaction or lack of satisfaction with the effects of schematic activity. If children placed one brick *on top of* another successfully, they would say *there* (240 instances). Alternatively, if the brick fell off they would say *oh dear* (320 instances). Similarly, the word *no* was used to signify that an aim had not been achieved or that objects had not behaved as expected. The word *no* was used 149 times when the child could not achieve his or her aim because of the actions of other people. For example, one child said *no* when an adult closed the lid of a tape-recorder he was trying to open. Another child said *no* when the adult wanted to put a particular lid on a box and he wanted to put a different one on.

The general factor behind the *oh dear* and *no* responses is the mismatch between what was anticipated and the actual outcome (Lock and Fisher, 1984, p. 89). Infants 'know' that schematic action performed on objects can bring about a desired state. Confirmation is expressed by *more*, which encodes the fact that a plan is to be repeated (1984, pp. 91–2). Disconfirmation is expressed by *no* or *oh dear*. Later these expressions are applied to more general events that are not the result of direct action: *more*, for instance, was used to mark the fact that two objects were similar.

This work seems to support Piaget's claim that the first mental representations are the results of internalized actions. Enough schematic, sensorimotor actions have been performed to set up anticipations. The anticipations show a continuity with skilled action and the effect of action. Early speech does arise from sensorimotor schemas, as Piaget claims, but more as a commentary on the effects of action rather than directly from the actions themselves.

8

Speech and Writing in Relation to Schemas

'A word is only as good as the knowing structure which uses it' (Furth, 1969, p. 111). The Froebel project findings give support to the 'cognition hypothesis of language acquisition' in that speech used by project children reflected prominent schemas as well as the content assimilated to schemas.

'The cognition hypothesis for language acquisition' (Cromer, 1979, cited in Lee, 1979), corresponds to the constructivist position on the relationship between speech and cognition, the early stages of which have been illustrated in Chapter 7 through Gopnic's work. The hypothesis is that speech is acquired in synchrony with acquired meanings. To the constructivist, speech is a necessary but not a sufficient condition for the construction of logical operations. Language is important but as part of a more general cognitive organization that has its roots in 'action'. 'Language is one of the elements of a cluster of signs resting on the semiotic function and in which symbolic play, deferred imitation and mental imagery participate' (Inhelder, 1980, p. 133). One implication of the 'cognition hypothesis' for teaching is that the language used by adults must be sufficiently elaborate to support and 'flesh out' advances in children's thinking.

The cognition hypothesis has been mainly supported by research on children over the age of 6 where speech forms alter to match increasingly complex concrete-operational thought structures. Before a child acquires *seriation* he or she will use speech that reflects *absolute size* notions, such as 'I am big, you are little'. As *seriation* proceeds towards greater differentiation, speech extends and *comparative terms* are used, such as 'I am bigger than you'. Similarly, when a child becomes able to think in *hierarchical categories* he or she will be able to make statements such as 'All sparrows are birds and all birds are animals and all animals are living beings' (Piaget, 1972a, pp. 78–81).

Sinclair-de-Zwart (1969) studied the relationship between speech and *conservation*. She found that 90 per cent of *non-conservers* used *absolute* rather than *comparative* terms to describe quantity. Conservers were able to *co-ordinate* two sentences *when they were able to* co-ordinate two dimensions *cognitively*. They would say, as well as understand, that 'This is short but it is also wide'.

Support for the natural order of thought preceding language comes also from attempts to train non-conservers into becoming conservers by the use of speech. Children were given *comparative terms* in order to accelerate *comparative thinking*. Even when children successfully learnt the verbal expressions they rarely advanced conceptually. Similar results were found when attempts were made to generate *seriation* structures through speech training (Inhelder, 1969, p. 232; Tamburrini, 1982).

Not only do children not advance conceptually through verbal means alone but they also actually transform test questions to fit in with their existing level. Piaget calls this 'distorting assimilation'. *Pre-ordination* children were asked to give more sweets to one doll rather than another. They were then asked to repeat the question. They transformed the question into absolute terms, such as 'You said I had to give a lot to that one and a little to that one' (Duckworth, 1974, cited in Schwebel and Raph, 1974, p. 144).

The general route of development is from early gross generalizations towards progressive separations and finer differentiations (Jakobson, 1941, cited in Cromer, 1974). Early babbling developing into speech has been compared with early scribbling developing into drawing and writing. Several strands require a more detailed examination. Even symbolic play (which is widely accepted as important in early childhood education) has remained elusive when attempts have been made to measure its occurrence in an educational setting (Sylva et al., 1980). The route 'from action to thought' has aroused interest but has not been studied systematically and longitudinally. It is illustrated and given substance in Chapter 6 of this book. Early scribbling developing into drawing and writing is illustrated in Chapter 5.

As already stated, Piaget considers sensorimotor intelligence rather than language to be the true foundation of operational thought, with mental representation being the culmination of sensorimotor intelligence. Few people would deny that speech is the major vehicle in 'carrying forward' sensorimotor developments and learnings to symbolic levels of functioning. The problem has been how to document this hypothesized route.

One problem is that early 'two-word' utterances are ambiguous. After climbing in and out of holes in hollow wooden boxes for some time, Kamal (2 years old and still in the main an Urdu speaker) made a construction from a part of a cardboard egg box. He described it as 'two holes'. Various schemas could be involved, such as *the salience of the circle* (the shape of the hole), *going through the boundary, two-ness*, and so on, but cognitive features are difficult to abstract from such short utterances. Because of this difficulty many project observations were coded at a motor level though they may have contained a symbolic component.

Intention and meaning were clearer when utterances were made in context. What young children say usually relates directly to what they do and see. As speech use and comprehension increased, ambiguities decreased. Support for the cognition hypothesis in the Froebel project findings is almost too obvious. A random inspection of any schema illustrated in Chapters 5 and 6 will show the close relationship between schema and speech use. Professionals and parents could work together in order to facilitate the necessary links between forms of thought, the content of thought and appropriate speech. As already mentioned in Chapter 4, there were relatively few symbolic representations of project children that did not involve speech – indicating that children like to talk about what they are doing.

FROM MARKS TO WRITING

There are different views on when writing begins. It is generally held that writing is writing when another person can read what is written without too much difficulty. Looking at writing from a developmental point of view, it could be said that the origins are to be found soon after birth when the infant distinguishes things that move from objects that are static. Both the perception and production of writing can be seen in these terms. Print as a product appears to be made up of *fixed patterns*. Writing as a process gives information on the *movingness of writing*: 'The moving finger writes and having writ moves on.

The Froebel project children's early writing was consistent with early symbolic representations in general. The movingness of cars or planes was represented, as was the movingness of writing as a continuous movement of the pencil across paper. There were not many instances of this pretend, cursive writing but the few examples that were produced were usually called 'a letter' or 'a shopping list'. Several writers have drawn attention to the ubiquity of the 'shopping list' in early writing (Temple et al., 1982, p. 33; Payton, 1984, p. 37; Sanderson, 1987, p. 3). Perhaps shopping lists and letters as instances of writing in action are produced mainly in homes. The few instances of this kind of imitation on the part of the project children may reflect a paucity of writing in the home.

As most print in the general environment is fixed and does not contain information on the writing process, the project teacher made a point of writing, in the presence of the children, about things that were happening. The intention was to convey the message that reading and writing are everyday activities. Parents soon joined in with this and 'home books', containing positive messages about matters of interest, were carried back and forth between home and school.

Several project children represented the *linear configuration* of writing with short *horizontal lines* or with strips of sticky paper. Most of the project children's highly specific representation of what they called 'writing', 'letters' and 'names were consistent with the graphic schemas they used for drawing other objects that shared a figurative similarity.

Pretend writing started with rows of discrete marks, such as short *vertical lines, crosses* and *circles*. Therefore, the project children's early writing, in a general sense, reflected both action and figurative schemas. When the children became interested in *circular* things in the environment and they were able to reproduce *circular* things in their drawings, the letter 'O' was singled out for reproduction rather than, say, the letter 'Z'. Letter shapes, like other shapes in the environment, were consistently assimilated to existing levels of mark-making. When *grid-like* marks were made, *grid-like* letters appeared, as did other *grid-like* configurations, such as cages, cranes, scaffolding, hammocks, the Eiffel Tower, railings and train tracks. Teachers and parents tend to show enthusiasm when standard letter forms appear. When an adult admired, at some length, a 4-year-old's upper-case 'H' the boy said, somewhat annoyed, 'It's a clothes line with two props'.

When project children were able to co-ordinate *vertical lines* with the *open semi-circle* they made a major step forward in the production of letter formations. This was achieved after much time-taking effort. Figure 5.18 shows Randolph's attempts to copy his mother's writing of his name. 'R', 'P' and lower-case 'A' are tackled with co-ordinated *line* and *semi-circle*. The *oblique line* has hardly started to emerge from the earlier *core and parallel radials*. Figure 5.19 shows the striking similarity between the graphic schemas used for letters and the drawing of a man.

Almost a year later, Randolph is still working spontaneously on all the letter forms needed for his name. 'The glasses' show a connection between two *core and curved radials* (Figure 5.13). The *curved radials* (arcs) are used five times in the spontaneous writing of his name. He now connects an *oblique line* correctly for his upper-case 'R'. From this time onwards, Randolph had no difficulty in representing the upper-case letters, 'A', 'M', 'K', 'V' or 'W'.

The similarity between general graphic schemas and letter forms is apparent in developmental studies of children's drawing and yet the similarity has often escaped notice. Eng (1959) gave enough illustrations from her niece, Margaret, to show the obvious link between letter and drawing forms but, as already discussed in Chapter 4, seeing commonalities requires attention to form rather than content. When Margaret managed to draw the *triangular* form (Figure 5.54) she not only drew an upper-case 'A' and 'M' but she began to draw *triangular* houses, groups of people wearing *triangular* capes, a sitting figure, a *zig-zag trajectory* behind a sledge, a dog kennel with a *triangular roof*, and so on.

The *open continuous triangle* (the zig-zag) opened up opportunities for the representation of zig-zag phenomena, such as 'steps', 'teeth', 'waves', stegosaurus and so on. Letter forms represented at this time were 'W', 'M', 'Y' and 'Z'. Figure 5.62 shows that Shanaz is able to draw all the letter forms needed for her name but she is not yet able to orient the letter 'Z' on a horizontal plane.

However, particular enthusiasm for 'letter-like' forms need not preclude valida-tion for other graphics, which also have a future. *Arrows pointing in different directions, spirals, helixes,* and many spatial orders are not related to the forms and directionality of reading and writing but they can be very important in science, mapping and mathematics, not to mention painting and drawing. As each graphic form emerged in the Froebel project each was admired and the various uses were discussed. The teacher would comment on the use of marks by point-ing out that *a curve* had been used for drawing an arch, a boat, a cup and a 'c'. The children gave enthusiastic responses to these comments, Adults can over-emphasize early writing but they can also miss it. Shirley Payton asked her 3-year-old, 'Are you drawing a lovely picture?' The child replied, 'No, I'm writing "S" for Sally'.

As the project children acquired graphic forms they used them to represent known objects, which included letters and words. The children also combined marks and by so doing created new graphic forms that included letters. *Connecting a vertical line* with a *semi-circle* allowed '9', 'P', 'B', 'b', 'D' and 'd' to be constructed. Varying motor actions that lead to variability in mark-making are instances of accommodation. Clay (1975) has named this a 'flexibility principle'.

The spontaneous repetitions of each new form in drawing and writing are instances of assimilation. Assimilation, as repetition, has the main function of 'practice makes perfect'. Clay (1975) describes this as the 'recurring principle'. Of greater interest than repetition per se is the way in which instances of assimila-tion can be used as indications of cognitive level. There is, for instance, a great developmental difference between the repetition of circles and crosses and repeated words or repeated sentences. Knowledge of levels of assimilation is syn-onymous with knowledge of stage levels.

Progress from early to later learning is illustrated in Chapters 5 and 6. It seems likely that the advanced reading scores of the Froebel project children were related to the procedure adopted in the project of paying minute attention to each observed increment in each child's learning over two years. The significant differences between the project children's scores and those of their older siblings indicate that the early education received in the project facilitated later develop-ment in reading.

CONTINUITY BETWEEN DYNAMIC SCHEMAS AND EARLY WRITING

Thirty-seven examples of early writing were collected from Sarah over three years (from age 4 to 7) by her teacher, Margaret Palladino, at Eveline Lowe Primary School, London. Her teacher selected examples in order to show developments in Sarah's writing as discussed in the literature on early writing.

Only one aspect of Sarah's writing will be considered here in order to show a continuity between the cognitive form and content of earlier schematic behaviours illustrated in Chapter 6 of this book and the cognitive form and content of much early writing. Of the 37 examples of Sarah's writing, 25 show this continuity. Many of the examples consist of simple *forward trajectories* with *one or two end-points,* such as:

- 'This is me going to the shops'.

- 'Mummy comes to tell Kelly's got to go home'.

- 'This is a lady getting married and the people watching and the car to take them home. Penny and Paul take the baby for a walk'.

- 'Snow White went to a little house. She looks after them in the woods'.

- 'My name is Sarah. I've got blue eyes and blond hair. I go to school in my dad's car. Debbie picks me up. When I get home I play out. Then I go in I have my dinner. I get undressed. I watch the telly. Mummy says go to bed now Sarah'.

- 'One day it was a girl's birthday. She got a puppy dog. She named it Sibar. She took it out for a walk. Her mum said she had to come in. She went in. She was tired and went to bed with her puppy dog. The end of the story'.

- 'One day a girl said can I go out? Yes said the mum take the dog. Alright said the girl. When she got there she picked blackberries and strawberries. Time to go home the girl said to the dog, so they went'.

This last example shows a simple *trajectory* and *return* but *the end-point* of the *trajectory* includes *collecting* two types of berries. In other words, there is now a co-ordination between the *spatial trajectory* and a *logical classification* (two types of berries).

The following is a written sequence of nine events that is equivalent, but at a higher level of symbolic functioning, to the action and speech representations of earlier development:

> *One day daddy and mummy went out for the day. Let's have a picnic said mummy. I have brought some sandwiches so they had a picnic and then they went blackberry picking. Then they went home and had their dinner and watched telly and went to bed and they went fast asleep.*

The next example contains co-ordinations of schemas of *inside/outside, enveloping space, rotation* and *trajectories:*

> *This is the story of the horse. His name is Sandy. She is brown all over. Sandy belongs to a farmer and he lives in a stable. Sometimes the farmer lets him out in*

the field because he doesn't like being stuck in the stable all day. Out in the field Sandy runs about and rolls in the sand.

The following sequence of five cooking events consists of four actions of *placing inside,* one action of *rotation* and one action of placing *on top of*:

I made some pastry.

I put the flour into the bowl.

I put the water into the bowl.

I put the milk into the bowl and we stirred it. And we put the pastry onto the tray.

The functional dependency understandings of the following example are twofold: the figurative effects of ball and flat shapes are *functionally dependent* upon different kinds of *rotation* and cakes not sticking are *functionally dependent* on *greasing the surface* of the tin: 'I rolled the dough into a ball. I rolled it out then I cut out shapes. And then I greased the tray and put the cakes into the tray'. Cutting out shapes involves *going through* boundaries.

In the following, some of the processes of baking that were included in earlier written accounts are now left out. This may illustrate a 'speeding-up' of 'thought'. First written (and previously spoken) accounts include many actions in sequence but once the sequence is internalized, and thoroughly assimilated, some details become redundant:

We picked blackberries. We washed them. We made pastry. You need flour, margarine and water. I put it in a bowl and mixed it with a wooden spoon. I put it in the tray and put the blackberries on top and put the pastry on top of the black-berries and I put it in the oven for an hour.

9

Continuity Between Schemas and Concepts

Early education will never be accepted as a necessary part of lifelong learning until it is realized that later concepts are built on the schemas and experiences of the early years. This chapter is an attempt to trace through some of these cognitive continuities. Parents and professionals experience few difficulties. Politicians often do not see even the surface characteristics of young children's thinking, much less the cognitive structures underlying such content.

In 1995 a review of different areas of the curriculum was published by the School Curriculum and Assessment Authority (SCAA, 1995). There was a Foreword by Sir Ron Dearing in which he stated that the purpose of the review was to simplify assessment. The publication, entitled *Consistency in Teacher Assessment: Exemplification of Standards*, gives examples of different levels of thinking from real children; these were meant to illustrate Key Stages, each stage having six different levels. The complexity of assessment had got out of hand, and this was a real attempt to simplify the process of development and assessment. The examples given in support of different stages and levels were recognizable to most primary school teachers because they unintentionally illustrated the development of 'forms of thought'. These had been the main concern of many primary school teachers, arising from constructivism, during most of the twentieth century.

Most of the examples are accompanied by bland generalizations about attainment targets at different levels and attempts to externalize the learning of the children detracts from the real developmental value of the examples. Consider the example of 'Connecting Towns' shown in Figure 9.1. The task given to the children (ages are not given) is to find the shortest length of railway line which connects all towns. This task is classified unhelpfully as being at Key Stage 2, level 4 with the following comment on what is supposed to be level 4's defining factor: 'One aspect of this level is that children find and use strategies that can be

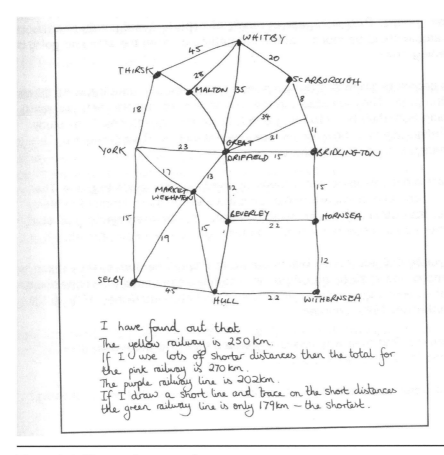

Figure 9.1 'Connecting towns.'

generally applied.' This can be applied to human beings from birth to adulthood. Specifically, and related to this particular example, they write: 'At first, Anne adopted a random approach to solving the problem. She then developed a more sophisticated strategy by deciding to use colour for the different railway lines' (SCAA, 1995, p.10). (This example was first used at a conference at Pen Green and later reproduced in an article in *Early Childhood Practice*, Athey, 2002, p. 13.)

A more helpful analysis might have included 'Anne found that the line coloured green was the shortest route connecting all towns'; or 'the green line represented 179 kilometres'. Developmentally speaking, this task requires the organization and measurement of:

- 26 routes (trajectories);

- 13 stopping off points;

- each route represented by a railway line;

- each line connected by two points (the beginning and the end of the route); and

- Each route (trajectory) given as a measurement in kilometres.

But this is not all that can be said about this example. Connecting points in space within trajectories has a past which starts in early infancy. The developmental route, from a schematic point of view, goes something like this:

- Infants in the first month track objects which move between points. They also gaze at points of departure and points of arrival.

- Infants under a year spend a lot of time throwing things from the pram. They are making 'vertical displacements' from A to B.

- Toddlers displace themselves by toddling from point A to point B. The points of departure can be moveable or static objects, such as people. The point of arrival is usually a fixed place or object.

Children can find their way round the garden, or any safe area, at a sensory and motor level before they can represent those displacements symbolically. Trajectories can be horizontal, vertical or circular. Later they can be oblique:

- Barbara (just turned 3) dropped toy airplanes from a height saying 'The aeroplane has fallen down'.

- Amanda, at 4, observes ' You know leaves ... they fall off the tree onto the ground [pause] and acorns fall off the tree'. (She has an early set of things that move vertically).

- Randolph, after hearing 'Hickory dickory dock' re-told it. He said: 'There was a mouse and it ran right up the inside of a clock'. This is a vertical trajectory fleshed out with nursery rhyme content.

At around 4 years there are endless chasing games, as well as the ubiquitous picnic. Such trajectory play has great possibilities for extension. Early trajectories increase in complexity and spontaneously become more and more linked with the external aspects of the curriculum. The example of 'Connecting Towns' illustrates a stage in a developing system of concepts which consists of trajectories, stopping-off points, different distances and number.

Many children's stories have interesting events happening at stopping-off points as their basic structure. For instance, the spatial structure of the story *Sam Who Never Forgets* (Rice, 1977) is to do with an habitual trajectory with stopping-off points. Sam, the zookeeper, transports appropriate food to a whole range of animals in the zoo. The story suggests that he may have forgotten the poor old elephant. The listener accompanies Sam on his rounds at the zoo where he has habitual stopping-off points. Co-ordinated with this spatial organization there is a logical classification of animal foods with a one-to-one mapping between food and animal. There are also possibilities for extending 'enveloping spaces' by naming animal enclosures:

> *He sets off transporting food in his wagon. He delivers:*
> *Green leaves to the giraffe.*
> *Bananas to the monkeys.*
> *Fish for the seal.*
> *Red berries for the bear.*
> *Food for the crocodile.*
> *Food for the long-legged ostrich.*
> *Fresh meat to the lion.*
> *Oats for the zebra. (Rice, 1977)*

At the end of his round the wagon is empty. All the animals are very concerned when a tear begins to fall from the elephant's eye. Then Sam reappears and shouts: 'I never forget!' He produces a whole wagon full of hay. Sam and the elephant hug each other. Here, Sam's action at each stopping-off point had the effect of lessening the amount of food left (subtraction) until there was nothing left – or so it seemed.

CO-ORDINATION OF SCHEMAS NECESSARY FOR LINEAR MEASUREMENT

The following example shows two levels in the understanding of length, both of which are based on the co-ordination of schemas acquired during early education.

Two 6-year-old boys were given the task of measuring the woodwork bench – the bench is only 'content', anything measurable would do. They used a pencil as a rough-and-ready standard. They came up with different answers. The teacher checked that they measured the same thing with the same measure, and then asked: 'How did you arrive at different answers?' Both boys understood that equivalence of outcome was to be expected from equivalence of procedure, and so they did the measuring again under the teacher's supervision. The first boy started at the edge of the bench; he put a finger at the end of the pencil to get his next starting point and continued doing this until he reached the end of the bench, counting each unit as he went.

The second boy did the same, except that he did not connect one increment of length with the beginning of the next, instead he left a gap between each step. He had a cluster of three schemas, but he should have had a cluster of four. Each schema has its roots in earlier schemas and experiences, and correct linear measuring requires:

1 Co-ordinating the end points of lines.

2 Making equidistant points on a line.

3 Leaving no gaps between points.

4 Applying a number system to three spatial ideas.

The co-ordination of schemas in early education develops into the integration of higher-order concepts which are taken forward into primary education. In Figure 9.2 James (age 1:6:20), a Froebel Project child, has discovered that pushing down on a top makes an item move in a circular direction.

Here there is a co-ordination of vertical and circular trajectories (I push down, it turns round).

Figure 9.3, Alistair (4:1:5) made a model of ' A train on a track'. He pointed to part of the model and said, 'That's where you wait and it goes round'. His mother said teasingly, 'I've never seen a platform go round'. Alistair said firmly, 'Well this one does!'

The idea of the revolving train platform is interesting as it seems to illustrate Piaget's theoretical construct of 'distorting assimilation'. Alistair was applying his 'rotation' schema with abandon. His mother was trying to wean him away from the idea of a rotating platform because she viewed it as a wrong idea and, as far as Alistair's intentions were concerned, she was probably right. When Mrs B (the teacher) and the present writer pointed out that such things existed, as with the Round House in North London used in the past for reversing trains, Alistair was not only absorbed, he was jubilant and triumphant.

In the level-crossing example in Figure 9.4, Al and John were using rotation at a functional dependency level in that the forward trajectory of the cars was functionally dependent on the gates being opened and the forward trajectory of the train functionally dependent on the gates being closed.

Figure 9.2 James (1:6:20) 'pushing down on top.'

Figure 9.3 Alistair (3:9:8) made 'a train on a track.'

Figure 9.4 Al and John – cars going forward functionally dependent on gates being opened.

Figure 9.5 'My spring – you push it down and then it jumps up.'

Figure 9.6 'Make something which will travel across a table top without being pushed or pulled.'

The representation in Figure 9.5, 'My spring – You push it down and then it jumps up', is described in SCAA documents as Key Stage 1, level 1. However, the earliest knowledge about force arises from actions performed in early education of pushing, pulling and pressing on. The child who drew and wrote about the spring probably knew that when force is applied to a spring the compression increases the speed of the upward trajectory. Early play forms consist of 'Jack in the box' and playing with pogo sticks and stilts that have springs attached to them and through this is learned the co-ordination of horizontal and vertical trajectories without physically pushing or pulling.

Figure 9.6 demonstrates clear progression and continuity from early education to primary education. The task is to make something which will travel across a table top without being pushed or pulled. The 'something' has to stop at the edge. Two children make this model. One boy writes: 'This piece of string must be as long as the table is high. When the wood reaches the floor it stops the cart' (Williams and Jinks, 1985, p. 13). The cluster of schemas or concepts required for this 7-year-old's solution to the given problem in 'design and technology' includes several that can be acquired before the age of 5. These include rotation, connection, vertical and horizontal trajectories, going through and round boundaries (as in making knots) and equivalence between three pairs of end-points (height and length of table and string).

FROM TRAJECTORIES TO ASPECTS OF ECONOMIC GEOGRAPHY

Figure 9.7 features Maurice and Mathew, both 6 years old.

These two boys were not set a task. They were the first in class to finish their 'work' (work cards all to do with the three Rs). This meant that they were free to choose. The teacher was marooned at her desk with two long queues, one queue to read one page from a reading book and one queue for the correct spelling of a word. The two boys started by building a simple intersection of bricks which represented two main roads. Both of the roads were crammed with toy cars representing traffic jams. During this construction they talked about real traffic jams and the consequences in terms of time wasted. They finally arrive at the conclusion that it would be more economical to transport corn through a tunnel to the river, where they can take the corn by boat to the cereal factory.

This road and river system could easily have been represented with a two-dimensional map. Places on maps, of course, can be found more easily if their location is known on a set of horizontal and vertical co-ordinates. The teacher remained unaware that something of value was taking place between Maurice and Mathew. The boys did not attempt to discuss their model with the teacher.

Figure 9.8 shows 8-year-old's development of force and trajectories when they made 'A missile launching base'. The task was to create something with two

Figure 9.7 Maurice and Mathew (both 6) arrive at 'aspects of economic geography'. **Figure 9.8 'A missile launching base.'**

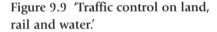

Figure 9.9 'Traffic control on land, rail and water.'

Figure 9.10 'The bridge is raised to let the water transport through and lowered to let the road transport over the bridge.'

different movements. The children made a heavy weight fall onto a wooden lever which made the missile shoot up in an upward trajectory. One child wrote: 'I am going to make a wood base with a wooden tower. The pulley goes at the top of the tower. A weight will fall on a wooden lever and the rocket will go up'. When tackling this task, the children focused on the serious side of levers, pulleys and equivalence of weight. They were learning about two out of four basic kinds of movement:

- *Linear movement*, that is, motion in a straight line in one direction.

- *Reciprocating motion*, that is, motion in a straight line. But, what goes up also comes down, hence the fascination with see-saws, scales and levers and pulleys. These children are exploring early principles of physics.

Many humorous situations in literature are based on play with pulleys, levers and weight and dynamic trajectories in general. For instance, children who have found that hauling objects upward is a function of vertical leverage find Paddington Bear's attempts to lever a bucket up on a rope very funny. The weight of the bucket pulled Paddington up in the air (Bond, 1976).

The task in Figure 9.9 required some 11-year-olds to make a model, which they named: 'Traffic control on land, rail and water'. These children developed a 'multiplicity of relations', which involves the co-ordination of concepts such as seriation (or ordering) of time and speed, in three different transport situations. The group built a model of a level-crossing which had flashing red lights to indicate to road transport that the barriers were down and it had to remain stationary. The grids and intersections were controlled by computers, just as they are in the real world.

For the task in Figure 9.10 a group of 11-year-olds made a bridge: 'The bridge is raised to let water transport through, and lowered to let road transport over the bridge'.

FROM TRACKING TO MAPPING

Throughout this book reference has been made to patterns of action that lead to subsequent action representations (Chapter 6), and behaviours of looking or gazing which lead to iconic or figurative representations (Chapter 5). A map may suggest an iconic picture of fixed points in space, and examples are given of early representations of fixed locations in Chapter 6. However, it would appear that early maps are primarily records of action.

Britton captures the configurational and the action basis of 'recalled space'. He and his brother would set out from their home on the outskirts of town:

> *I could walk into the country. On Saturdays we did, my brother and I. As we explored the area we drew a map of this precious bit of countryside, and I can recall one name on it … there was a long winding lane called Hobbleythick Lane. With the name comes a picture of a tall, ragged hawthorn hedge: one only, though I suppose there may have been a hedge on the other side also.* The map was a record of our wanderings. *There were other representations … my brother certainly used to stop occasionally and make a drawing of something he had seen. Neither the drawing nor the map was Hobbleythick Lane: each was a representation, and each representation was differently related to the thing itself. Each was in a different way a record of experience and each was capable, in a different way, of setting up or reviving expectations about the area. The map, we might say, was a more general representation, the drawing more particular. (1970, p. 11: my italics)*

The developmental route of mapping is from tracking, and the displacements of toddlers to being able to find one's way about familiar neighbourhoods because of having developed a mental map. Actual maps are graphic representations of trajectories in relation to fixed points. These are sometimes drawn by children as young as 3.

There is a sound basis for studying the local environment in early education because children have been spontaneously exploring location and states from birth. Primary school can provide continuity in that the study of space and place requires a co-ordination of motor action and the perception of things encountered at various points. Although the iconic or figurative features of places help to fix them in the mind, it would appear that the most important aspect of neighbourhood studies is action. In recent years an important finding has been made in studies of the brain: London taxi drivers who studied 'The Knowledge' (the gruelling course one has to take to become a registered London cab driver) have developed a larger part of the spatial part of their brain than is usual – through action.

Also, an anatomical study of Einstein's preserved brain showed the area associated with maths was bigger than normal (Carter, 1999). Evidence is accruing that 'thought' really is 'internalized' action (Raley, 2001). This is at the heart of constructivism.

London taxi drivers were scanned while they reported the complex route they would take to get from one area of London to another. The area that was activated by this navigation task was the hippocampus (Maguire et al., 2000). In addition, the researchers compared the structure of the taxi drivers' brains with that of non-taxi drivers. There were significant differences between the hippocampus size of the London taxi drivers and the non-taxi drivers: the posterior hippocampus was larger in taxi drivers. Furthermore, its size was related to the time the person had been driving taxis, suggesting that its size depends on how much a person uses their spatial memory (Maguire et al., 2000; Blakemore and Frith, 2000). In other words, we become good at the things we do the most.

In an otherwise excellent book on curriculum development in 'the study of places' (ILEA, 1981, p. 6), the importance of pictures in learning about the environment needs qualifying. The book states that 'The teacher must encourage the children to extract the maximum information from each picture' (1981, p. 6). It is doubtful whether important information can be extracted from pictures unless they are figurative reminders of personal experience, as with Britton's brother. The difference in interest and information between other people's holiday snaps and one's own is well known: 'The figurative aspect of knowing does not have an intrinsic development but remains ever in close dependence on the operative developmental stages' (Furth, 1969, p. 58).

The close dependence of the figurative and operative in 'mapping' is found in an example of good nursery-school practice given by HMI (DES, l989b, p. 13). Children under 5 were taken out walking in the locality. Buildings in the area were photographed, as well as children standing by their own front doors. A board game was devised by a group of children showing the various routes taken by different children from home to school. These were drawn by the children, and showed how routes passed well-known landmarks represented by the photographs. The children drew plans and pictures showing streets, shops and other features. The children's photographs were used to represent the players.

One intelligence test item, at a $4\frac{1}{2}$-year-old level, requires an ability to hold in the mind for a short time three trajectories, three end-points and three actions to perform at the end-points. In this test the child is instructed to put a pencil on a chair, open a door and fetch a box (Terman and Merrill, 1976, p. 164). Success requires a mental map, albeit temporary, of three trajectories connected with three end-points. The tasks to be performed at each end-point are related to earlier spontaneous behaviours, such as placing things on top of other things, opening doors (going through boundaries) and being intrigued by enveloping spaces such as boxes. Where the earlier transporting behaviours of toddlers have been supported by adult speech, the children will be more proficient in carrying out such instructions.

If 'maps are about the space we use' and intelligence tests contain questions about space from the early years right through to the highest adult level, which they do, it is important to encourage consciousness of space, and the objects that define positions in space, from the earliest years (Gerhardt, 1973; Bailey and Burton, 1982).

THE MATHEMATICS OF MOVEMENT IN A STRAIGHT LINE

Mathematically, 'motion in a straight line' without any change of direction is a translation. Various mathematical activities can be based on this early concern … A child sees these movements every day on the roads and in his own actions. (Williams and Shuard, 1980, p. 106)

Three-year-olds like to thread beads, stack bricks and line up toys. This spontaneous behaviour of making horizontal and vertical linear patterns is there for all to see. The problem is to trace the origins, diagnose the potential in the present and predict the future of such behaviours all from the point of view of extending cognitive form with worthwhile curriculum content. Connecting bricks into lines is an early stage of a synthesis of displacement and additive partitioning, which leads to a true concept of measuring (Inhelder et al., 1974, Preface, p. ix).

One of the earliest space concepts is connection. When children connect squares, they either describe their action ('I put these together') or they describe the figurative effects that such actions have ('this is a pavement'). These descriptions lead to functional dependency relationships when they observe that connecting more results in getting bigger or longer. Early schemas have been co-ordinated into new, higher-order concepts and can lead, in turn, to tessellation. In the following example, the mathematical actions of connecting with noted effects are clearly articulated (Schools Council, 1974, p. 23).

A roadway of bricks was constructed by a group of boys:

J: *Look at how long it is.*
P: *We can make it much longer. There are lots more bricks yet.*
A: *Yes, let's make it longer and longer till it touches the wall. [Note that 'more' (the unconnected bricks) can be imagined as being connected and thus adding to the length of the road.]*
J: *It's too long, we'll have to make it shorter.*

They removed three blocks at the closed end. As the boy is using the operation of subtraction on length he could be shown an economical way of representing his subtraction with symbols.

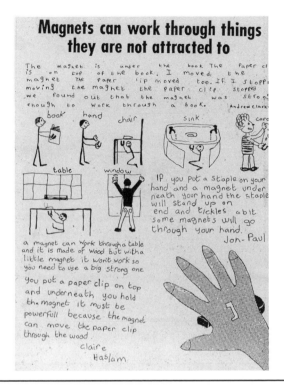

Figure 9.11 'Going through boundaries with a magnet'.

GOING THROUGH BOUNDARIES WITH A MAGNET

The example shown in Figure 9.11 is taken from 7-and 8-year-olds' primary Science in Sheffield. The task was to: 'make something move without physically pushing or pulling directly'. These children made trajectories using magnetism, based on earlier motor schemas of 'on top of', 'underneath' and 'going through', but now these are done by the remote control of magnetism. One child wrote: 'The magnet is under the book. The paper clip is on top of the book. I moved the magnet, the paper clip moved too. If I stopped moving the magnet the paper clip stopped. The magnet was strong enough to work through a book'.

Williams and Shuard suggest that one of the most useful purposes of a magnet is that children are experiencing a force they cannot see. Although earlier experiences suggest that force can be exerted as either a push or a pull, a magnet shows pushing and pulling within an invisible context. Magnetism can therefore be a good introduction to the force of gravity.

FROM TRAJECTORIES TO CLASSIFICATION

Dynamic trajectories are practised and played with in early education. These early happenings often become conceptualized later as different forms of travelling. Seven-year-olds are encouraged to study how their classmates travel while

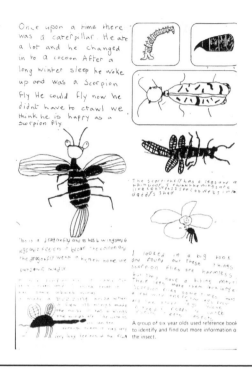

Figure 9.12 'Six-year-olds from Sheffield – small creatures travel in two ways: some crawl, some fly.'

on holiday. One girl subdivided travelling into 11 categories: walking, taking a taxi, taking a ferry, taking an aeroplane, a train, a car, a canal boat, a motor bike, a coach, a caravan, a bike. She designated one sticky square for each family (one-to-one correspondence) and made a graph of the situation. Twenty-four families travelled by car. Only one family went by canal boat and motor bike. No family walked or went by bike.

In Figure 9.12, some 6-year-olds in Sheffield were working on small creatures. Apart from 'transformations' from one state to another, small creatures are seen to travel in two ways: some creatures crawl and some fly. These movement aspects are co-ordinated with variation in their static configurations.

GRIDS ARE NOW USED AS ANALOGIES

In describing wings, one child wrote: 'Their wings are like cobwebs seen in daddy's shed' Another child wrote: 'Their wings are like net curtains'. A Froebel Project child, at 3, working with her mother, made a book of all the grid shapes in the home. Net curtains were included. By the age of 6, children have come a long way from simple grid patterns consisting of a few crossed lines. Each stage is accompanied by expressions of satisfaction.

Wherever children have plenty of material and freedom of choice in early education, schematic behaviours will be obvious to the aware observer. Teachers in Cleveland, for instance, found that their perception of children's behaviour was illuminated by some of the Froebel findings (see Nicholls et al., 1986). Although schematic behaviours are obvious, worthwhile curriculum extensions do not immediately suggest themselves. In some of the constructivist programmes examined by Forman and Fosnot (1982), teachers were able to observe children creating and inventing while using open-ended materials such as sand, bricks, boards, rollers, levers, pulleys and so on. The teachers frequently admitted to being 'stuck' for appropriate follow-up ideas. This means that there are great opportunities for teachers to work individually or together on curriculum extensions. What is needed particularly is evidence on whether 'offered' curriculum extensions have actually been 'received'.

The following few observations were selected from many collected by teachers in Sheffield (Sharp, 1987; Nutbrown, 1988).

- Carl (3:9) pointed out cement-mixers and wheels at the building site. When he returned to school he said he wanted the see-saw to go round and not up and down.

- Betty found that the bowl containing dough would spin. She tried to spin the dough without the dish. She placed the dish with dough on an old record-player and spun it round for about four minutes. She found a clock and rotated the hands. Outside she ran round the climbing frame five times before she climbed the ladder and slid down the slide.

- Four boys took selected wheels from the wheel box and began to roll them down planks.

- Emma rolled the rings along the carpet. Her mother joined in. Other shapes were tried out. Emma rolled the shapes to her mother and laughed when she discovered that only the cylinder worked. Emma jumped up and began to twirl round. Her mother said, 'Stop it, you'll be dizzy'. The teacher sang, 'The wind blows high, the wind blows low, round and round the windmills go'.

There are many ways of extending dynamic circular or rotation schemas. All the 'ring' nursery rhymes with their actions can be taught, such as 'Here we go Round the Mulberry Bush' and 'Ring-a-Ring o' Roses'.

In children's literature there is a wide range of situation comedy that depends on understanding functional dependency relationships. When Paddington Bear, for instance, decides to be an interior decorator, he uses an electric rotator to mix the paint. To the child with appropriate concepts, this has predictable, disastrous and hilarious results (Bond, 1976).

Informed adults notice different degrees of understanding in children and can extend these in various ways. An important starting-point is to validate existing knowledge by acceptance. Some kinds of extension require professional initiation but can involve non-professionals. For instance, a teacher observed children rolling out dough. She wanted to know whether the children had perceived any relationships between the action of rolling and the figural and transformational effect on the dough, so she asked a 'functional dependency' question. Knowledge of the correspondence between actions and the effects of action lie behind all Piaget's conservation experiments. Examples of this level of extension are not difficult to find in the literature because of the link with conservation. For instance, the Schools Council (1974, p. 23) gives the following example of diagnosis and extension.

Four-year-olds are making pastry for jam tarts. Ian (4:6) says, 'I have more than you'. Stuart (4:4): 'You've just rolled yours more' (has he noticed the effect of rolling?). Glen (4:3): 'But Ian can make more tarts so he must have more.' The teacher suggested that the children roll their pastry into balls again in order to compare the size. They did so and agreed on the initial equivalence of the balls of dough. Teacher: 'If they are the same, how could Ian make three tarts and you only two?' Glen: 'Ian spread his thinner.' The teacher's intervention was in the direction of conservation of quantity. Glen, at 4:3, knows that the figural effects of extra rolling signifies differences in thickness and not differences in quantity.

There are many functional dependency relationships based on rotation in mathematical and scientific literature. For instance, in the Bullock Report (DES, 1975) an example is given of a mystery object that stimulated junior-aged children to use a great deal of language in the process of discovering that the object was a land-measuring tape. They arrived at the exciting conclusion that distance was functionally dependent on rotation (1975, p. 56). Trundle wheels of various sizes are useful in demonstrating that each rotation has a specific distance that is functionally dependent on the rotation and diameter of the wheel.

The example from Nicky (4:4:3) in Chapter 6 of this book (who lists rotating objects) makes it clear that there is no need to delay the introduction of cog-wheels, sand wheels, water wheels, food-mixers, land-measuring tapes and so on until statutory schooling.

When, at the end of the Froebel Project, the writer began to visit primary schools, the schematic bases of speech, writing and all other kinds of representation stood out as never before. On the very first visit to a school in Richmond, a middle-class area on the outskirts of London, a videotape was made of a 5-year-old boy, Tom, who began a conversation with his teacher: 'Do you know that the earth goes round the sun in little balls?' The teacher made a fist and said: 'Suppose this is the sun, show me what you mean'. Tom made a circular and rotational movement with his finger around the fist. He proceeded to talk about night and day and the seasons with a high degree of accuracy.

ROTATION IN TECHNOLOGY

Wherever there are young children and cars and other vehicles, the children will be representing the movement aspects of the vehicles from the simple representation of trajectories along roads to more complication variations based on speed differences. At a certain stage children ask whether speed differences depend on the size of wheels or the angle of the slope the vehicles are going down.

In Figure 9.13, 'Ramp runners', children ask themselves two 'functional dependency' questions: Given the observed difference in speed, are these differences due to the size of wheels or the different angles of slopes?

In Figure 9.14, children were enquiring into 'how to make a motor turn'. One child expressed what he had done with a cluster of schemas. To paraphrase : 'I pressed the switch which made the current go through the wires to the motor. The motor rotated, which made the paper-clip move in a vertical direction. Doubling the energy made the motor run faster'. The five cognitive factors which are co-ordinated with each other are: speed (speed is a co-ordination of time and distance), rotation, dynamic, vertical and multiplication. Each of these schemas are being explored by very young children. Appropriate early education helps to 'flesh out' schemas with worthwhile curriculum content.

This brings us to the thorny question of what is worthwhile content in education. During the 1960s, a debate took place in which different cultures were compared. Certain aspects of some cultures came out as 'bog standard' when compared with aspects of a *crème de la crème* culture. Snow and Leavis hotly debated the two cultures of science and art. Professor Bantock compared bingo

Figure 9.13 'Ramp runners.'

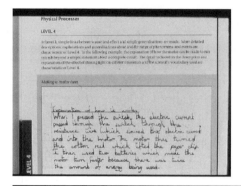 

Figure 9.14 'How to make a meter turn.'   Figure 9.15 'This is a tank with guns on the top' (they rotate).

with Bach, and he knew which was superior. At about the same time Bruner wrote that just because a child had a schema of rotation, there was no need to teach him or her the history of thumb screws.

Endless debates go on in the world about such issues, particularly whether children should be allowed to play at gun fights. What children are allowed to represent from their culture can raise temperatures all round. How should the representation Figure 9.15 be regarded?

Child: This is a tank with guns on the top – they rotate.
Teacher: Why do they rotate?
Child: So they can kill people all around.

So, killing people or, more accurately, knocking down anything that surrounds a rotator, are picked off by the rotational properties of the guns.

One parent got into a real state because she believed her daughter was constructing nooses. She was relieved to hear that she was simply practising her 'going through' schema with string, the end-product being knots to connect objects better. (Personal communication with Cath Arnold at PenGreen).

ROTATION IN MOVEMENT AND DANCE

Shanaz's mother, who spoke less English than other Asian mothers, was clearly very pleased and supportive of the 'dance' and rotation. However, Shanaz went next to an area where tools were used and snatched a screwdriver from an Asian boy. Her mother was shocked. Three-year-old Pakistani girls are encouraged to dance, but not to use screwdrivers or to push little boys! To recognize a schema does not entail embracing it if it clashes with the norms and mores of a society: there are cultural constraints and gender constraints. We tried but failed to get fathers in the home area to do things such as washing, ironing or rotating the handle of the mangle.

Figure 9.16 'Shanaz (3:5:13) starts her dance by rotating her whole self.'

Figure 9.17 'With difficulty she climbs into a wooden box with circular holes.'

Figure 9.18 'She makes the lorry move in a circular direction.'

Figure 9.19 'She rotates her hands

Figure 9.20 'She rotates her hands and arms, which are covered with bracelets.'

DEVELOPMENTS IN CORE AND RADIALS

All schemas have a past and a present. Like life in general, the precise nature of the future of schemas and concepts is less predictable. At the age of 2, a child will put a radial into a core shape and call it something appropriate such as 'an apple' or 'a lollipop'. Later they will represent a range of experienced content such as 'flower' or 'sun' using developments of a core-and-radial configuration.

In the following representations from primary science in Sheffield, 6- and 7-year-olds have applied their 'core-and-radial' configurations with good effect to 'Plants and growing'.

In Figure 9.21 a 6-year-old writes 'a spider plant has dark green and light green leaves and yellow and white leaves. It has babies. It is called a spider plant because it looks like a spider'.

In the Froebel Project, children initially used little dabs of pencil or paint to represent things in the world that had a similar configuration. Figure 9.22 illustrates a child of 7 who has differentiated between some seeds and others. She has written: 'Lettuce seeds are like little crumbs, beetroot seeds are like the tops of oranges. Radish seeds are like bird food'. She has also used horizontal and vertical co-ordinates to represent different kinds of seeds on paper.

FROM STRUGGLE THROUGH PRACTICE TO PLAYFULNESS

All schemas and concepts can go through a complete range of psychological process from struggle to playfulness, through not, of course, if mere 'competence' is seen as an end-point to knowledge. 'Struggle' as used here is self-motivated and is not imposed from the outside world. The process from struggle to play is a human characteristic of learning. The process starts with the desire to master some perceived problem. Although people differ in their persistence in problem solving, most will soldier on until competence is achieved and many will go 'beyond competence to fun'.

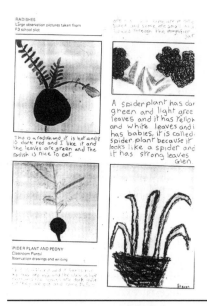

Figure 9.21 'A spider plant is called a spider because it looks like a spider.'

Figure 9.22 'Lettuce seeds are like little crumbs. Beetroot seeds are like the tops of oranges.'

Under the surface features of most psychological theories lurks either survival, gloom ('as ye sow so shall ye reap', in other words Struggle with a capital 's') or possibly the theory reflects a lighter-hearted approach which, at a certain stage of competence, reflects playfulness. Evolutionary psychology focuses too much on the survival aspect of Darwinism for it to be of particular use to teachers and parents. Darwin himself was aware of this deficiency in the survival aspects of his theory and tried through his 'baby biographies' to find examples of playfulness and humour under the umbrella of 'survival'. He could not do it.

BEYOND COMPETENCE TO FUN

Several important thinkers have embraced the idea that the processes of thought occur on a learning continuum – not a developmental continuum as in cognitive stage levels, but on a psychological continuum. This continuum starts with struggle (accommodation to the new). Everybody knows from personal experience the struggle which accompanies new learning. With practice, the struggle lessens and competence and confidence takes the place of struggle. Everybody knows the saying 'Practice makes perfect'. The final part of the learning process, which is sometimes left out of schooling, is the part when children can have some fun with their knowledge.

Philosophers and psychologists who have written at length about the process of learning going from struggle through practice to playfulness and fun include Immanuel Kant (the father of modern philosophy), Karl Buhler (who invented the term 'function pleasure' to describe the function of humour), Freud and Piaget, Arthur Koestler (in his book *The Act of Creation*), Huizinga (who wrote a book called *Homo Ludens* (playful man) in 1949) and Chukovsky (1966).

Chukovsky, in his wonderful little book *From Two to Five*, described the end of this continuum at its most simple and direct. He described the position of playfulness in relation to the other aspects of learning: 'When the child has become so sure of truths that he can even play with them' (1966, p.103). Well-assimilated concepts can be thought of as 'toys of the mind'. This is his 2-year-old grand-daughter's first intentional joke: 'Oggie-miou' (a doggy mious). Here are two known elements put into a new, playful co-ordination.

Figure 9.23 demonstrates a seriation joke with 'Bottle breaking ship'. It topsy-turvies, or reverses, everything we know about size and strength. It is the bottle that is supposed to break. On any series of size or strength the ship is very large and tough and the bottle is tiny and fragile.

Seriation and classification have their origins in early motor actions which are applied to a wide range of objects and events. The everyday world contains sufficient information to feed universal cognitive structures such as size, height, weight, strength, temperature, porosity, number and so on. Even if children did not go to school they would still make statements such as 'I'm taller than Charlie' or 'I have more marbles than Jenny'.

Figure 9.23 'Bottle breaking ship – a seriation joke.'

Before children acquire seriation structures they tend to think in absolutes, so they will say 'I'm big and he's little' or 'I've got a lot of marbles, she hasn't'. An important role for the teacher is to feed the spontaneous cognitive structures inside learners at different stages with worthwhile curriculum content.

Most 6-year-olds show an obsession with organizing things in the world within a size continuum. What varies is the amount of worthwhile content that some children assimilate to existing schemas and concepts compared with other children.

Most children in western culture have experienced the delight of The Three Bears story where the chairs, the beds and bowls and the bears themselves are given significance through size. There is also one-to-one correspondence between the sizes of the bears the sizes of the chairs and so on. One 5-year-old (5:3) responded to the 'bottle breaking ship' exercise with great interest but not a hint of humour. He said: 'Well, they banged the bottle and crashed the boat '(pause while he seriously studied the cartoon) 'There must have been a little crack somewhere there'. He is making a great 'effort after meaning' and 'cracks' do tend to be noticed by children with a 'grid' schema, but his size and strength series, required for understanding this cartoon, do not seem to have reached a playful stage.

In The Three Little Pigs story there is a seriation of house strengths which correlate with the different IQs of the three little pigs: clever, sensible and silly.

Knowledge of size leads to a great enjoyment in the fun aspects of 'Trouble at the laundrette with the shrinking and stretching of clothes'. Here are two 6-year-olds:

Jane: You have a long jersey and you are going to wash it and it shrinks. Oh dear, my jersey has shrinked [loud laughter].

Kate: Yes, you would have to give the jersey to a little baby [screams of delight from both of them].

Around 9 there is enjoyment in taking seriation jokes and riddles beyond limits. A popular riddle is: 'What is the definition of a skeleton? A striptease that's gone too far!' Children's minds gradually become capable of structuring events in the external world along those lines of the cartoon 'bottle breaking ship' The results can be either catastrophic or comic, both enjoyable.

The 'Ball and chain' cartoon in Figure 9.24 could be used as a playful end-point in response to a task in design and technology. If the task were 'how could a convict with a ball and chain escape from prison without climbing a high wall?', this cartoon could be offered as a playful suggestion. It shows rotary motion providing enough momentum to carry an object high in a curved direction, where gravity then plays some part in the landing.

Centrifugal force can lead to a perfect poached egg in that the simmering water is stirred to create a centrifuge. The egg is dropped in the middle of the whirl and this stops the outside of the white from spreading too thinly. Stuart, aged 4, pointed out the whirl made by water going down the drain when his bathwater was let out. Centrifugal force also separates cream from milk and takes excess moisture from wet clothes in the spin drier.

Figure 9.25 'Microscope', demonstrates play with magnification. Chukovsky pointed out that children's literature is full of examples of such fun events as where the most puny insects are attributed the characteristics of enormous beasts (1966, p. 101).

Andrew (5:11) looked at the array of objects on an interest table. He picked up one of the objects and looked through it. He said to the teacher: 'Look miss, things look all funny ' ... [unusual], Miss, what is this?' The teacher replied: 'It's a magnifying glass.' 'Look, Miss – it makes things all big.' This is exploration before playfulness.

Garvey (1977) related an instance of playfulness with magnification. After exploring many objects with a magnifying glass, a 5-year-old boy picked up a hat. He examined it with the glass and chanted 'That's the biggest hat I ever saw in my life.' He continued in this playful mode for some time.

Figure 9.26 'A black eye' illustrates a comic functional dependence relationship due to rotation. Three co-ordinations of cognitive structures (schemas) are required for seeing the joke:

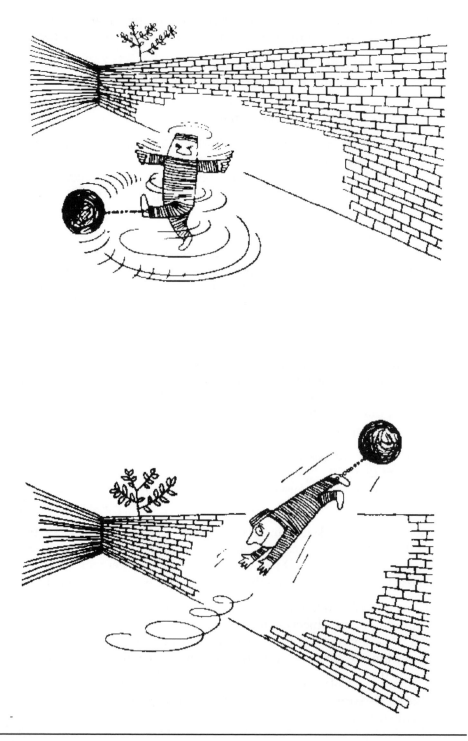

Figure 9.24 'The ball and chain demonstrates rotary motion and gravity.'

Figure 9.25 'Microscope, demonstrates play with magnification.'

Figure 9.26 'A black eye – rotation and its functional dependency relationship.'

1 A schema or concept of rotation.

2 A concept of distance.

3 A concept of length.

These are all mathematical notions. There is another psychological ordering required which ranges from happiness to misery.

I asked some children what they thought of this cartoon:

■ One child said: 'They're all dizzy.' She had noticed the effect of rotation. This response is not incorrect, just partial.

- Another child said: 'She's got a black eye and they are going round and round.' Both correct statements, but without the functional dependency relation between those two aspects.

- A third child, Laura, said: ' Why did she get that black eye? Why are those happy and why is she sad?' She laughed and said, 'Oh, I see.' She made an accommodation and the accommodation consisted of a new co-ordination of two concepts to make a third.

10

Parental Participation and Extended Experience

As part of the enrichment programme, Project families were taken on 71 visits to places of interest one morning each week in the project bus accompanied by Project staff and students: 19 visits were within the grounds or departments of the Froebel Institute; 12 visits were from outside people coming to the Project, including police, doctors, a dentist and a book publisher; and 40 visits were organized to places of interest outside the Froebel Institute.

The psychological process of 'experiencing' or 'acquiring knowledge' cannot be observed directly. Therefore, a simple if laborious method was adopted of assessing the experiences of the Project children by the 'content' of what they chose to represent: 'The whole problem is to find out how the subject records the data of experience' (Piaget, 1953, p. 360). To this end, every symbolic representation was analysed in order to find out whether it had a connection with project visits or whether the content could have been equally well acquired in the home or neighbourhood. Two examples will make these two criteria clear:

- During a visit to the police stables, Jock (2:6:6) saw a policeman mount and dismount his horse several times. Later, Jock climbed a metal structure, cocked one leg over the top and said, 'Me policeman 'orsey'. This representation was repeated several times.

- Amanda (4:2:1) painted a *rectangle*, filled it in and said, 'This is a window with curtains across.'

The first example was classified as an action representation arising from a Project event. The second example was classified as a figurative or graphic representation that could have risen from experiences at home.

'Experiencing' contains at least two important factors: The 'content' being experienced; and the 'concept' or 'schema' (cognitive form) to which content is assimilated. Carrying out a 'content' count as a measure of experience was separate from the analysis of the cognitive forms to which experiences were assimilated. (Chapters 5 and 6 illustrate the relationships between form and content.)

RESULTS OF THE CONTENT ANALYSIS OF SYMBOLIC REPRESENTATIONS FOLLOWING PROJECT VISITS

There were 1,968 clear, unambiguous representations of content: 1,191 (60.5 per cent) were related to project visits and related events that included preparation and follow-up work in the Project organized by the teacher; 777 (39.5 per cent) could have been experienced in the home setting. These figures offer some support for the critical importance of first-hand experience in providing the content of representation. Experience thought of in this way could be called the 'stuff' or 'content' of mind, as opposed to the 'form' or 'structure' of mind.

EXPERIENCE IS WHAT 'FEEDS' SCHEMAS AND EXTENDS THEM

The visits that stimulated the greatest number of representations were: the zoo (11.7 per cent), boat trips up the River Thames (9 per cent), London Airport (6.6 per cent), trips to the common or park (6.6 per cent), the railway (4.5 per cent), the police (with dogs and horses) (3.5 per cent) and swimming (2.6 per cent).

Figure 10.1 'Horse with legs.'   Figure 10.2 Lois (4:5:12), 'This is the back of a horse. He's carrying things on his back.'

All the places visited were sufficiently 'rich' to be experienced at different schematic levels. Lois displayed two different levels of representation. After a first visit to police stables, Lois (3:5:5) represented 'Horse with legs' (Figure 10.1). After a second visit, when she was 4:5:12, she painted another horse (Figure 10.2). She called this painting 'This is the back of a horse. He's carrying things on his back'. A careful examination of her early representations showed her interest in content that could be expressed with *gridlike* graphic schemas. In the later representation she shifted to a *projective space* concept, where objects are represented from different points of view. She used the semi-circle (*an open curve*) that emerges later than *grid*. (It is worth mentioning at this point that speech use reflects schematic concerns as well as describing content.)

Even when some offered experiences appear to have less potential than others (Westminster Abbey compared with the zoo), the children found situations that 'matched' their existing schemas. Children who were drawing or making clay models of *semi-circles* absorbed the *semi-circular* structures in the abbey and represented 'arches'. Children who had started to represent objects from different points of view (*projective space*) represented *horizontal* statues.

As the Project progressed, the professionals became increasingly skilled at predicting the aspects of environment on which certain children would focus during visits. Parents became engrossed in this aspect of their children's learning.

Project visits provided an important continuity where adults were able to refer back to shared experience. This kind of continuity is expressed most clearly in the question, 'Do you remember when …?' Another important aspect of continuity lay in the different levels of reality being received by the children. For instance, sensory and motor experiences, gained during a visit to a helter-skelter, provided a basis for the further study of the *helix*. Scientific toys were introduced with this kind of extension in mind. Continuity is a vital component of conceptual development.

THE DEVELOPMENT OF PARENT AND PROFESSIONAL COLLABORATION

At the start of the Project a conceptual gulf existed between parents and professionals on issues such as play, creativity, messing about with raw materials, individuality, self-regulation, reading readiness, and so on. This was due to many factors, none of which were to do with 'high-handed' attitudes of staff or cognitive deficits of parents, but rather to a lack of previous shared experiences typical of disparate groups of people who start to work together. The process of the growth of shared understandings developed during the Project and was linked with the search for schemas.

During initial home visits and the early days of the Project, the parents treated the professionals with too much reverence. They were seen as experts on child development. Early interactions can best be described as tentative explorations of shared meaning. The Project could be described as a physical environment in which parents and professionals worked together within a developing symbolic system that changed as people accommodated to the ideas, views and attitudes of other people. Initial differences became less and less important in the search for shared areas of agreement on how to help individual children.

At first the teacher concentrated mainly on interacting with the children, but it became clear that it would be more economical in time, and of greater use to parents, if she focused on interactions between parent and child. As parents became more confident they tended to be over didactic and unnatural, but this soon changed.

Throughout the two teaching years of the programme, children's interactions with adults were considered together with useful interpretations from educational and psychological literature. Information passed on to parents from a wide range of writers on education was usually prefaced by 'They say ... '. What 'they' had said provided much of the substance of daily discussions between the researcher, the teacher and the parents.

There was much discussion on the importance of adult speech, particularly speech that accompanied the children's motor actions, together with the effects of those actions on materials. Adult speech support from the start was focused on what the children were doing.

The ongoing analysis of the interactions between parents and children inevitably involved some kind of theoretical assessment. Trying to establish this process required an attitude of reciprocity between professionals and non-professionals, not present at the start of the project but developed in action.

A genuine 'open-ended' type of enquiry was encouraged, with everyone working together to find patterns of cognition. The parents were genuinely respected and recognized as experts on their own children in that they had had them full-time from birth and therefore knew them better as individuals than anyone else. This knowledge did not include what they had in common with other children. The professionals were better equipped to initiate, to manage and to assess this aspect of the inquiry throughout.

The search for commonalities of behaviour necessarily relied on highly specific instances of behaviour. Most observations were made in the Project or on visits and some were made in the home by parents. Each child had a 'home book' for the exchange of noteworthy information between home and school. Apart from the educational advantages of exchanging information, it made reading and writing both meaningful and affectively satisfying for the children. The usefulness of home observations depended on the degree to which parents became increasingly involved and informed.

Initially the Project was too unfamiliar for the parents to understand what was entailed in helping with the education or research. Creative collaboration had to be carefully cultivated. Parental confidence required evidence of professional knowledge, but the most important feature of the 'ongoing' collaboration was a genuine and, where possible, a clearly articulated interest in the children.

There were four main categories of parental participation (PP). These categories, with their absolute and relative frequencies, are:

1 No PP (2,026 instances ; 38 per cent of observations). In most of these cases the parent was not present at the Project when an observation was made.

2 Parent listening to, or copying, the project teacher (849 instances; 16 per cent).

3 Parent recognizing, or trying to extend, the child's learning by making reference to content or material (1,188 instances; 22 per cent).

4 Parent recognizing or trying to extend the child's learning with knowledge of the child's prevailing schemas (1,189 instances; 22 per cent).

Table 10.1 shows a decrease over time in the level of help described as 'listening to or copying the teacher'. During the first term, most parental help was at this level. In the sixth term there were very few cases. In the early days the teacher invariably initiated an interaction with a child, usually about what the child was doing. The teacher would make a comment such as: 'This looks interesting, would you like to talk to me about it?' If the child continued with his or her action but remained silent, the teacher would describe the actions and the per-ceptual results of the action. For instance: 'I see that you are squeezing that piece of clay. You can make it into different shapes, can't you?'

Table 10.1 Frequency of different levels of parental participation over six terms

Project terms	2	3	4	Total
1	274	134	30	(438)
2	152	289	145	(586)
3	94	187	224	(505)
4	122	258	202	(582)
5	124	169	325	(618)
6	83	151	263	(497)
	(849)	(1,188)	(1,189)	(3,226)

By this simple approach the teacher was validating the action for the child and parent as well as employing a central aspect of constructivism: to assist the developmental route from 'action' to internalized action, which becomes thought (Piaget, 1952, p. xi). Throughout the Project the children were helped to become aware of two important aspects of learning:

- the specific nature of the actions they were using; and

- the transformations or displacements that actions produced on objects, materials and events.

Table 10.1 also shows an increase of category 4 instances (the highest level of parental participation) over six terms. There were only 30 instances in the first term; this rose to 263 cases in the sixth term; this increase reflects the success of the second aim of the Project, which was to search for schemas. The parents became increasingly skilled at recognizing and extending schematic behaviour after they had been identified by the professionals.

The numbers of category 3 cases do not differ systematically over the six terms. This is to be expected as 'help with content and material' is a 'common-sense' type of help typical of most adult–child interactions in home and school. This type of help probably becomes more skilled, but it is difficult to assess the level of skill. It is also difficult to convey the considerable excitement experienced by all the adults involved in the day-to-day exploration of these fundamental patterns of behaviour in the children.

Although the number of families involved in the Froebel Project was small, the parents are typical of larger populations in inner-city areas. The amount, level and commitment of Project parents is an indication of the great source of untapped ability and energy that exists in working-class, multiracial communities. This waste of potential, actual and created, is likely to become less as the legislation under 'Every child matters' is implemented.

One term after the official end of the Project, the parents called a meeting in one of their homes in order to discuss how the children had settled in school. The home consisted of one room and a kitchen. Many issues were discussed at the meeting including what the children were focusing on now that they were at school and the different degrees of encouragement school staffs had given in response to offers of help from most mothers. In the main, schools were over-cautious about letting the parents in: where parents were allowed to help, it was almost always with narrowly prescribed tasks.

Some of the parents were critical of the schools, but in a good-natured way. One mother had astutely grasped the mechanism of a self-fulfilling prophesy. In her child's school the parents were put into a hut in the playground and were asked to make things for the school jumble sale. With such trivial occupations there was some back-biting and parental 'drop-out'. She noted humorously that the staff had taken this to be an instance of parent unreliability. She said she would be interested to see how many teachers would 'survive' the jumble-sale course.

The strength of the parents' interest and involvement can be measured by their attendance at the meeting. All mothers except one unsupported mother were present, including the Asian mothers with very little English. Three fathers who had helped in the Project whenever they could also attended the meeting.

Examples of the highest level of parental participation are given below to illustrate the way in which project parents used their developing knowledge of schemas to identify instances and to extend in various ways. Jock's father demonstrated the *up and down* movement of the toy crane to match Jock's (2:7:7) *dynamic vertical* schema.

- Lois (4:0:7) made 'traffic lights' (Figure 10.3) and referred to the *sequence* in which the lights came on and what they signified. Mother reported playing the 'traffic light' game, which consisted of the question, asked at every set of lights, 'Which one comes on next?' Lois (4:7:12) was *connecting*, naming three parts in her model, and always got the sequence of events right. Her father took her to the library for a book on insects. They studied the drawings together and named the parts. The next day Lois reported to her teacher, 'I just saw an ant'. Earlier, when she was 4:4:15, she wrapped a piece of paper round a straw and stuck a piece of green paper onto this base and named it 'Traffic light' (Figure 10.4).

- Shanaz (3:11:9) described a picture she had drawn as 'Big, big flowers growing up in a big, big house and the girl going down that' (pointing to a drawing of a ladder). Her mother who spoke very little English, understood Shanaz's powerful *'grid'* schema. Together they made a book at home that contained cut-out pictures and drawings of all the *grid-like* objects in the home.

Figure 10.3 Lois's (4:7:12) 'traffic lights' – she referred to the sequence.

Figure 10.4 Lois (4:4:15) wrapped a piece of paper round a straw – she named it 'traffic light.'

- Linda (3:6:28) walked round an *enclosure* in the park and reported to her mother, 'The ducks can't get out of there'. This led to a shared examination of various kinds of *enclosures*. The next day Linda made 'An island' (Figure 10.5) and surrounded it with green paint, which she said was 'the sea'. Linda's mother reported that she could not get her (3:9:2) past a junk-shop window because she was so absorbed by an old bed-spring. This led to an exploration of *helix* and *spiral* shapes. Linda's mother began to talk with interest about what was on the classroom walls of the school where she was a cleaner.

- Brenda (3:9:16) showed her mother two straws she had interwoven, and said that the pattern was a *spiral*. Two days later she pointed out the 'pattern on a jelly mould' and said it was *spiral*. Later she drew the *spiral* 'stair case' she had seen at Kew Gardens.

- Alistair's mother maintained that he really did understand the true nature of 'four'. She said that long after Alistair (4:1:10) had eaten three biscuits he demanded the other one. When she teased him by saying he had had them all, he held up four fingers. She also reported that he had an understanding of 'five' because he had put five seats in his model boat and told her who the seats were for.

- Stephen's mother reported the following instances that, in each case, she helped to develop further. Stephen (3:4:30), having examined their underground tickets, said, 'Your ticket is thick and mine is thin'. Stephen (3:5:3), standing in a bus queue, observed, 'There are three men and one lady in this queue'. Stephen (3:5:27) said, 'I like the dolls with the happy faces best'. His mother related this comment to the *semi-circle* mark he had started to use in drawing. Figure 10.6 shows Stephen's mother pointing out the semi-circle configuration of a horse's hoof. When Stephen mistook a shoe for a handbag in a picture, his mother suggested that the source of his confusion might be related to the fact that they were both *containers*. While walking along the river bank, Stephen (whenever possible) varied his base level by, for instance, walking on top of walls. Stephen's mother knew that he had been paying attention to *height* and asked teasing questions, such as 'Who is the *tallest* now?' Stephen always referred to the *height* he was standing on.

The final example, 'Enactive Son, Iconic Mum' is given in greater detail to show that communication between Jack (3:11:4) and his mother demonstrated two different kinds of symbolic functioning. Jack was mainly 'enactive', his mother mainly 'iconic'. These differences provided substance for communication between parent and professional. Bruner (1974, pp. 314–24) uses the term 'enactive' to describe schemas that are abstractions from actions, as opposed to 'iconic' schemas.

Figure 10.5 Linda (3:6:28) 'An island' surrounded with green paint and she said that was the sea.

Figure 10.6 Stephen's mother pointing out the semi-circle configeration of a horse's hoof.

Jack had had meningitis and his paediatrician was anxious for him to be included in the Project because of under-functioning. During the early days of the Project, Jack was given concentrated help by Miss D, a third-year teaching-practice student. She was implementing the Project policy of accompanying the children's actions with speech. As Jack played with a model train, the student used a range of space words in context, such as *up*, *under*, *on top of*, *over*, *near* and *round*. Jack's mother was very interested in this, and communicated with Jack in a similar way.

The next day Jack accompanied his actions with speech. For instance, as he moved a toy car he said, 'Now it's going *straight*, now it's going *up*, now it's *going down*'. This rapid accommodation to the appropriate use of speech probably indicates the depth of his need. It may also explain the startling increase in his test scores. In two years, Jack's IQ increased from 75 to 112. His scores on the English Picture Vocabulary test increased from 91 to 126.

Although Jack's mother picked up Miss D's 'enactive' speech in the example just given, picking out these features of events did not come naturally to her. An analysis of encounters between mother and son shows an interesting mismatch that seemed to be due to her 'iconic' view as opposed to his 'dynamic' approach to objects and events. For instance, when Jack was 3:9:12, his mother was show-ing him shapes and giving him the names. She said, 'This is a *circle*'. Jack replied, 'A *circle goes round*'. When she said, 'This is a *triangle*', Jack followed one of the lines with his finger and said, 'That goes *up there*'.

Jack's mother loved painting and drawing and often painted pictures for the Project. Jack never painted. He spent much of his time playing action games, such as chasing and hiding (*trajectory* games).

In the following situation, which was video-taped, the mismatch between the enactive and iconic approaches is clear, although there was some accommoda-tion on both sides. The discussion was over features of a model farm provided by the teacher in preparation for a visit to a real farm. The interaction between mother and son can be described as 'Enactive Son, Iconic Mum':

Mum:	*What are these animals called? [Request for Jack to name].*
Jack (3:11:4):	*The animals are going in there [his hand indicates the route between the animals and the enclosure].*
Mum:	*[Accommodating to Jack's reply and expanding on it]: Yes, they are going in there for a drink, aren't they? What are they called?*
Jack:	*They're pigs.*
Mum:	*And what is in this little enclosure? [this is a request for naming and identifying, but his mother has recognized that Jack has a strong schematic interest in enclosures].*
Jack:	*It's a lamb.*

Mum looks closely at the very small model with genuine interest and asks, 'Oh, is it?' At this Jack becomes very animated. As he speaks he moves the toys about as an action illustration of what he is saying: 'Yes! You open the gate and let the lambs out and they go get a wash. They go in the water and get back.' In this example, three connected schemas are being described and enacted with gesture: opening and shutting (or connecting and disconnecting), in and out and going through a boundary. Mum shifts attention to another part of the farm and asks, 'Do you know who that man is?' (request for naming and identifying):

Jack:	*He's holding those baby lambs [the man is defined in terms of what he is doing].*
Mum:	*What sounds do cows make?*
Jack:	*I don't know.*
Mum:	*[In encouraging tone] Yes you do.*
Jack:	*[Using a circular hand gesture]: They go running round the other [the animals are defined in terms of movement].*
Mum:	*How do they talk?*
Jack:	*[Accommodating obligingly] They go mooing [at this point Jack gets in a quick sentence that reflects his inside/outside schema: 'outside the farm that man was'].*
Mum:	*What is this lady doing? [This is her first action-based question, which is asking about the imagined movement of the farmer's wife.]*
Jack:	*That lady's going and getting the buckets. That's her house [Jack makes a clear statement that matches the question].*

Just to confuse the issue of enactive versus iconic, which seemed fairly clear and which Jack's mother found extremely interesting, at the age of 6 Jack started to draw a great deal and became very good at it. It is difficult to know how to account for this change in emphasis.

The over-zealous parental help, already mentioned, developed into natural play-ful and teasing communication. An instance of this is as follows: Jack's mother asked two boys what they expected to see when they visited the zoo. The boys started a playful conspiracy of silence. 'Well,' she said casually, 'I know what we are going to see.' She allowed a suitably long pause: 'We are going to see cats and dogs.' This triggered a stream of disagreement from the boys, followed by an interesting discussion on the difference between *tame* and *wild*.

Parents and professionals can help children separately or they can work together to the great benefit of the children. Parents can give practical help in classrooms (as many already do), but perhaps the greatest benefit to teachers in working with parents is the spur towards making their own pedagogy more conscious and explicit.

One of the most important outcomes of the project was that all the adults watched and listened with ever-increasing interest to what the children were saying and doing. Nothing gets under a parent's skin more quickly and more permanently than the illumination of his or her own child's behaviour. The effect of participation can be profound.

Appendix: The Froebel Early Education Project

GENERAL AIMS OF THE FROEBEL PROJECT

The initial general aims of the Froebel Early Education Project reflected generalities rather than the search for 'minute particulars' of cognitive functioning. The 'search for schemas' quickly took over as the main motivation for parents and professionals because the findings of the one-year pilot study had led to certain conclusions. The pilot study was of deprived children from a residential nursery who were unwanted, neglected, damaged and/or abandoned. The difference between those children and normal children was startling.

The main evidence of improvement in the children was the sort that practitioners could see with their own eyes. There seemed to be progress in the children's ability to co-operate with other children and adults, and in their representational behaviour both in physical action, drawing and language.

There were no means of describing, much less analysing or generalizing, the nature of the improvements for a wider professional and reading audience. None of the professionals involved in this first pilot project had either the concepts or the language to describe more detailed improvements. There was no way of applying formative evaluation procedures to the data of the first project. Formative evaluations document how earlier, less adequate forms of thinking and behaviour in children develop into later, more adequate forms of thinking and behaviour. The difficulties of formulating formative progress without a systematic system of developmental theory was , and still is, one of the reasons why, throughout the world , researchers still rely so heavily on standardized tests.

Attempts to analyse the large number of observations made during the first pilot study made one thing crystal clear. It is one thing to make observations, but quite another to interpret observations in ways that are illuminative, useful or even interesting. Examples from children however detailed need to be embedded in a system of appropriate, useful and internally consistent interpretative theory. It was realized that such a system was not available and would have to be constructed.

THE PEDAGOGY OF CONSTRUCTIVISM IN THE 1960s

Enoch Powell's 'Rivers of blood' speech on 20 April 1968 was expedient in the obtaining of funds for programmes linked with the avoidance of future social unrest.

A great deal of research of an experimental nature was carried out during the 1960s by educationalists and psychologists who had adopted Piagetian theory. It was estimated that during the twentieth century, up to 80 per cent of all research into child development in France, Britain and the USSR was carried out within a constructivist conceptual framework. Piaget called himself a 'genetic epistemologist', but the term was never adopted in the UK or the USA. Nowadays, the term 'genetic' has been restricted to the mechanisms of heredity in the English-speaking world, and so it is better to use *a developmental theory of knowledge* (Cambell, 2002, p. 6). Many eminent Americans before Weikart, such as Hunt (1961), Bruner et al. (1966), Skeels et al. (1938) and Bloom (1964) contributed to the evidence that if worthwhile experiences were made available to children in the critical period from birth to 4 years of age, significantly improved cognitive functioning could result, especially in children who were under-functioning in the first place.

Skeels and colleagues (1938) from Iowa deserve a special word of praise for their courage in maintaining and persisting that there had been an increase in IQ in the young children they were studying as a result of an unintended enriched environment. The infants had to share housing with adolescent girls with low IQs; the girls thought that this was the greatest thing that had ever happened, and they loved, played and talked with the infants.

The Iowa team's claim that the infants' IQ had altered as a result of this enriched environment sent shock waves through the psychometric world. This was almost equivalent to Nietzsche's proclamation that God was dead. These are such important shifts away from shared beliefs that they are candidates for illustrating Kuhn's 'paradigm shifts'. Nothing is quite the same again.

Leading psychometricians of the time and professionals in power, such as Florence Goodenough, vigorously opposed the Iowa researchers' finding that human intelligence was sufficiently flexible to improve as a result of increased stimulation in early childhood.

Politically, implying an unfixed IQ was probably viewed by some as an inconvenient research finding as it cut across the norms and assumptions of a firmly stratified society and education system. Flexibility of cognitive functioning is more difficult to provide for than a society where the rich man is in his castle and the poor man is at his gate, or where a fixed elite go to university and the future minimum-wage workers do not.

THE MAIN PROJECT (1972/76)

A dramatic change of priorities had occurred in society around the time of the end of the Froebel pilot study. Unwanted children were no longer a social problem; in fact, the birth control pill led to a shortage of children for adoption. Attention shifted from individual neglected children to a more widespread problem of the under-functioning urban poor. Research funding was affected by this shift of emphasis and the funding of the Project determined the selection of the families who were approached to join the Project.

Mrs Walch, the head teacher of the first pilot study, suggested an area of London agreed by all concerned as suitable for the subsequent Project; it was thought that the planned Project bus journey from Wandsworth to Roehampton would not tire the children. Local playgroup leaders, health visitors and staff of the local primary school suggested families who would be suitable for, and interested in, joining the Project. The families were visited and, with a few exceptions, they constitute the group who started at the Project on 24 September 1973.

There were invisible hands guiding some events. An Asian health worker made sure that the Asian families approached would be likely to work together harmoniously and that they were all Urdu speakers. This silent help was not realized and therefore not sufficiently appreciated at the time.

PRELIMINARY HOME VISITS

A battery of standardized tests were given, mainly in the children's homes, before the families began to attend the Project. Four visits were made to each family (approximately 45 visits all together). Tina Bruce, the appointed teacher, joined the visits from the middle of August. Her experience with young deaf children was invaluable in interpreting what the children were saying in response to the standardized testing. Most of the children were approaching their third birthday. An attempt was made to reflect the ethnic mix as existed in the local school.

A slightly modified version of the questionnaires used in the Swansea Schools Council Study 'Just Before School' helped to establish that the new target group fell within the remit of the new aims and criteria of the project's experimental group of children and families. Summative tests include the Stanford-Binet, the Reynell Verbal Comprehension and Expressive Language Scale. These were used for establishing what later became known as 'baseline assessments'.

There are fundamental problems involved in using standardized tests for the purpose of showing educational gain. IQ tests have been modified over the years to show consistency rather than change of scores. An assumed stability of scores from year to year is at the heart of psychometrics. Before comprehensive education, children were sorted for different kinds of education. Given that one of the aims of education is to produce improvement in all children, it is bizarre, and may go down as a curio of educational research history, that researchers have to use measures which were invented and constantly modified to show stability rather than change in IQ scores. For instance, at one point it was discovered that girls did better than boys in the tests, so the items which showed these differences were changed. It was called making the test more fair. As someone remarked cynically, 'more fair for boys and less fair for girls'.

Another problem with summative evaluation is that if there is a change for the better in IQ scores, there is no indication as to what brought the improvement about. Educational research needs to concern itself with how progress is made from an earlier to a later stage of development.

However, in spite of these difficulties, with the lessons of the first pilot study in mind, it was considered expedient to use a battery of summative evaluation procedures in case the invention of formative evaluation procedures should prove too difficult.

BASELINE SUMMATIVE ASSESSMENTS

The initial scores of five standardized tests given to the Project children and the Ibstock 'comparison group' children during the summer of 1973 illustrated the wide differences between two groups of children from different social groups. These differences had been found in other studies. However, findings on the same tests given at the end of the first year showed a narrowing of the gap. A preliminary analysis showed that project children made significant gains on all the tests. As tests are unreliable when used on very young children, a wider analysis was carried out. All siblings of Project and comparison group children were also tested. During the home visits, four standardized tests were given to the children.

The Asian children were tested in English and Urdu. Mariam Abbas, a second-year student from the Froebel Educational Institute (FEI) gave willingly of her time in order to help in this and in many other ways. She explained that test items introducing little pink pigs into Moslem households was equivalent to introducing mangy old rats into traditionally wetsern households. Cows were immediately substituted. After the end of her training, Mariam set up her own nursery school in Karachi. She now has several.

THE EDUCATIONAL PROGRAMME

The Projects' educational programme involved keeping close and detailed daily records on every child. These records were studied frequently for information on sequences in the formation and evolution of concepts. Categories of space, time, classification and ordering have long been thought of as fundamental categories of thought. These categories figure in studies of thinking in children from the age of 6 or 7.

Universal, or even widespread, categories of thought between the ages of 2 and 5 years of age had not been described or observed in existing studies. In spite of constant reiteration in the literature that the behaviour of young children was unsystematic, it was a stated Project assumption that behaviour was bound to be systematic but that we did not, as yet, understand the system. If there were patterns of behaviour underneath the content of experience, they seemed to be invisible to parents and professionals alike at that time. In the light of emerging evidence of systematic behaviour discovered during the Project, which was consistently discussed with parents, the parents became increasingly involved in the educational process. Parents were not given token or peripheral roles which, in earlier days, often passed for parental participation.

The work of Rosenthal in the USA had made it clear that the teachers' expectations must be kept high if high achievements in children were to be reached. Strenuous efforts were made to keep the aspirations of all concerned with the Project as high as possible. With this in mind, a plan to involve staff and children in the Ibstock Place Kindergarten was devised.

EARLY DAYS OF PARENTAL PARTICIPATION

The non-stop sun and heat of the summer of 1973 highlighted the need for children who lived in the concrete, highly industrial part of London to have access to fresh air and play facilities with other children in a constructive, adult-protected environment. Project mothers (with their babies), a few fathers, aunts and some grandparents, came to the Project regularly on the Project bus with their children. The Project driver, a former London bus driver known as 'Uncle Frank', was always helpful and popular but strict. He was particularly strict about children not eating in his bus, especially crisps. Khaliq was so impressed by this that, at three, he drew a picture called: 'Crisps falling in the bus'. Professionals and parents were excited by this example of what we saw at the time of the importance of first-hand experience. We did not initially interpret 'Crisps falling in the bus' as example of a vertical trajectory.

Tina Bruce adopted a diagnostic role as much as possible, but direct intervention was necessary in some cases. It is important to record that parental participation was not immediate or spontaneous, it had to be created. Tina and the present writer gave a constant, even relentless, feedback on the children's learning to parents, particularly via the video. This was sufficiently like television to have immediate appeal. The educational aim was to show small increments of learning and to invest them with educational significance. Great significance was given to steps forward in individual children. For instance, when children first drew a complete circle there were congratulations and discussions about all the representation that would now be possible. Children would now be able to draw all the 'round shaped things' they knew about. Parents made sure that their children's experience of round things was extended.

As a result of the focus on these small increments in learning, a collection of detailed, developmental studies through written records and specific examples were built up. As well as collecting data, it was a useful educational strategy to construct tentative educational significances and to include parents in this process. It was not easy to break down the 'expert' versus 'non-expert' division and to replace it with a more useful shared, ongoing exploration.

ATTENDANCE AND INVOLVEMENT OF WHOLE FAMILIES

The parents soon began to be invaluable in helping to identify specific instances of learning related to the general 'schemas' (patterns of behaviour) initially identified by project staff.

Play-group leaders, health and social workers working in the vicinity of the estate where the families lived began to express increasing interest, with requests to visit the Project. Information seemed to have been disseminated from Project parents to the wider local community. An exchange of visits and information between the Project staff, College staff and Kindergarten staff began.

A wide range of college staff organized educationally worthwhile events for all the siblings who attended the Project during the schools holidays. One morning each week, the present writer would observe and video comparison group children in the Ibstock Kindergarten. Tina Bruce arranged project visits every Wednesday. Every parent accompanied their children on these visits to the airport, river, Teddington Lock, Natural History and Science Museum, London Zoo, swimming baths and travelling on the Underground, a helter-skelter specially opened on a fairground site near Westway, and Westminster Abbey. All these experiences provided the content which was assimilated to existing schemas.

THE SEARCH FOR SCHEMAS

The ongoing identification of repeatable schemas began to provide an extra excitement for everybody concerned with the study. Discussion with parents took on a new higher level. A shared and entertaining discussion point was: 'What have a visit to a school for the deaf, a helter-skelter and Kew Gardens hot-house got in common?' This was suggested, playfully, as a new kind of experiential intelligence test question. A possible answer which could be discussed with the children was, among other things: 'A helter-skelter has a spiral you sit on and slide down. A hearing aid has a spiral inside it and Kew hot-house has a spiral staircase.' We would say to each other: 'Any of our 4-year-olds could tell you that.'

The sheer volume of 'content specific' representation following project visits provides evidence that neither an extreme child-centred pedagogy nor a largely custodial programme can provide the wide experiences needed for extending cognition in the early years.

Froebel said many years ago that education must be concerned with making 'the inner outer' and 'the outer inner'. In tackling problems of 'representation', there is now a thriving literature on 'internalism' and 'externalism'.

EXAMPLES OF CO-ORDINATIONS OF FORM AND CONTENT IN CHILDREN'S REPRESENTATIONS

Following one visit and after playing with a simulated lock in the classroom, Stuart (4:7 – that is, 4 years and 7 months) drew a few simple lines that looked like two shallow stairs (see Figure 6.7). He said: 'This is Teddington Lock. First level, gate, second level, gate, third level.' Stuart used the mathematical concept of 'ordination': first, second and third. Deficit theory maintains that children of four can think only in absolutes: 1, 2 and 3. He is using his graphic horizontal and vertical line 'grid' schema appropriately.

Clare (4:7), after the same visit, drew parallel circular lines with a straight line joined to the circumference of the circle (see Figure 5.46). She said: 'It's a lifebelt and the rope. A big one, another rope. Clare was recorded on video tape at Teddington Lock having a discussion with her mother about what lifebelts are for. Clare is using a 'core and radial' graphic schema to represent the content of lifebelt, but a higher level of cognitive functioning is revealed in the recorded conversation and that is to do with the function of a lifebelt.

PARENTAL PARTICIPATION

The increase in the quantity and quality of the parents' participation in the children's learning over two years was largely due to the ongoing excitement and satisfaction of the search for and understanding of schemas. The fact that children used 'core and radial' schemas to represent such a disparate array of content such as 'clock', 'apple with a stalk' 'lifebelt', 'face with hair', 'deer with antlers' and so on brought significance and illumination to what had been perceived as unsystematic drawing at its best and random scribbles at its least valued. We realized that we had rescued young children from the 'pejorative flitting' to the 'cognitive fitting'. All those objects can be represented by a core and radial schema or graphic form.

FUNDING FOR DATA ANALYSIS AND FOR A FURTHER PROJECT

During 1974 to 1975 something of great importance occurred to the present writer, already a Leverhulme Research Fellow. The Leverhulme Trust renewed the research fellowship at a principal lecturer's level for a further two years. However, in spite of promised support from several distinguished people, the FEI application to the

Social Science Research Council (SSRC) for money to initiate another action research project failed. Members of the Project steering committee perceived this as bad news.

The inside story of the failure of the application for funds will never be known, but there was a suspicious aspect to the whole process of application, delivery and denial of delivery leading to eventual refusal. The document had involved so much labour that the present writer delivered it by hand into the letter box of the SSRC headquarters in the City of London one Sunday evening. After several weeks they said they had not received it. Another copy was delivered by hand, which they then said must have been lost during a move. With hindsight, it would appear that the SSRC itself was being disbanded.

In the Project minutes it was stated:

> It would be possible to re-apply to the SSRC and/or to apply to the Schools Council as the findings of the project will have important implications for the curriculum of the pre-school. However, in view of the present economic plight of the country and the unusual upheavals in the education world it seems wiser to let the coming publications mark the official end of this particular five year project.

This meant that the extended fellowship would allow time for a detailed examination of the mountain of data, the statistical analysis of the data and the painstaking job – largely unrecognized in the research world except by researchers – of stitching together tiny fragments of theory and observations from a wide array of books and journals, to provide an internally consistent theory sufficiently powerful to explain the significance of the data in hand. This would not have been possible if time had been used up on another action project.

THE LAST DAY FOR THE FAMILIES

Thursday, 10 July 1975 was the last day of attendance for the Project families. The parents expressed both depth of feeling and a high level of appreciation for the educational opportunities that had been given to them and their children over the two years. There was a unanimous opinion shared by both parents and professionals involved in the Project, that parents and teachers can and must work together to further the educational process in individual children. The key issue, and possibly the main reason for the success of the Project, has been to draw parents into an ongoing dialectic on what the educational process consists of in relation to children from 2 to 5 years of age.

IN DEPTH ANALYSIS OF DATA

It was clear, even before in-depth computer analysis, that there was nothing random in the behaviour of individual children. The records showed a persistence in pursuing particular concerns. The explorations seemed to be as systematic and ubiquitous as babies throwing things out of the pram or hotly pursuing a desirable, newly permanent object. Each instance of recorded behaviour was examined, however trivial or idiosyncratic it appears to be at first sight. What became clear was that there were schemas which united a wide range of apparently different instances and which manifested themselves over a wide range of different material.

One such persistent concern was in the exploration of space. The beginning of this scheme appeared in Lois when she drew a face using her most advanced repertoire. Mother and teacher were very pleased. Lois then scribbled all over it (the adults were disappointed). She then made a pancake out of clay which she carefully wrapped up. (A mother had wrapped real pancakes a few days earlier so that the children could hold them). Lois said: 'I've wrapped it up so the children won't burn their hands'.

At this time Lois became totally absorbed in stories which had anything to do with any type of container. All drawings and paintings at this time were scribbled over.

- She made a model of a train with sliding doors.

- She made a model of a house with covered windows and said 'because it's dark outside'.

- She carefully wrapped up her mother's shoes at home and posted the parcel in the rubbish bin. Although this made the family late for school, her mother was delighted with this particular example of the 'enveloping' schema.

- On a visit to the park she became absorbed with peeling the bark off twigs.

- She made a model bus, said: 'This is a bus with a steering wheel and all the people are inside'.

- She found a worm and covered it with sand and said: 'At night he'll be asleep … you know they live under the sand'.

- She made a small hole in her home book and peeped through it. (Her mother was embarrassed and carefully mended the book.)

- She painted her first square and said: 'It's a square shape'.

- She drew a square grid and said: 'This is a gerbil in a cage'. (Enveloping space is now extended to include open grid-like structures.)

- She dressed up all morning in a long dress which completely covered her.

- She made a model of a boat and said: 'That sail is wrapped round that there' (the mast).

- To her brother who was painting: 'I'm sorry to see you haven't got your pinafore on'.

- She painted a figure carrying a large bag and called it : 'Mummy going shopping'. She drew a picture of a cage and said: 'It's raining inside the cage'.

- She told a long story about her cat, the persistent theme was of the cat going inside and outside her house. The naughtiness of the cat going inside and outside the dustbin. Bringing what is inside the dustbin to the inside of the house and so on.

It is difficult to capture the excitement experienced by all the adults during this continuing 'search for schemas'. When a schema has been identified, it has an obviousness, even inevitability about it, which generates an excitement that both sustains future searching and reinforces the partnership between teacher and parent. The partnership is based on the search for ongoing processes in cognitive development.

PROJECT RESULTS OF SUMMATIVE TESTS

School holiday time during Easter 1978 was spent re-testing the children. Most were at the end of their infant school period and were about 7 years old. It was interesting, and pleasant, to visit the families in their homes again. About half the families had been re-housed and their new circumstances had generated extra confidence and feelings of wellbeing. All the re-housed children could play outside, many in special play areas. Three families had their own gardens. Tina Bruce had become well-informed on successful procedures regarding re-housing and had passed this knowledge on to parents during day-to-day discussions.

The results of intelligence testing over five years are given below. The number on the left is the mean age for the group; the enclosed number is the mean intelligence quotient for the group:

3:0 (90)   3:11 (105)   4:8 (117)   7:4 (115)

As can be seen, the children made steady gains during the Project years and they sustained the very highly significant mean gain of 25 IQ points.

It is usual in research projects of this kind to take the final scores two years after the end of the venture as the most important evidence of success or failure. The sustained gain of 25 IQ points therefore can be taken as an important and objective measure of the success of the educational programme carried out over two years at the FEI. It might be said that the mean lQ of 90, the results of the first test, could reflect an unreliability of the test at its lowest age level. However, the mean IQ of the children's older siblings, tested during the first year of the project, averaged 93. This shows an initial equivalence of children within families, which indicates that 90 was probably a fair measure of the initial scores of the younger children.

No such equivalence was demonstrated when four project babies were tested at the mean age of 2:11. They had a mean IQ of 108. Their older siblings, at 3:1 (measured before the Project began) had a mean IQ of 86. The babies had attended the project from birth.

In the most recent tests, the four Project babies, at average age 5:6, scored mean IQ 123. Their older project siblings at average age 7:4 scored mean IQ of 112.

In brief, the children from the low socio-economic group made outstanding gains in all areas of functioning tested by standardized tests:

- Average intelligence quotients (Stanford-Binet) increased from 90 to 117.

- 'Listening vocabulary' (English Picture Vocabulary Test) increased from 101 to 110.

- 'Language comprehension' (Reynell Developmental Language Scales) increased from –25 below the normal population to +1.1 above the normal population.

- 'Expressive language' (Reynell) increased from –1.0 below the normal population to +18 above the normal population.

At the end of the Project the children who were educated at the FEI had higher intelligence quotients than their older brothers and sisters. Project children with older siblings finished with an average IQ of 113. Their older brothers and sisters had an average IQ of 93. The four babies included in the Project group finished with higher intelligence quotients than the rest of the family. This is a complete reversal of the usual statistical trend, where, in unstimulating cultural conditions, intelligence quotients decrease with age within families.

Large increases were made on the Goodenough 'Draw-a-Man' test. Initial average standard scores were 80.9. These increased to 94.9. A third-year student at the FEI compared a group of Project children at the end of the experiment with a group of children from a playgroup serving the area from which the Project children were originally drawn. The two groups were matched for age, sex and ethnic background. The two groups of children were given the English Picture Vocabulary Test and the Goodenough 'Draw-a-Man' test. The Project children scored 101 on the 'Draw-a-Man' test and 111 on the EPVT. The playgroup children scored 74 on the 'Draw-a-Man' test and 97 on the EPVT.

No significant gains were made by the comparison group of 18 children of high socio-economic status attending Ibstock Place Preparatory School. These children presumably had been helped to learn effectively from birth by their well-educated parents. They were not under-functioning at the start of the Project.

The main conclusion rising from the FEI research is that poor cultural conditions are associated with intellectual under-functioning in children. This under-functioning is clearly shown in test scores as early as 3 years of age. Early education can facilitate higher cognitive functioning, particularly if parents participate in the programme. The situation as it now exists with project families can be summed up by saying that the younger the child within the family, the higher the IQ. This unusual state of affairs is probably due to a combination of factors such as the extremely stimulating environment of the Project and the parents' extra focused attention on their infants during the early critical years. There was considerable evidence that what the parents were learning, they were practising on their infants.

The Project group were 20 IQ points ahead of their older siblings at the end of the project. This difference is, again, dramatically demonstrated in the results of the reading tests given to all children. The project children were six months ahead of their chronological age in reading accuracy and three months ahead in reading comprehension. Eight children had older siblings who fell within the age range covered by the reading test. These older siblings lagged 14 months behind their chronological age in reading accuracy. There was an equivalent lag in their reading comprehension.

A similar pattern of sustained gain, and large differences between older and younger children, were found in the vocabulary test scores and the Draw-a-Man test. The older siblings were lagging 22 points behind the project children in their vocabulary scores. This was a dramatic difference and most of the project parents became uncomfortably aware of the difference although test results were never disclosed or hinted at. There was also some evidence that the older brothers and sisters became aware that their performance was being compared unfavourably with that of their younger siblings. This is just one of many social difficulties which beset people involved in compensatory education projects.

The final findings of the project must be viewed against what is generally known of the issues being discussed, intelligence quotients, language development and so on. All large-scale studies of children within families have demonstrated statistically that first-born children have an advantage over their younger siblings both mentally and physically.

This particular project culminated in the project publication *Extending Thought in Young Children: A Parent–Teacher Partnership*, written by the present author and published in 1990.

Bibliography

Ahrens, R. (1954) Beiträge zur Entwicklung des Physiognomie und Mimikerkennes, *Zeitschrift fur experimentelle und angewardte Psychologie, 2,* in T. G. R. Bower (1977a), op. cit., p. 79.

Alexander, R. (2004) Still no pedagogy? Principle, pragmatism and compliance in primary education, *Cambridge Journal of Education,* Vol. 34, No. 1, March 2004.

Anderson, R. C., Spiro, R. J. and Montague, W. E. (1977) *Schooling and the Acquisition of Knowledge,* Lawrence Erlbaum Associates, Hillsdale, NJ.

Arnheim, R. (1972) *Art and Visual Perception,* Faber and Faber, London.

Arnold, C (2002) *Georgia's Story,* Paul Chapman Publishing, London.

Arnold, C (2003) *Observing Harry,* Open University Press, Buckingham.

Athey, C. (1977) Humour in children related to Piaget's theory of intellectual development, in A. J. Chapman and H. C. Foot (eds) op. cit., pp. 215–18.

Athey, C. (1990) *Extending Thought in Young Children: A Parent–Teacher Partnership,* Paul Chapman Publishing, London.

Athey, C. (2002) Extending thought in young children, *Early Childhood Practice: The Journal for Multi-Professional Partnerships.* Vol 4, No. 1, pp. 8–16.

Athey, C. (2004) Early learning and the brain, *Early Childhood Practice: The Journal for Multi-Professional Partnerships.* Vol 6, No. 1, pp. 7–17

Bailey, R. A. and Burton, E. C. (1982) *The Dynamic Self,* C. V. Mosby, London.

Baldwin, A. L., Kalhorn, J. and Breese, F. H. (1945) Patterns of parent behaviour *(Psychological Monograph,* Vol. 58, No. 268), in M. V. Hunt (1961) op. cit., p. 279.

Bartholomew, L. and Bruce, T. (1993) *Getting to Know You: A Guide to Record Keeping in Early Childhood Education and Care,* Hodder & Stoughton, London.

Bartlett, F. C. (1932) *Remembering: A Study in Experimental and Social Psychology*, Cambridge University Press, Cambridge.

Bayley, N. and Jones, H. E. (1937) Environmental correlates of mental and motor development; a cumulative study from infancy to six years, *Child Development*, Vol. 8, pp. 329–41.

Beadle, M. (1971) *A Child's Mind: How Children Learn During the Critical Years from Birth to Age Five*, MacUibbon & Kee, London.

Beilin, H. (1972) The status and future of preschool compensatory education, in J.C. Stanley (ed.) op.cit., pp. 165–81.

Bereiter, C. and Engleman, S. (1966) Teaching disadvantaged children in the preschool, originally published by Prentice Hall and reproduced in *Deprivation and Disadvantage (Educational Studies)*, Open University Press, Buckingham (1973) E262, Block 8, pp. 52–8.

Berman, P. W., Cunningham, J. G. and Harkulich, J. (1974) Construction of the horizontal, vertical and oblique by young children: failure to find the oblique effect, *Child Development*, Vol. 45, pp. 474–8.

Bernstein, B. (1974a) *Class, Codes and Control* (Vol. 3), Routledge & Kegan Paul, London.

Bernstein, B. (1974b) Class and pedagogy: visible and invisible, in W. B. Dockrell and D. Hamilton (eds) op. cit., pp. 115–39.

Bertram, T. and Pascal , C. (2000) The OECD Thematic Review of Early Childhood Education and CARE. Background Report for the United Kingdom. www.oecd.org/copyr.htm/w.

Blackstone, T. (1971) *A Fair Start: The Provision of Pre-school Education*, Allen Lorne, London.

Blakemore, S. J. and Frith, U. (2000) The implications of recent developments in neuroscience for research on teaching and learning. A paper given out at a seminar at the Royal Institution in 2000.

Blenkin, G. M. and Kelly, A. V. (eds) (1988) *Early Childhood Education: A Developmental Curriculum*, Paul Chapman Publishing, London.

Blenkin, G. M. and Whitehead, M. (1988) Education as development, in G. M. Blenkin and A. V. Kelly (eds) op. cit., pp. 32–60.

Bloom, B. S. (1964) *Stability and Change in Human Characteristics*, Wiley, New York, NY.

Bond, M. (1976) *Paddington Decorator*, Fontana, London.

Bower, T. G. R. (1974) *Development in Infancy*, W. H. Freeman, San Francisco, CA.

Bower, T. G. R. (1977a) *A Primer of Infant Development*, W. H. Freeman, San Francisco, CA.

Bower, T. G. R. (1977b) The Perceptual World of the Child, in J. Bruner, M. Cole and B. Lloyd (eds), Fontana, Glasgow.

Brearley, M. and Hitchfield, E. (1966) *A Teacher's Guide to Reading Piaget*, Routledge & Kegan Paul, London.

Brierley, J. K. (1987) *Give me a Child until he is Seven: Brain Studies and Early Childhood Education*, Falmer Press, Abingdon.

Brimer, M. A. and Dunn. L. M. (1962) *English Picture Vocabulary Test (EPVT)*, Educational Evaluation Enterprises, Marsh St, Bristol 1.

Britton, J. (1970) *Language and Learning*, Penguin Books, London.

Brown, B. (1978) *Found: Long Term Gains from Early Intervention (Selected Symposia Series)*, Westview Press, Boulder, CO.

Brown, R. (1973) *A First Language: The Early Stages*, Allen & Unwin, London.

Bruce, T. (1987) *Early Childhood Education*, Hodder & Stoughton, London.

Bruce, T. (2004) *Developing Learning in Early Childhood*, Paul Chapman Publishing, London.

Bruner, J. S. (1971) The growth and structure of skill, in J. S. Bruner (1974) op. cit., pp. 245–69.

Bruner, J. (1972) Nature and the uses of immaturity. *American Psychology*, Vol. 27, No. 8.

Bruner, J. S. (1974) *Beyond The Information Given*, Allen & Unwin, London.

Bruner, J. S. (1980) *Under Five in Britain* (Oxford Pre-School Research Project – OPRP), Grant McIntyre, London.

Bruner, J. S., Olver, R. R. and Greenfield, P. M. et al. (1966) *Studies in Cognitive Growth*, Wiley, New York, NY.

Butterworth, G. and Jarrett, N. (1982) Piaget's stage 4 error: background to the problem, *British Journal of Educational Psychology*, vol. 73, pp. 175–85.

Cambell, R.L. (2002) *Jean Piaget's Genetic Epistemology: Appreciation and Critique*, http://hubcap.clemson, edu/-camber/index.html.

Cane, B. and Schroeder, C. (1970) *The Teacher and Research*, NFER/Nelson, London.

Carle, E. (1969) *The Very Hungry Caterpillar*, Puffin Books, London.

Carter, R. (1999) *Mapping the Mind*, London, Weidenfeld and Nicolson.

Central Advisory Council for Education (1967) *Children and their Primary Schools* (The Plowden Report), HMSO, London.

Chalmers, N., Crawley, R. and Rose, P. R. S. (1971) *The Biological Bases of Behaviour*, Harper & Row, London.

Chapman, A. J. and Foot, H. C. (eds) (1977) *It's a Funny Thing Humour*, Pergamon Press, Oxford.

Chomsky, N. (1980) On cognitive structures and their development: a reply to Piaget, in M. Piattelli-Palmarini (ed) op. cit., pp. 35–54.

Chukovsky, K. (1966) *From Two to Five*, University of California Press, Berkeley, CA, (first published in the Soviet Union in 1925).

Clark, D. (1999) www.nwlink.com/~donclark/hrd/history/history.html.

Clay, M. (1975) *What Did I Write?*, Heinemann Educational, Oxford.

Cratty, B. (1973) *Intelligence in Action*, Prentice-Hall, Englewood Cliffs, NJ.

Cromer, R. F. (1974) The development of language and cognition: the cognition hypothesis, in B. Foss (ed.), op. cit., pp. 184–252.

Curtis, A. (1986) *A Curriculum for the Pre-School Child*, NFER/Nelson, London.

Curtis, A. (1987) The education of four year olds in school, *Update: Current Issues in Early Education, Organisation Mondiate pour Education Prescolaire. UK Nat. Committee.* No. 16, February.

Damasio, A. (1999) *The Feeling of What Happens: Body, Emotion and the Making of Consciousness.* Heinemann, Oxford.

Darwin, C. (1877) Biographical sketch of an infant (Doddy), *Mind*, Vol. 2, pp. 28–294.

Davies, M. (2003) *Movement and Dance in Early Childhood*, Paul Chapman Publishing, London.

DES (1972) *Education: A Framework for Expansion*, HMSO, London.

DES (1975) *A Language for Life* (the Bullock Report), HMSO, London.

DES (1983) *Teaching in Schools: The Content of Initial Training* (HMI discussion paper), HMSO, London.

DES (1985) *The Curriculum from 5 to 16 (Curriculum Matters 2)*, HMSO, London.

DES (1987a) *National Curriculum: Science Working Group. Interim Report*, DES and Welsh Office, HMSO, London.

DES (1987b) *The Task Group on Assessment and Testing: A Report*, DES and Welsh Office, HMSO, London.

DES (1989a) *Aspects of Primary Education: the Education of Children under Five*, HMSO, London.

DES (1989b) *National Curriculum: From Policy to Practice*, Publications Despatch Centre, DES, Honeypot Lane, Canons Park, Stanmore.

DES (1989c) *Statistics Bulletin No. 7. Pupils Under Five Years in each Local Authority in England, January 1988*, Publications Despatch Centre, DES, Honeypot Lane, Canons Park, Stanmore.

Dockrell, W. B. and Hamilton, D. (eds.) (1980) *Rethinking Educational Research*, Hodder & Stoughton, London.

Dodd, B. (1972) Effects of social and vocal stimulation on infant babbling, *Developmental Psychology*, Vol. 7, pp. 80–3.

Donaldson, M. (1978) *Children's Minds*, Fontana, Glasgow.

Duckworth, E. (1974) The having of wonderful ideas, in M. Schwebel and J. Raph (eds) op. cit., Chapter 12.

Duffy, A., Chambers, F., Croughan, S. and Stephens, J. (2006) *Working with Babies and Childen under Three*, Oxford: Heinemann Harcourt Edition.

Earwaker, J. (1973) R. S. Peters and the concept of education, *Proceedings of the Philosophy of Education Society of Great Britain*, Vol. 7, No. 2, pp. 239–59.

Elkind, D. (1969) Piagetian and psychometric conceptions of intelligence, *Harvard Education Review*, Vol. 39, No. 2, pp. 319–37.

Elkind, D. and Flavell, J. H. (eds) (1969) *Studies in Cognitive Development: Essays in Honour of Jean Piaget*, Oxford University Press, Oxford.

Eng, H. (1959) *The Psychology of Children's Drawings*, Routledge & Kegan Paul, London (first published in 1931).

Fantz, R. L. (1961) The origin of form perception, *Scientific American*, Vol. 204, pp. 66–72.

Ferreiro, E. and Teberosky, A. (1982) *Literacy Before Schooling,* Heinemann Educational, Oxford.

Fodor, J. (1980) On the impossibility of acquiring 'more powerful' structures, in M. Piattelli-Palmarini (ed.) op. cit., Chap. 6, pp. 142–62.

Fodor, J. (1998) *When Cognitive Science went Wrong.* Oxford University Press, Oxford.

Forman, G. E. (ed.) (1982a) *Action and Thought: From Sensorimotor Schemes to Symbolic Operations,* Academic Press, New York, NY.

Forman, G. E. and Fosnot, C. T. (1982) The use of Piaget's constructivism in early childhood education programs, in B. Spodek (ed.) op. cit., Chap. 9, pp. 185–211.

Foss, B. (ed.) (1974) *New Perspectives in Child Development,* Penguin Books, London.

Furth, H. G. (1969) *Piaget and Knowledge: Theoretical Foundations,* Prentice-Hall, Englewood Cliffs, NJ.

Garvey, C. (1977) *Play,* Harvard University Press, Cambridge, MA.

Gerhardt, L. (1973) *Moving and Knowing: The Young Child Orients Himself in Space,* Prentice-Hall, Englewood Cliffs, NJ.

Gesell, A. (1971) *The First Five Years of Life,* Methuen, London.

Gopnik, A. (1984) Words and plans: early language and the development of intelligent action, in A. Lock and E. Fisher (eds.) op. cit., pp. 83–101.

Gopnik, A., and Meltzoff, A. (1987) Early semantic developments and their relationships to object permanence, means-end understanding, and cateogorisation', in Child Language, K. Nelson (ed.), vol. 6, Lawrence Erlbaum Associates, Hillsdale, N.J.

Gopnik, A., Meltzoff, A., and Kuhl, P. (1999) *How Babies Think,* Weidenfeld and Nicolson, London.

Greene, M. (1971) *Curriculum and Consciousness* (reprinted in G. Esland et al. (1977) *Schooling and Pedagogy,* Unit 6, The Open University Press, Buckingham.

Greenfield, S. (2006) in the *Guardian* from an interview by Juliet Rix, Saturday 25 March.

Gura, P. (ed.) (1992) *Exploring Learning: Young Children and Blockplay,* Paul Chapman Publishing, London.

Harlen, W., Darwin, Sr. A. and Murphy, M. (1977) *Match and Mismatch: Finding Answers,* Oliver & Boyd for the Schools Council, Edinburgh.

Harris, D. B. (1963) *Children's Drawings as Measures of Intellectual Maturity: A Revision and Extension of the Goodenough Draw-a-Man Test,* Harcourt, Brace & World, New York, NY.

Harris, P. L. (1975) Development of search and object permanence during infancy, *Psychological Bulletin,* Vol. 3, No. 82, pp. 332–44.

Hayes, P. J. (1979) The naive physics manifesto, in D. Michie (ed.) op. cit, pp. 242–70.

Held, R. and Hein, A. (1963) Movement-produced stimulation in the development of visually guided behaviour, *Journal of Comparative Physiology and Psychology*, Vol. 37, pp. 87–95.

Hohmann, M., Banet, B. and Weikart, D. (1979) *Young Children in Action*, High/Scope Educational Research Foundation, Ypsilanti, MI.

Hubel, D. H. (1963) The visual cortex of the brain, in N. Chalmers, R. Crawley and P. R. S. Rose (eds) op. cit., pp. 122–32.

Hubel, D. H. and Wiesel, T. N. (1962) Receptive fields, binocular interaction and functional architecture in the cat's visual cortex, *Journal of Physiology*, Vol. 160, pp. 106–56.

Hubel, D. H. and Wiesel, T. N. (1965) Receptive field and functional architecture in two non-striate visual areas (18 and 19) of the cat, *Journal of Neurophysiology*, vol. 28, pp. 229–89.

Hubel, D. H. and Wiesel, T. N. (1971) Aberrant visual projections in the Siamese cat, *Journal of Physiology*, vol. 218, (1), pp. 33–62.

Huizinga, J. (1949) *Homo Ludens: A Study of the Play Elements in Culture*, Routledge & Kegan Paul, London.

Hunt, J. McV. (1961) *Intelligence and Experience*, The Ronald Press, New York, NY.

Hutchinson, T. (1969) *Wordsworth Poetical Works*, Oxford University Press, Oxford.

ILEA (1981) *The Study of Places in the Primary School: Curriculum Guidelines*, Publishing Centre, Highbury Station Rd, London NI 1SB.

Inhelder, B. (1969) Memory and intelligence in the child, in D. Elkind and J. A. Flavell (eds) op. cit., pp. 337–64.

Inhelder, B. (1980) Language and knowledge in a constructivist framework, in M. Piattelli-Palmarini (ed) op. cit., pp. 131–41.

Inhelder, B. and Piaget, J. (1964) *The Early Growth of Logic in the Child: Classification and Seriation*, Routledge & Kegan Paul, London.

Inhelder, B., Sinclair, H. and Bovet, M. (1974) *Learning and the Development of Cognition*, Routledge & Kegan Paul, London.

Isaacs, S. (1960) *Intellectual Growth in Young Children*, Routledge & Kegan Paul, London (first published in 1930).

Jensen, A. R. (1969) How much can we boost IQ and scholastic achievement?, *Harvard Education Review*, vol. 39, No. 1, pp. 1–123.

Katz, D. and Katz, R. (1936) *Conversations with Children*, Routledge & Kegan Paul, London.

Katz, L. (1984) Lecture given at the National Children's Bureau, London, 10 May.

Kay, K. (1974) IQ tests fiddled to get stable scores, The *Times Educational Supplement*, 25 January.

Kellogg, R. (1968) The biology of aesthetics, in *Anthology of Impulse. Annual Contemporary Dance 1951–1966*, Dance Horizons, Brooklyn, NY.

Kellogg, R. (1969) *Analyzing Children's Art*, National Books, Palo Alto, CA.

Koestler, A. (1964) *The Act of Creation*, Dell, New York.

Kohlberg, L. (1968) Early education: a cognitive-developmental view, *Child Development*, vol. 39, pp. 1014–62.

Kohlberg, L. and Mayer, R. (1972) Development as the aim of education, *Harvard Educational Review*, vol. 42, pp. 449–96.

Lee, V. (ed.) (1979) *Language Development*, Croom Helm, Beckenham.

Leehey, S. C., Moskowitz-Cook, A., Brill, S. and Held, R. (1975) Orientational anistropy in infant vision, *Science*, vol. 190, No. 4217, pp. 900–2.

Liebschner, J (1991) *Foundations of Progressive Education: The History of the National Froebel Society*, The Lutterworth Press, Cambridge.

Light, P. (1979) *The Development of Social Sensitivity*, Cambridge University Press, Cambridge.

Ling, B. C. (1941) Form discrimination as a learning cue in infants, *Comparative Psychology Monographs*, vol. 17, pp. 1–66.

Lock, A. and Fisher, E. (eds) (1984) *Language Development*, Croom Helm in association with the Open University, Milton Keynes.

Lovell, K. (1959) A follow-up study of some aspects of the work of Piaget and Inhelder on the child's conception of space, *British Journal of Educational Psychology*, Vol. 29, pp. 104–17.

Lowenfeld, V. (1957) *Creative and Mental Growth*, Macmillan, New York, NY

Maguire, E. A. et al. (2000) Navigation-related structural change in the hippocampi of taxi drivers. Proceedings (8)of the National Academy of Sciences (USA) 97 (8) pp. 4398–403.

Mann, M. and Taylor, A. (1973) The effects of multi-sensory learning systems on the concept formation of young children, *Journal of Research and Development in Education*, Vol. 6, No. 3, pp. 35–43.

Matthews, J. (1984) Children drawing: are young children really scribbling?, *Early Child Development and Care*, Vol. 18, pp. 1–39.

Matthews, J. (1987) The young child's early representation and drawing, in G. M. Blenkin and A. V. Kelly (eds) op. cit., pp. 162–83.

Matthews, J. (2003) *Drawing and Painting: Visual and Visual Representation*, 2nd edn, Paul Chapman Publishing, London.

McCandless, B. R. (1970) *Children, Behaviour and Development*, Holt, Rinehart & Winston, London.

Meade, A. (ed.) (2005) *Catching the Waves: Innovation in Early Childhood Education*, NZCER Wellington Press, Wellington.

Meade, A. with Cubey, P. (1995) *Thinking Children*, Wellington, New Zealand Council for Educational Research, College of Education, Victoria University, Wellington.

Michie, D. (1979) *Expert Systems in the Micro-Electronic Age*, Edinburgh University Press, Edinburgh.

Moore, T. W. (1982) *Educational Theory: An Introduction*, Routledge, London.

Moyles, J. (2006) In the right direction, *Nursery World*. 26 January, p. 11.

Murray, J. (2005) Collaborating for effective early education and care: Can policy translate to practice. OMEP Update No. 118 (Winter).

Mussen, P. H., Conger, J. J. and Kagan, J. (1969) *Child Development and Personality*, Harper & Row, New York, NY.

Neale, M. D. (1966) *Neale Analysis of Reading Ability*, Macmillan Education, London.

Neisser, U. (1976) *Cognition and Reality*, W. H. Freeman, San Francisco, CA.

Newell, K. and Barclay, C. (1982) Developing knowledge about action, in J. Kelso and J. Clark (eds) op. cit.

Nicholls, R. (ed.) with Sedgewick, J., Duncan, J., Curwin, L. and McDougall, B. (1986) *Rumpus Schema Extra*, Teachers in Education, Cleveland, LEA, Cleveland, OH.

Norman, D. A. (1985) Twelve Issues for Cognitive Science, in A. M. Aitkenhead and J. M. Slack (eds) op. cit., pp. 309–36.

Nutbrown, C. (1988) The role of a teacher in the development of early writing skills and understanding of a group of three- and four-year-old children, unpublished paper for an in-service M.Ed., Sheffield Polytechnic, Sheffield.

Nutbrown, C. (1999) *Threads of Thinking: Young children Learning and the Role of Early Education*, 2nd edn, Paul Chapman Publishing, London.

Oates, J. (ed.) (1979) *Early Cognitive Development*, Croom Helm in association with the Open University Press, Buckingham.

Oldfield, R. C. (1954) Memory mechanisms and the theory of schemata, *British Journal of Psychology*, Vol. 45, pp. 14–23.

Oldfield, R. C. and Zangwill, O. L. (1942) Head's concept of the schema and its application in contemporary British psychology, *British Journal of Psychology*, Vol. 32, pp. 267–86 (part 1); Vol. 33, pp. 58–64 (part 2); Vol. 34, pp. 113–29 (part 3).

Olson, D. R. (1970) *Cognitive Development: The Child's Acquisition of Diagonality*, Academic Press, London.

Opie, I. and Opie, P. (1959) *The Lore and Language of Schoolchildren*, Clarendon Press, Oxford.

Payton, S. (1984) *Developing Awareness of Print: A Young Child's First Steps Towards Literacy, Educational Review* (off-set publication no. 2), University of Birmingham.

Piaget, J. (1951) *Judgement and Reasoning in the Child*, Routledge & Kegan Paul, London.

Piaget, J. (1953) *The Origin of Intelligence in the Child*, Routledge & Kegan Paul, London.

Piaget, J. (1959) *The Construction of Reality in the Child*, Basic Books, New York, NY.

Piaget, J. (1962) *Play, Dreams and Imitation in Childhood*, Routledge & Kegan Paul, London.

Piaget, J. (1965) *The Child's Conception of Number*, Routledge & Kegan Paul, London.

Piaget, J. (1968a) Quantification, conservation and nativism, *Science*, Vol. l62, pp. 976–9.

Piaget, J. (1968b) *Six Psychological Studies*, University of London Press, London.

Piaget, J. (1969) *The Mechanisms of Perception*, Routledge & Kegan Paul, London.

Piaget, J. (1970) *The Child's Conception of Movement and Speed*, Routledge & Kegan Paul, London.

Piaget, J. (1971a) *Biology and Knowledge*, Edinburgh University Press, Edinburgh.

Piaget, J. (1971b) *Science of Education and the Psychology of the Child*, Longman, Harlow.

Piaget, J. (1971c) *Structuralism*, Routledge & Kegan Paul, London.

Piaget, J. (1972a) *Psychology and Epistemology: Towards a Theory of Knowledge*, Penguin Books, London.

Piaget, J. (1972b) *The Child and Reality: Problems of Genetic Psychology*, Viking Press, London.

Piaget, J. (1972c) *The Principles of Genetic Epistemology*, Routledge & Kegan Paul, London.

Piaget, J. (1973) *Main Trends in Psychology*, Allen & Unwin, London.

Piaget, J. (1974a) *The Child and Reality*, Frederick Muller, London.

Piaget, J. (1974b) *Understanding Causality*, Norton, New York, NY.

Piaget, J. (1976) *To Understand is to Invent*, Penguin Books, London.

Piaget, J. (1977) *The Grasp of Consciousness: Action and Concept in the Young Child*, Routledge & Kegan Paul, London.

Piaget, J. and Inhelder, B. (1956) *The Child's Conception of Space*, Routledge & Kegan Paul, London.

Piaget, J. and Inhelder, B. (1969) *The Psychology of the Child*, Routledge & Kegan Paul, London

Piaget, J. and Inhelder, B. (1971) *Mental Imagery in the Child*, Routledge & Kegan Paul, London.

Piaget, J. and Inhelder, B. (1973) *Memory and Intelligence*, Routledge & Kegan Paul, London.

Piaget, J., Apostel, L. and Mandelbrot, B. (1977) *Logique et Equilibre (Etude D'Epistémologie Genetique)* ii, Presse Universitaires de France, Paris.

Piaget, J., Grize, J. B., Szeminska, A. and Vinh-Bang (1968) *Epistémologie et Psychologie de la Fonction, (Etudes D'Epistémologie Genetique, xxiii)*, Presse Universitaires de France, Paris.

Piattelli-Palmarini, M. (ed.) (1980) *Language and Learning: The Debate between Jean Piaget and Noam Chomsky*, Routledge & Kegan Paul, London.

Pinker, S. (1997) *How the Mind Works*, Penguin Books, London.

Plowden Report (1967) see Central Advisory Council for Education (1967).

Preyer, W. (1882) *The Mind of the Child*, Appleton, New York, NY.

Ratey, J. (2001) *A User's Guide to the Brain*, London, Little, Brown and Co.

Reggio Children (1996) *The Hundred Languages of Children*, Catalogue of the exhibition, Unipol Assicurazioni, Reggio Emilia.

Reynell, J. (1969) *Reynell Developmental Language Scales*, NFER, London.

Rice, E. (1977) *Sam Who Never Forgets*, Puffin Books, London.

Roberts, M. and Tamburrini, J. (1981) *Child Development: 0 to 5*, Holmes McDougall, Edinburgh.

Roberts, R. (2002) *Self-Esteem and Early Learning*, 2nd edn, Paul Chapman Publishing, London.

Rose, S. (1978) Molecular neurobiology: an examination of growing points in a new science, *New Scientist*, 6 July, pp. 31–3.

Rose, S. P. R. and Chalmers, N. (1971) The environmental determinants of brain function, in N. Chalmers, R. Crawley and S. Rose (eds) op. cit. pp. 246–7.

Rudel, R. G. and Teuber, H. L. (1963) Discrimination of the direction of line by young children, *Journal of Comparative and Physiological Psychology*, Vol. 56, pp. 892–8.

Ruff, H. A. (1978) Infant recognition of the invariant form of objects, *Child Development*, vol. 49, no. 2, pp. 293–306.

Rummelhart, V. E. and Norman, D. A. (1978) Accretion, tuning and restructuring: Three modes of Learning, in J. W. Cotton and R. L. Klatzky (eds), *Semantic Factors in Cognition*, Lawrence Erlbaum Associates, Hillsdale, N.J.

Sanderson, A. (1987) *The Early Years: How Children Develop as Writers*, Language Development Centre, Sheffield Polytechnic, Sheffield.

Sauvy, J. and Sauvy, S. (1974) *The Child's Discovery of Space*, Penguin Books, London.

SCAA (1995) *Consistency in Teacher Assessment Authority: Exemplification of Standards*, School Curriculum and Assessment Authority. Ref: Ma/95/291.

Schools Council (1974) *Early Mathematical Experiences* (EME), Schools Council, London.

Schwebel, M. and Raph, J. (eds) (1974) *Piaget in the Classroom*, Routledge & Kegan Paul, London.

Schweinhart, L. J. and Weikart, D. P. (1980) *Young Children Grow Up: The Effects of the Perry Preschool Program on Youths Through Age 15* (Monograph no. 7) The High/Scope Educational Research Foundation, Ypsilanti, MI.

Schweinhart, L. J. and Weikart, D. (1981) *High-Quality Early Childhood Programs for Low-Income Families Pay For Themselves* (research report) High/Scope Educational Research Foundation, Ypsilanti, MI.

Sharp, A. (1987) *The Learning and Development of Three to Five Year Olds: Schema*, City of Sheffield Education Department, Sheffield.

Sheridan, M. D. (1975) *Children's Developmental Progress from Birth to Five Years: The Stycar Sequences*, NFER Publishing, London.

Simon, B, (1985) Why no pedagogy in England? (Chapter Four in Simon (1985) *Does Education Matter?*, Lawrence and Wishart, London.)

Sinclair, H. (1971) Sensorimotor action patterns as a condition for the acquisition of syntax, in R. Huxley and E. Ingram (eds) op. cit. pp. 121–36.

Sinclair, H. (1974) From pre-operational to concrete thinking and parallel development of symbolization, in M. Schwebel and J. Raph (eds) (1947b), op. cit., pp. 35–40.

Sinclair-De-Zwart, H. (1969) Developmental psycholinguistics, in D. Elkind and J. H. Flavell (eds) op. cit., pp. 315–36.

Skeels, H. M., Updegraff, R., Wellman, B. and Williams, H. M. (1938) A study of environmental stimulation: an orphanage pre-school project, *University of Iowa Studies in Child Welfare*, vol. 15, no. 4.

Skemp, R. R. (1962) The need for a schematic learning theory, *British Journal of Educational Psychology*, vol. 32, pp. 133–42.

Skemp, R. R. (1971) *The Psychology of Learning Mathematics*, Penguin Books, London.

Slobin, D. (1973) Cognitive prerequiities for the development of grammar, in C. A. ferguson and D. I. Slobin (eds), op. cit. pp. 155–208.

Smith, L. A. H. (1985) *To Understand and to Help: The Life and Works of Susan Isaacs: 1885–1948*, Associated University Presses, London and Toronto.

Smith, N. R. and Franklin, M. B. (eds) (1979) *Symbolic Functioning in Childhood*, Lawrence Erlbaum Associates, Hillsdale, NJ.

Spodek, B. (1982) *Handbook of Research in Early Childhood Education*, The Free Press, London.

Stanford-Binet Intelligence Scale (1976) See L. M. Terman and M. A. Merrill (1976).

Stanley, J. C. (ed.) (1972) *Preschool Programs for the Disadvantaged*, Johns Hopkins University Press, Baltimore, MD and London.

Stern, W. (1924) *Psychology of Early Childhood up to the Sixth Year of Age*, Holt, Rinehart & Winston, New York, NY.

Stukat, K. G. (1976) *Current Trends in European Pre-School Research (European Trend Reports on Educational Research)*, NFER, London.

Sundberg, N. and Ballinger, T. (1968) Nepalese children's cognitive development as revealed by drawings of man, woman and self, *Child Development*, Vol. 39, pp. 969–85.

Sutton-Smith, B. (1970) The psychology of childlore: the triviality barrier, *Western Folklore*, Vol. 29, pp. 1–8.

Sylva, K., Roy, C. and Painter, M. (1980) *Childwatching at Playgroup and Nursery School* (Oxford Preschool Research Project), Grant McIntyre, London.

Sylva, K., Smith, T. and Moore, E. (1986) *Monitoring the High/Scope Training Programme, 1984–5* (final report), Department of Social and Administrative Studies, University of Oxford, Oxford.

Tamburrini, J. (1982) Some educational implications of Piaget's theory, in C. Modgil and S. Modgil (eds) op. cit., pp. 309–24.

Temple, C. A., Nathan, R. G. and Burris, N. A. (1982) *The Beginnings of Writing*, Allyn & Bacon, London.

Terman, L. M. and Merrill, M. A. (1976) *Manual for the Third Revision, Form L-M. Stanford-Binet Intelligence Scale*, Harrap, London (first published in France, 1916).

Uzgris, I. C. and Hunt, J. McV. (1975) *Assessment in Infancy*, University of Illinois Press, Urbana-Champaign, IL.

Vernon, M. D. (1955) The functions of schemata in perceiving, *Psychological Review*, Vol. 62, pp. 180–92.

Volpe, R. (1981) Knowledge from theory and practice, *Oxford Review of Education*, Vol. 7, no. l, pp. 41–57.

Vygotsky, L. S. (1962) *Thought and Language*, Wiley & Sons, New York and London.

Weikart, D. P. (1972) Relationship of curriculum, teaching and learning in preschool education, in J. C. Stanley (ed.) op. cit, pp. 22–67.

Weikart, D. P. (1983) Serving children: the High/Scope Foundation, *Concern* (National Children's Bureau), issue no. 49, autumn, pp. 23–31.

Weikart, D. P., and Lambie, D. Z. et al. (1969) Preschool intervention through a home tutoring program, in J. Hellmuth (ed.) op. cit.

Werner, H. (1948) *Comparative Psychology of Mental Development*, Follett, Chicago, IL.

Werner, H. and Kaplin, B. (1967) *Symbol Formation*, Wiley, New York, NY.

Westinghouse Learning Corporation (1969) The impact of Headstart: an evaluation of the effects of Headstart experience on children's cognitive and affective development, Westinghouse Learning Corporation, Ohio University, cited in J. C. Stanley (ed.) op. cit., p. 29.

Whalley, M. (1994) *Learning to be Strong*, Hodder & Stoughton, London.

Whalley, M. and the Pen Green Centre Team (2001) *Involving Parents in their Children's Learning*, Paul Chapman Pulishing, London.

Wheelan, Chris (2006) A Paper on Pedagogy written for a course at Pen Green in 2006. Personal communication.

Whitbread, N. (1975) *The Evolution of the Nursery–Infant School: A History of Infant and Nursery Education in Britain 1800–1970*, Routledge & Kegan Paul, London.

White, B. L. (1969) The initial co-ordination of sensorimotor schemas in human infants, Piaget's idea of the role of experience, in D. Elkind and J. H. Flavell (eds) op. cit; pp. 237–56.

Williams, E. M. and Shuard, H. (1980) *Primary Mathematics Today*, Longman, Harlow.

Williams, P. and Jinks, D. (1985) *Design and Technology 5–12*, Falmer Press, Lewes.

Wilson, P. S. (1969) Child-Centred Education, proceedings of the Annual Conference of the Philosophy of Education Society of Great Britain, January, pp. 105–26.

Wolde, G. (1975) *The Vacuum Cleaner*, Hodder & Stoughton, London.

Wolpert, L. (2000) *The Unnatural Nature of Science*, Harvard University Press, Cambridge, MA.

Wood, E. and Attfield, J. (1996) *Play, Learning and the Early Childhood Curriculum*, Paul Chapman Publishing, London.

Worthington, M. and Carruthers, E. (2003) *Children's Mathematics. Making Marks, Making Meaning*, Paul Chapman Publishing, London.

Young, J. Z. (1978) *Programmes of the Brain*, Oxford University Press, Oxford.

Author index

Subject index